FILIBUSTERING IN THE SENATE

FILIBUSTERING IN THE SENATE

By

FRANKLIN L. BURDETTE

NEW YORK
RUSSELL & RUSSELL · INC
1965

TO MY PARENTS

In Appreciation

FOREWORD

Hundreds of thousands of yellowing pages preserve the records of the United States Senate. One who dared to read them all would run again and again the whole gamut of human emotions. The business of the Senate, often important and at times critical, is transacted in a fashion and with a tempo which vary with the moods of distinguished legislators who are a law unto themselves. The subject of this volume is restricted to a phenomenon by which business is delayed rather than promoted, to the celebrated practice of filibustering.

It is amazing, when one contemplates the popular interest in filibusters, that hitherto not even a detailed history has been published. Perhaps the inevitable millions of uninteresting words which must be encountered have helped to deter both academic and literary adventurers. So many statements about filibustering have been inaccurate that even a bibliography would be misleading. Yet insurmountable difficulties confront an attempt to compile a complete and unchallengeable list of instances in which the Senate of the United States has been subjected to the tactics of delay. With motives hidden in the give and take of parliamentary battle, who can say whether a prolonged speech is a concealed design for obstruction or a sincere effort to impart information, whether garrulousness is more cunning than it seems? Undoubtedly there have been filibusters which will forever go unrecognized. Useful tools for identification are often to be found in the attitude of those who seem to delay proceedings, in occasional frank admission by participants, in general public recognition of a filibuster situation, and in relevancy of remarks. But such signposts must be viewed with caution. It must be remembered that the cleverest obstruction is often the least publicized and that, on the other hand, it is not difficult to spread rumors of a filibuster when none exists.

The chapters of this book are intended to present the story of Senate filibustering; to discuss the parliamentary devices utilized for restraint of the practice; and to survey the arguments both for and against the Senatorial privilege of virtually unlimited debate, a freedom of expression largely responsible for the prevalence of filibusterism in a body where dignity and statecraft are supposedly traditional. For the benefit of readers who would delve into the background, footnotes have been included. But to conserve space, citations to the most obvious repositories of data, the *Congressional Record* and its predecessors, have been omitted except where their absence might prove to be misleading.

Sources are available for many studies in legislative obstruction. To intensify the picture and to make the problem specific, the following pages are confined to the Senate of the United States and to the tactics which can be classified under the name "filibustering" without strain upon the terminology used in legislative circles. Other aspects of the wider term "obstruction," especially in standing committees and in conference committees, offer fruitful areas for investigation. Obstruction in the House of Representatives, in significance too little appreciated, is itself an inviting but unexplored field.

For the use of materials acknowledgment is gratefully made not only to the library of Princeton University, where most of the research has been undertaken, but also to the Library of Congress, the New York Public Library, and the libraries of the University of North Carolina and Duke University. To various members and officers of the United States Senate and to many persons who have helped with the details of inquiry and exposition, indebtedness is also acknowledged. In particular Professors William S. Carpenter, Edward S. Corwin, Alpheus T. Mason, William Starr Myers, and Harold H. Sprout of Princeton University have offered suggestions and assistance which have been invaluable. Parts of the text have had the benefit of the keen criticism of my friends Robert A. Horn and Donald C McVay, Jr. For the editorial suggestions of Marian Alexander Blake of Huntington, West Virginia, whose literary genius has transformed many an obscure passage, sincere sentiments of gratitude are expressed. My wife, Evelyn Page Burdette, has borne important responsibilities at every stage of the task. Without all this friendly assistance publication would have been long delayed. If errors and misinterpretations are present they accrue to the discredit of the writer alone.

FRANKLIN L. BURDETTE

Princeton, New Jersey,
Saturday, January 20, 1940.

CONTENTS

PAGE

Foreword   vii

I. The Art of
    Legislative Obstruction   3

II. An Instrument
    of Policy: Development   13

III. Filibustering Unrestrained   43

IV. The Modern Filibuster   83

V. Cloture at Last   127

VI. Turmoil   165

VII. The Dilemma   209

Index   243

CHAPTER I

THE ART OF LEGISLATIVE OBSTRUCTION

CHAPTER I

THE ART OF LEGISLATIVE OBSTRUCTION

WITH the death of Huey P. Long the Senate of the United States lost its most tempestuous filibusterer. The late Senator from Louisiana played upon the legislative stage with a bizarre humor which set a new mark for brazen obstruction. Only one man has held the floor longer than he, and no man in the United States Senate has exceeded his most celebrated feat of continuous and almost uninterrupted talking. For fifteen and one-half hours, in June 1935, Senator Long talked vociferously, energetically, and futilely in an effort to force an amendment to the proposed extension of a "skeletonized" National Recovery Administration.

"I desire to ask," he said, "that every Senator be made to stay here and listen to me, unless he has himself excused."

"In the opinion of the present occupant of the chair," ruled Vice President John N. Garner, "that would be unusual cruelty under the Bill of Rights."

Disgusted leaders of the Senate insisted upon strict enforcement of the rules. The Senator could yield only for a question, or he would lose the floor. If the majority could manage it by parliamentary technicality, they would stop the filibuster. Henry F. Ashurst of Arizona commented with pungent accuracy that "the Senator's present popularity is about as great as that of a cuckoo clock in a boys' dormitory at three o'clock in the morning." Yet some Senators objected to tactics too harsh. "While I am not a part of this filibuster," said Millard E. Tydings of Maryland, "I think the Senator is entitled to fair play."

The spectacular Senator from Louisiana made no pretense of relevancy or of restraint in his tremendous diatribe. His political enemies in and out of the administration were bathed in vitriol; such epithets as "pot-bellied politician," "scoundrel," and "chinch bug" were but characteristic of his angrier moments. His whimsical dissertations included comments upon the preservation of eyesight, biographical sketches of Frederick the Great and Judah P. Benjamin, and extensive quotations from Victor Hugo. Openly he invited suggestions from his auditors for topics of discussion. "I will accommodate any Senator tonight," he promised, "on any point on which he needs advice. . . ." Moreover, he would do more than that; he would dictate for the benefit of the *Congressional Record* recipes for cooking upon which his authoritative advice had been regularly in demand in Washington social circles. Once printed, the recipes could be more easily circulated. He then proceeded to tell the Senate at great length and in meticulous detail how to fry oysters. Nor did he omit a rambling discourse on the subject of "potlikker." "First let me tell Senators what potlikker is. Potlikker is the residue that remains from the commingling, heating, and evaporation— anyway, it is in the bottom of the pot!" It should be prepared, he said, by cooking turnip greens. With infinite patience, holding aloft a wastebasket to represent a pot, he told the Senate how turnip greens should be washed, seasoned with "side meat," and cooked. "I wonder if we could not print these recipes as a Senate document and send them out separately," he mused aloud. Several million reprints, each Senator being allotted a hundred thousand copies, "would do an immense amount of good." Indeed the idea so appealed to him that he forthwith presented to the Senate a third recipe—for Roquefort cheese salad dressing. It was a remarkable address with which he was favoring his fellow Senators, the galleries, and the country, he insisted. "Years from today there will be great jealousy over the fact that Senators will be claiming that they were among those who heard my memorable speech."

The demonstration by the inimitable Mr. Long was but an extreme example of the tactics to which the Senate is often subjected. The political showman from Louisiana added outrageous burlesque to grim purpose. In comparison, his predecessors and contemporaries, themselves not infrequent devotees of obstruction, were mere dilettantes in audacity. Yet their own exploits were not always accomplished with the politeness of the drawing-room.

Filibuster in its primary lexicographic sense is a noun used to designate an armed adventurer, on land or sea, who wages unauthorized and irregular warfare against foreign states or dependencies for plunder or power. The word came into use about the middle of the nineteenth century to describe marauders or freebooters in Central America and the West Indies. Before many years, certainly as early as 1863,[1] it was used in the United States as a term of reproach signifying flagrant legislative obstruction—though legislators knew how to employ the tactics long before they were favored with a satisfying name for them.

Filibustering to the politically minded is the use of dilatory tactics upon the floor of a legislative body. It is a device to delay business in order to defeat legislation or to force unwilling adoption as a price for time to consider other and perhaps much more important matters. Whether the underlying purpose is positive or negative the technique is designed to consume time. And in the matter of consumption of time, legislators often seem gifted far beyond the common man.

The record for continuous occupancy of the Senate floor was established in 1908 by the late Robert M. La Follette of Wisconsin when, for more than eighteen hours, he filibustered against the Aldrich-Vreeland Currency Bill. But the Wisconsin Senator was relieved during the course of his remarks by twenty-nine quorum calls and three roll-call votes on questions of order. Other filibuster speeches have been long and much discussed, although none has been so singular a feat of endurance as the June 1935 tirade of Huey Long.

As recently as the winter of 1937-1938, during consideration of an antilynching measure, Southern loquaciousness occupied the time of the Senate almost exclusively for six weeks. Allen J. Ellender sat in the place of the late Senator Long and, true to the modern Louisiana precedent, talked day after day for hours on end. Ellender

[1] cf. *Cong. Globe*, 37th Cong., 3rd Sess., p. 1437.

alone, in the course of discursive illustrations from the histories of peoples both ancient and modern, took over the business of the Senate for more than a week. Southerners talked in relays till both Senate and nation were weary of the ordeal, but no one found a way to force an ending of the long carnival of talk.

In its past, however, the famous legislative body had been racked by obstruction far more intense, more bitter, and even more prolonged. In 1893 a fierce struggle against the repeal of a silver purchase law was protracted for more than eight weeks, the hours of forty-six actual business days being dissipated by dilatory tactics. An earlier and only slightly less prolonged fight against a Federal Elections or "Force" Bill occupied Senate attention in 1890-1891 for fifty-six days, thirty-three of them spent in the throes of filibuster. In 1881 a parliamentary battle against the election of Senate officers obnoxious to the Democrats was won after forty-one days, twenty-six of them devoted to obstruction.

But perhaps the United States Senate, with all its reputation for speeches of tremendous length, has no fair claim to a record for continuous personal verbosity. It is said that in 1908 E. G. Senter of Texas talked for twenty-nine consecutive hours in the Senate of that State in an attempt to force a legislative investigation of charges against United States Senator Joseph W. Bailey. Sustained by hot coffee every thirty minutes during his long exertions, Mr. Senter was still speaking when the furious legislators abandoned their rules and voted him off his feet.[2]

Legislative filibustering is made possible at least partly by the nature of rules of procedure. In the United States Senate, aside from a few precepts in the Constitution, authority to make the rules rests in the Senate itself. And those rules would almost seem to have been contrived to encourage the stubbornness and daring of obstructionists. Under ordinary conditions no measure before the body can reach a final favorable disposition until every Senator has had an

---

[2] See letter from Senter in *New York Times,* June 23, 1935. For instances of long speeches abroad, see Georg Jellinek, "Parliamentary Obstruction," *Political Science Quarterly,* Vol. XIX (Dec. 1904), at p. 581.

opportunity (which of course he need not utilize) to speak upon it for as long as he wishes. Prior to 1917 no rule had ever existed to limit the flow of Senatorial eloquence, however extended or unnecessary it might become. In that year, after filibuster episodes which enraged the country, a much qualified rule for delayed limitation of debate was adopted. It is called the rule for cloture, or closure; and under it a motion may be introduced at any time, if signed by sixteen Senators, to end discussion on any pending measure. But an entire day must elapse before a vote on the motion is required, and even then it can be carried only by a two-thirds majority. Even after the adoption of a motion for cloture every Senator is entitled to speak for one hour.

The provision authorizing cloture has had less effect on filibustering than might have been anticipated, for it is difficult to apply as a matter of practical politics. Despite repeated efforts, in more than twenty years the Senate has actually employed cloture only four times. Though filibusters have blocked the business of the Senate by day and by night, and though at times a meager minority of obstinate Senators has defied the will of a tremendous majority, usually the time has been too short or the necessary votes have not been available to close debate.

Under ordinary circumstances the Senate rules are not strictly enforced. The tradition of that body encourages laxity of regulations in deference to the importance and therefore to the convenience of its members. Moreover any business can be conducted and almost any arrangement can be made by unanimous consent. Even debate is thus frequently limited. But in times of urgency or keen controversy the rules are likely to be more rigidly enforced. On such occasions there may be employed one technical limitation of debate aside from cloture: the restriction that no Senator may speak more than twice upon the same question in any one day without leave of the body. While it has been said that there have been many men in the Senate who have found it easy to occupy a day without speaking even twice, in reality the term *day* has been so interpreted by long precedent that it has a special meaning: *legislative day*. A legislative day, which is terminated by an adjournment but never by a recess, may last for many weeks. When the Senate ends a sitting to allow its members a few hours of rest, it may adjourn or it may recess. If it adjourns, the next sitting of the body must be opened with routine formalities, such as reading the journal, presentation of petitions, and introduction of bills—all of which can be avoided if a recess instead of an adjournment is voted.

Since, then, a legislative day continues until the Senate decides to adjourn rather than to recess, the limitation upon Senators to speak only twice upon the same question in one day might become decidedly inconvenient. But Senatorial adeptness has found a way around even this difficulty: every amendment is held to constitute a separate question, and Senators who have exhausted their speaking privilege on the main question may begin again upon an amendment.

Several parliamentary devices may be employed by the resourceful filibusterer. Within the framework of the Senate rules the techniques are talk, dilatory motions, yea-and-nay votes, quorum calls, quorum breaking through absentations, points of order and appeals, "baiting the opposition" in the hope of inducing it to reply and thus to assist unintentionally in consuming time, and, finally, the interjection of other business. No Senate session is ever quite free from the possibility of filibuster, and occasionally the much feared system of delay springs into action like the sudden eruption of a long quiet volcano.

Of the implements for filibustering, wearisome, long-continued talk is most commonly utilized. Each Senator is permitted to be the sole judge of the relevancy of his own remarks, without regard for pertinency. If he chooses to discuss the fate of the Aztecs or fur trading in Alaska while the Senate is considering an antilynching bill, such comments are on the subject if he says they are. Cole L. Blease of South Carolina often read to his colleagues historic sketches about Confederate heroes, and in 1936 Rush Holt of West Virginia entertained the august assemblage with Aesop's Fables.

The existence of filibustering in America today is evidence of a compromise between the authority of the many and the rights of the few. The principle of leadership is tinctured with restraints.

Liberty in America, despite its heritage from afar, has developed in its own peculiar mould. Perhaps in no other portion of the world does stable government present so many indications of instability. To the political theorist legislative obstruction, for instance, is a symbol of immaturity; it comports neither with the need for action nor with the dignity of power. Charitable scholars have predicted that its excrescences will be outgrown, that long experience will teach calmer and more settled ways. On the other hand, to the politician interested in practical use of the doctrine of inalienable rights, obstruction is a recourse of more than passing value. It is an effective if incalculable defense against oppression and overbearing authority. It may lie unused for years and then, in a moment of emergency, serve to good purpose in the cause of freedom. It may defeat the hand of greed or the ambition of irresponsible officials without resort to more violent means.

Such are the schools of thought which in America have provided a century and a half of argument about the merits and the evils of filibustering. Obstruction is a weapon, and like all weapons it is dangerous. Yet in the lives of nations as of men there are times when weapons are a safeguard, and it is indeed a high degree of civilization in which they are useless.

CHAPTER II

AN INSTRUMENT OF POLICY: DEVELOPMENT

CHAPTER II

AN INSTRUMENT OF POLICY: DEVELOPMENT

MODERN as is the term *filibustering,* dilatory tactics are no new legislative practice in the world. Even the renowned Roman Senate had its persistent obstructionists. In the English Parliament, extended obstruction was known long before the brilliant Irish leader, Charles Stewart Parnell, employed the strategy of delay to such purpose and effect that an exasperated Speaker of the House of Commons closed debate and put the main question on his own initiative.[1]

Obstruction which newspapers of today would call filibustering was certainly known in our colonial legislatures. George Mason of Virginia said in the debates upon the Constitution in the Federal Convention of 1787 that beneficial results might come from systematic quorum breaking practiced by members of the legislature. In Virginia, he remarked, an undesirable issue of paper money had once been prevented by those tactics.[2]

Indeed, the very issue of ratifying the Federal Constitution resulted in a famous though unsuccessful filibuster in the Pennsylvania one-house legislature. Proponents of the new document, exulting in the weight of their numbers, undertook to rush through a measure for calling a state convention to deliberate formally upon the new Constitution. Opponents of the proposal promptly managed to break a quorum by deserting the legislative session and by

[1] See Robert Luce, *Legislative Procedure* (Boston, 1922), pp. 277-83; Carl Joachim Friedrich, *Constitutional Government and Politics* (New York, 1937), pp. 391-3.

[2] James Madison, *The Debates in the Federal Convention of 1787,* Hunt and Scott ed., (New York, 1920), p. 376.

defying the summons of the sergeant at arms for attendance. Thereupon friends of the Constitution visited representatives of the recalcitrant minority, carried them forcibly to the legislative hall, and held them in their seats while the majority voted through the proposal for a state convention.

Under the Constitution, filibustering found its place in the very first Congress. Representative Fisher Ames of Massachusetts wrote in June 1790 of a wrangle in the House which unquestionably bears the filibuster stamp. Congress was sitting in New York; but in a controversy regarding the city in which the legislators should later assemble, the House had voted for Philadelphia. The Senate, with the vote of a Senator brought to the hall in a sick bed, rejected the proposition. On a rainy day, when it was known that the ill Senator could not be brought, Representatives attempted to carry the motion once more in the House and send it to the Senate; but Gerry of Massachusetts and Smith of South Carolina delivered long speeches and made dilatory motions which prevented a vote that day.[3] The question of a new residence for Congress brought the threat of filibuster even to the exclusive Senate. The querulous Senator William Maclay of Pennsylvania wrote in his *Journal* that William Linn (a chaplain to Congress) had told him that "the design of the Virginians and the Carolina gentlemen was to talk away the time, so that we could not get the bill passed." And when the Senate next met, Maclay recorded, "every endeavor was made to waste time."[4]

Tactics patently obstructive, however, were characteristic of the House long before they became common in the Senate. That fact may be ascribed to the small membership of the early Senate and to the dignity and polished politeness with which its proceedings were conducted; but it also must not be overlooked that, prior to the Jacksonian era, it was in the House rather than the Senate that political prestige was greatest, and it was in the House that the hardest legislative battles were fought. Moreover, there were individuals in

[3] *Works of Fisher Ames* (Boston, 1854), Vol. I, pp. 79-80.
[4] *Journal of William Maclay* (New York, 1890), p. 158.

the House whose temperaments prompted them to extended speech and dilatory maneuvers. John Randolph of Roanoke, erratic Virginian of marked abilities, acquired in the House such a reputation as an adroit designer of delay that in 1810 ex-President Jefferson, in a personal letter, referred to "a John Randolph" as a generic term symbolizing one who might protract the proceedings of Congress.[5]

Barent Gardenier of New York, in his brief service of two terms in the House from 1807 to 1811, developed such an amazing propensity for holding the floor that his perplexed colleagues became convinced that curbing action must be had. A favorite proposal provided for use of the "previous question," a technical motion which in modern times has come to mean that, if adopted, all debate shall end and a vote shall be taken on the main question. Thomas Jefferson wrote from Monticello to suggest to his son-in-law John W. Eppes, member of the Virginia delegation in the House, that debate be closed and a vote had on the pending question at eight o'clock in the evening, whenever the House should remain so long in session. This expedient he regarded as less inconvenient than long night sessions or the use of the previous question.[6] Actually, the House voted that the previous question should be used to close debate.[7] But mere limitation of debate is not sufficient to avert effective filibusters when other dilatory tactics are available, as long experience in the House has shown. Not until 1890, when Speaker Thomas B. Reed counted a quorum even if members present would not answer their names upon a vote—and when he also refused to entertain dilatory motions[8]—were drastic measures taken to abolish obstruction on the floor of the House.

Since the subjugation of the House by Speaker Reed, spectacular and long-continued scenes of filibuster have been confined to the Senate. The practice is not dead in the House, but it is not followed so readily or for such extended periods as in the Senate. Yet it re-

[5] *The Writings of Thomas Jefferson,* Ford ed., (New York, 1892-99), Vol. IX, p. 280.

[6] *ibid.,* pp. 267-8.

[7] *Annals of Cong.,* 11th Cong., 3rd Sess., pp. 1092, 1106-7.

[8] 21 *Cong. Record,* pp. 948-60, 996-1001.

mains a weapon of value for the wily and the adept. In the present House, strictly limited in debate and to germaneness, filibustering demands parliamentary finesse in offering amendments, forcing votes or quorum calls, and in making appeals. In the Senate, finesse is an asset; but endurance and obstinacy are often as effective.

For many of the proceedings of the early Senate, as in the case of the early House, historians are dependent upon contemporary commentaries and upon private records left by the members. Debates in Congress were often scantily reported, and in the Senate they were secret till 1794. Not until 1873 did there originate the official *Congressional Record,* reporting verbatim speeches in both Houses. The earlier *Annals of Congress, Register of Debates,* and *Congressional Globe,* printed as commercial undertakings and including verbatim accounts of only parts of the proceedings, leave the searcher without adequate clues to many possible parliamentary maneuvers.

In any event, it seems likely that there were no major or extended filibusters in the dignified Senate prior to the advent of the remarkable John Randolph of Roanoke. Elected in 1825 to fill an unexpired term, he had long before attained in the House of Representatives a tremendous reputation for great ability, unusual loquacity, and extreme eccentricity. Possessed of one of the most sarcastic tongues ever heard in the Senate, Randolph was too crabbed to spare either friend or foe from the vitriol of his language. It is recorded that once, while addressing Vice President John C. Calhoun in the chair, he forgot momentarily that he spoke in the Senate rather than in the House and said, "Mr. Speaker! I mean Mr. President of the Senate and would-be President of the United States, which God in His infinite mercy avert."[9]

In his Senatorial service of less than two years, Randolph occupied the floor day after day, talking for hours at a time without the slightest reference to the business at hand. His dreary monologue, broken only at times by violent language, drove Senators one by one from a scene of harangue rather than of action; and the Senate

---

[9] Ben: Perley Poore, *Perley's Reminiscences of Sixty Years in the National Metropolis* (Philadelphia, 1886), Vol. I, p. 64.

would finally adjourn without a quorum, a situation, as one of Randolph's biographers sets forth, till then unknown to an assembly of suave and unvarying courtesy. The long and rambling discourses of the Virginia Senator went unreported and unrespected. His friends pardoned him as one half insane; his enemies ascribed his irrationality to drink; and a charitable biographer wrote that an ungovernable temper had driven him to the verge of madness.

Hezekiah Niles, an editor of prominence, after listening to the Virginian for thirty-five minutes, wrote in his *Register,* "I had been told that the bankrupt bill was before the senate—but, during the time stated, he never, to the best of my recollection, mentioned, or even remotely alluded to it, or any of its parts, in any manner whatsoever." For five minutes the Senator had described a scheme for founding a bank, then discussed Unitarians in religion and politics, attacked the President and the administration, expressed his disgust for "family Bibles"—though he thought no family would flourish without a Bible—and his distrust of any book in an American edition. He referred briefly to the presses of the Universities of Oxford and Cambridge and their accuracy in printing: "they would be fined 10,000 £ sterling, if they should leave the word *not* out of the seventh commandment. . . ." Soon he passed to Shakespea , drubbing some one soundly for having had the impudence to publish a "family Shakespeare." Then he vehemently disavowed all connection with the American "Protestant Episcopal Church." He declared that he belonged to the church of Old England and had been baptized "by a man regularly authorized by the bishop of London who had laid his hands upon him [laying his own hands on the head of the gentleman next to him]." Referring again to the Episcopal church, he quoted "Them that" as beginning a part of its service, "reprobating its grammar, and implying that no good man could belong to a church which used such language! Suddenly, he spoke about wine—it was often mentioned in the Bible, and he approved of the drinking of it—if in a gentlemanly way—at the table—not in the closet—not in the closet; but as to whiskey, he demanded that any one should shew him the word in the Bible—it was not there. No sir, you can't find it in the whole book. Next, or shortly after this, he spoke of his land, saying that he held it by a *royal* grant, with which he seemed greatly pleased—but, in a minute or two, was speaking of the 'men of Kent,' in England, saying that Kent had never been conquered by William the Conqueror, but had made terms with him, and, in consequence, when the militia of England are called to the field, the men of Kent are entitled to the front rank." He spoke of a song on the men of Kent, and evidently he said that he would give a thousand pounds to have written it.

Apparently Senator Randolph was about to rehearse the song or sing it when Editor Niles hastily left the chamber to relieve his feelings in print: "Nine-tenths of his long speeches just as well apply to a discussion about the constitutional powers of congress to make a road, as to the case of John Smith, or the long disputed claim about Amy Darden's stud-horse. . . . He talks with so much ease, that, unless for want of 'meat, drink or sleep,' one would suppose that he might speak twelve months without stopping; though he freely stops to rest himself, and keeps the senate waiting, when he pleases. A greater part of the time that I heard him, he was leaning, or lolling . . . and the careless ease with which he delivered himself brought to mind the 'Arabian Nights Entertainments,' because of their fluency—they, however have a regular design, which his speeches have not."

Mr. Niles concluded that "it is generally felt, and pretty freely acknowledged by many of the senators themselves, that their body has lost a large portion of their own respect for it, and of the respect of the people, through Mr. Randolph's incessant talking. If every other gentleman spoke as long as he does . . . a three years perpetual session would not do the *business* of a week. . . ."[10]

There were Senators who thought that the chair should call to order the abusive speaker. But Vice President Calhoun insisted that the right to call to order on questions of latitude or freedom of debate belonged exclusively to the members of the body, not to the

[10] *Niles' Weekly Register*, Vol. XXX (May 13, 1826), pp. 186-7.

chair.[11] The duty of the Vice President was argued in the press, and soon there appeared in the Washington *National Journal* under the name "Patrick Henry" letters attacking Calhoun's alleged neglect to enforce the Senate rules. It was widely believed that President Adams, stinging under the denunciations of Randolph and resenting the serenity of Calhoun, was himself the author of the letters; and to this day there is some uncertainty whether the attacks actually were written by Adams, by one Philip Richard Fendall (a government clerk), or by an unknown hand. The Vice President, in reply, earnestly defended his position by sending to *The National Intelligencer* letters under the name "Onslow." If Randolph's tirades were filibusterous, he had a protector, though by no means necessarily an abettor, in the Vice President.

One who remembers the reputation of this same Randolph in the House, and who is aware of the bitter opposition of the caustic Virginian toward the administration of John Quincy Adams, may well doubt whether these unfettered diatribes were altogether purposeless. They certainly did the administration no service, and they aided in obstructing the enactment of its policies. When all the circumstances are considered—the past reputation of John Randolph, the resentment of the administration and its friends, and the fact that no one claims that the Virginia Senator was altogether deranged or even altogether lacking in genius—one is inclined strongly to suspect that the Senate's first extended and spectacular filibusters were staged by that Southern opponent of the Adamses.

It might have been anticipated that the Senatorial career of John Randolph would have encouraged other men to forget or ignore the dignity of the Senate and to disrupt its business for personal or partisan advantage, but such seems not to have been the case. If men filibustered in the years immediately following, they at least did so with gravity and beneath the cloak of relevancy.

But in 1837 the Senate calm met profound disturbance as the result of a resolution to expunge from the journal a long-standing censure of President Jackson, a condemnation proposed by Henry

[11] *Register of Debates*, 19th Cong., 1st Sess., pp. 572-3.

Clay and voted in 1834 after the President had succeeded in withdrawing the federal deposits from the Bank of the United States. Jacksonian supporters had served notice upon the Senate and the country that they would never rest until the hated resolution had been revoked. Men loyal to Jackson considered the censure an unforgivable outrage, and the question became one of the burning issues in American politics. Many state legislatures instructed Senators, whom they had previously elected, to vote in favor of expunging the resolution, and in the two years between 1835 and 1837 at least six states replaced anti-Jackson Senators with men determined to vindicate the President. The final and successful drive of the proponents of the expunging motion was pushed on Monday, January 16, 1837, a continuation of consideration from the close of the preceding week. Undoubtedly there was at least an incipient filibuster against it. The staunch Jacksonian Thomas H. Benton, Senator from Missouri, said of Webster, Clay, Calhoun and other enemies of the pending motion, now in the minority: "It was evident that consumption of time, delay and adjournment, was their plan." But the Senate was to be held in continuous session, if possible. Expecting a protracted session, Jacksonian Senators fortified themselves with an ample supply, ready in a nearby committee room, of cold hams, turkeys, beef, pickles, wines, and cups of hot coffee.[12]

Opponents talked and talked; only a few spoke on the side of the expunging resolution. As night drew on, the great chandelier lit a crowded chamber, the lobbies and galleries filled with spectators of the sullen contest. Near midnight the opposition faltered. Calhoun and Clay had already denounced the proposal; Webster concluded the opposing argument. The resolution was passed, 24 to 19, and anti-Jackson Senators contented themselves with stalking out of the chamber before the expunging order could be carried into effect. But of the spectators in the galleries, many were bitterly hostile to the President; and his friends were uneasy, if not actually alarmed. Some Senators, recalling vividly an attempt two years before to

---

[12] Thomas H. Benton, *Thirty Years' View* (New York, 1854-56), Vol. I, p. 727.

assassinate the President, in the Capitol itself, sent out for arms. And when the original journal of 1834 was brought for the expunging act, hisses and groans broke out in the galleries, to be suppressed only by the most energetic action on the part of the sergeant at arms.[13] In the strained situation a single violent motion might have turned the staid legislative body into an arena of tumultuous disorder.

On this occasion, at least, the dignity of the Senate, caution in partisan opposition, or unwillingness for an exhausting trial of physical endurance—perhaps a combination of reasons—had prevented an embattled minority from prolonging the contest into an intense filibuster of the dramatic type which was to take place upon the Senate scene in later years. Indeed, the Senate experience with filibustering four years later was less dignified: the year 1841 saw two extended attempts to hinder measures before the body by tactics which can be called little else than purposely obstructive.

When the Senate met in special session at the beginning of the 27th Congress, March 4, 1841, the Whig majority determined to rid the body of its official printers who had been elected in spite of protests on February 20 by the then Democratic majority. For what reason had William Henry Harrison and his Whig supporters come into power if their party should not control the government? The new session had scarcely convened when Senator Willie P. Mangum of North Carolina moved to dismiss the printers. The motion was considered from the 5th till the 11th of March, though the Senate was in session but five calendar days during that period; and debate resolved itself into a prolonged and acrimonious contention, relevant to the subject but spun out by the Democrats through lengthy arguments based on grounds of constitutionality and expediency.

Among the most noted of the Democratic arguers were James Buchanan of Pennsylvania, later to become President of the United States, John C. Calhoun of South Carolina, Thomas H. Benton of Missouri, Silas Wright of New York, Levi Woodbury of New

13 *ibid.*, pp. 730-1; *Cong. Globe,* 24th Cong., 2nd Sess., pp. 99-100.

Hampshire, and William R. King of Alabama. But the Whigs were not content, as majorities determined to break prolonged opposition may well be, to let the opponents carry all the burden of talking; they joined in the arguments with lengthy and sometimes heated defense.

On one occasion Henry Clay and King engaged in a personal exchange of scathing terms, and Clay became so offensive in his tones that before the day was over Senator King challenged him to a duel. The challenge, presented by Senator Lewis F. Linn of Missouri, was promptly accepted; and the duel was prevented only when official interposition brought the three Senators before a magistrate, who placed each of them under a peace bond.[14]

But, despite brave words, the force of the obstruction was wearing down. On the 10th of March Senator Ambrose H. Sevier of Arkansas admitted that sometime before the first of June the printers would be dismissed. Limits to the obstruction, however, were reached with far greater rapidity than the Arkansas Senator had implied; for on the very next day the Whig motion was carried by 26 yeas against 18 nays. The filibuster, though it had never reached a stage which might be called intense, ended with defeat for those who undertook it. As a matter of fact it was a mild demonstration; but hitherto the Senate had seen no more prolonged or more partisan obstruction.

Within four months the Senate was subjected to another, and far more famous, demonstration of delay. The first session of both Houses of the 27th Congress convened on May 31, 1841; and on June 21 Henry Clay rose in the Senate to report from a select committee a Fiscal Bank Bill. It was a measure dear to the hearts of the Whigs. Clay and his friends had for years fought unsuccessfully against Andrew Jackson and the Democrats in behalf of a national bank. The power of Jackson had prevented recharter of the second Bank of the United States, and the long arm of his influence had continued to hold the Whigs in check. The election of William Henry Harrison had seemed to assure victory at last for a bank, but

14 *Newark Daily Advertiser*, March 11, 1841.

now Harrison was dead and John Tyler sat in his place. Would the Virginian, so suddenly elevated from the Vice Presidency, support the program of the Whigs who had elected him? His background was strange: he had been no friend of Jackson; but, as Democratic journals were eager to point out, he had opposed a national bank. Yet Clay and his followers pressed on; they would send a bill to the new President and put his sentiments to the test. To the annoyance of the Whig leaders, however, Senators insisted upon discussing the measure at great length.

On July 15 Clay made a waspish announcement that it would be necessary to lay aside other matters for a time and take up for immediate consideration a loan bill to relieve a Treasury with only enough money to pay expenses of the government for a fortnight. Calhoun, doubtless expressing the opinion of the minority, objected to the precipitation with which measures were being hurried before the Senate, and Clay instantly waxed indignant. Regarding the remarks of the South Carolinian as arising from a spirit of obstruction, the Kentucky leader asserted that he would act to allow a majority to control the business of the Senate, that he would offer a measure to that end, and that he believed a limitation of debate would be approved. Senator King of Alabama retorted that the majority itself had consumed most of the time, and he demanded to know whether the Senator actually intended to introduce a gag measure.

Said Mr. Clay: "I will, sir; I will."

Mr. King, defiantly: "I tell the Senator, then, that he may make his arrangements at his boarding house for the winter."

Never before had the Senate listened to so plain an avowal of the intention to filibuster. Nor did the storm subside with the threat of the Alabama Senator. Benton, at length, denounced the "design to stifle debate," roaring: "Sir, this call for action! action! action! . . . comes from those whose cry is, plunder! plunder! plunder!" Calhoun, crying that here was "a palpable attempt to infringe the right of speech," declared that if a gag law were attempted he would resist it to the end.

Mr. Clay did not present his rule for limitation of debate. According to Benton, some of the Whig Senators, realizing the ill feeling now sure to be engendered by such a proposition, refused their support to Clay's plan and left the Kentucky Senator, much to his chagrin, without the votes to undertake a revision of the rules.[15] Nor did the obstruction of Mr. Clay's bank measure cease. It was necessary to consider the loan bill until the 19th of July, when the Senate program was cleared by its passage; but debate upon the bank bill continued till the 28th. On the 26th, Clay, in a much more conciliatory humor, admitted that his side had occupied its share of the time; it was imperative now to be diplomatic and perhaps even to compromise to get enough votes for the bill. On the 28th the Senate finally passed the measure. The filibusterous delay had not been fatal even if it had been provoking. In the House the Whig measure was obediently passed, and the controversial issue was presented squarely to the President.

Tyler delayed his decision. It was a question of tremendous political consequence. In his hands rested a power which filibusterers had been unable to wield; he could kill the bill, for two-thirds majorities could never be found to override his veto, yet he might darken irrevocably his own political future. But Tyler's convictions rose to the occasion, and the Whig dream of a national bank ended beneath the weight of Presidential disapproval. The President had broken with the leaders of his party, and his name and fame have never fully recovered from the blow. Disgruntled Whigs in the Washington populace assembled outside the White House and jeered him. The following night they burned him in effigy. The Democrats, of course, were jubilant; they believed that Tyler had befriended the people and had attested the wisdom of Jackson.

Obstruction had been used to oppose the Whigs, but it had not been the cause of their defeat. Not yet was filibusterism so organized that it could completely paralyze the program of the Senate. The threat was often present; the use was occasionally undertaken; but

15 Benton, *op. cit.*, Vol. II, p. 257.

the utter and indefinitely continued disruption of the Senate business by filibustering was a practice still essentially unexploited. In the two succeeding decades the Senate witnessed troublous scenes, and in some of the protracted contentions there were indications of filibuster. Rarely, however, were dilatory tactics openly admitted.

In 1846 a resolution to serve a year's notice of termination of "joint occupancy" of Oregon with Great Britain, recommended in a message from President James K. Polk, was considered during most of the session hours from February 10 to April 16. Since a treaty of 1818, renewed in 1827, the Oregon country had been open on equal terms to citizens of the United States and of Great Britain. As Americans moved westward, however, there arose a great public demand to place Oregon under the sovereignty of the United States. Polk agreed with that sentiment and undertook negotiations to carry it out. As part of his program he proposed to give to Great Britain the required notice ending treaty arrangements about Oregon. The Senate was deeply divided upon the issues involved, and speech after speech obstructed a decision. There were men who feared the danger of war from hasty action; others distrusted the policy of Polk; many counselled caution and delay. In spite of dilatory verbosity lasting more than two months, the Senate eventually passed the resolution to third reading by 40 yeas to 14 nays; immediately afterward, without a formal division, came final passage. The House concurred and the President transmitted the notice to Britain, thereby hastening a peaceful settlement of the Oregon boundary and garnering for his administration a diplomatic victory.

Even before negotiations over the Oregon question had been completed, the United States on May 13, 1846, declared the existence of war with Mexico. President Polk, an ardent annexationist, hoped that Mexico would ultimately be willing to cede territory to the United States, and he believed that he should have available a sum of money sufficient to make an initial payment for such territory if necessary. Consequently he asked Congress to authorize an appropriation of $2,000,000. The House, in voting compliance, attached as a condition the famous Wilmot Proviso, moved by Representative

David Wilmot of Pennsylvania, stipulating that slavery should never exist in territory acquired from Mexico. The appropriation measure with the highly controversial Proviso was considered in the Senate shortly before noon on the 10th of August, the hour already fixed for final adjournment. Dixon H. Lewis of Alabama moved to strike out the antislavery condition, and John Davis, a conservative Whig from Massachusetts, began a lengthy protest.

Davis had been one of two Senators to vote against war with Mexico; he wished an early peace, he was dubious of the need for additional territory, and he favored retention of the Wilmot Proviso if more territory must be annexed. Lewis and other Senators were impatient for the speech to end. If the Proviso should be stricken from the appropriation by vote of the Senate, it must be done in time for the House to concur. "I promise the gentleman that I will stop before the time for adjournment arrives," said Davis. Yet his remarks went on, and the session neared its end. "Pass this bill," he predicted, "and the President of the United States will feel justified in prolonging the war until . . . additional territory is acquired. . . ."

In the meantime the House adjourned. According to report, its clock was faster than the one in the Senate. If the bill should become law by vote of the Senate, it must now include the disputed Proviso; since the House had ended its labors, the Senate must accept the appropriation without amendment or let the measure die. Disgusted Senators took no further action. Davis had talked the whole proposition to death. "Should the war be now protracted," wrote President Polk, "the responsibility will fall more heavily upon the head of Senator Davis than upon any other man, and he will deserve the execrations of the country."[16]

When Congress reconvened in December, Polk again asked for money; he would provide a means to acquire territory if he could. Bills were introduced in both Houses to appropriate $3,000,000 to meet possible needs as foreseen by the President, but around the whole issue there again raged violent storms of dissension. In the

[16] *The Diary of James K. Polk* (Chicago, 1910), Vol. II, p. 77.

Senate, from the 4th of February till the 1st of March, 1847, fierce debates prevented a vote. The causes and the conduct of the war were critically examined, the sincerity and good faith of the President were questioned by many Whigs, and the legislative halls were filled with defense and denunciation of slavery. Should an antislavery condition such as the Wilmot Proviso be incorporated as part and parcel of the appropriation? Should the money, to be used for the dismemberment of Mexico, be voted at all? Senatorial delays, artfully protracted for more than a month, finally ended in approval of the bill without reference to an antislavery condition. The House added its sanction and Polk had his way. When peace was established in 1848, the funds appropriated were applied as part payment for the vast territory acquired from Mexico, an area extending from the Rio Grande westward to the Pacific.

Slavery was once more the critical issue in the extended debates upon the Compromise of 1850, and particularly upon that part of it dealing with the admission of California into the Union. But the entire session, lasting for nearly ten months, was tense with strained emotions.

On the 17th of April, 1850, during a caustic speech by Henry S. Foote of Mississippi, Senator Benton of Missouri lunged suddenly from his chair and advanced threateningly toward the speaker. The diminutive Senator Foote backed hastily down the aisle, levelling a pistol at the belligerent Missourian. In a moment almost every Senator was scrambling to his feet, clamoring for order and rushing toward the angry pair. Over the confusion Benton, struggling with Senators who sought to restrain him, was heard to shout, "I have no pistols! Let him fire! Stand out of the way! I have no pistols! I disdain to carry arms! Stand out of the way, and let the assassin fire!" Even when Benton had been pushed to his seat and Foote had surrendered his pistol, there ensued a noisy debate with Benton contending that a scoundrel had attempted to assassinate him and with Foote asserting that he had acted in self-defense.

The specific compromise proposals as suggested by Henry Clay, reporting from a select Committee of Thirteen, were subjects of active wrangling from May 13 to July 31. Clay believed that the proposals which he advocated would settle the slave controversy for many years, and because of the long debates he complained bitterly: "To postpone, to delay, to impede, to procrastinate, has been the policy of the minority in this body. . . ."[17] Finally, at the end of July, the admission of California and other proposals were stricken from an omnibus bill which had been drafted to include several of the compromise recommendations. On August 1 the measure passed the Senate simply as an act to provide territorial government for Utah. Because of cumulative opposition to specific items, it was recognized that the omnibus bill could not be passed: the propositions must be introduced in separate form. Senator Stephen A. Douglas of Illinois immediately asked that there be considered a bill intended solely to admit California. That measure produced stubborn resistance which, though less prolonged, was even more clearly filibusterous. Dilatory motions to adjourn, postpone, lay on the table, amend, and so on were employed, although by no means exploited to their full possibilities. On the 7th, Senator David L. Yulee of Florida declared that he would use "every proper parliamentary means to avert so great a calamity as . . . is to be forced upon the country and upon mankind"; and he proceeded to talk at length. But the opposition could not or would not continue indefinitely, and on the 13th the bill for California's admission was passed 34 to 18. Before the end of the session, all of the compromise measures had been adopted.

Similarly, the question of slavery was a bone of prolonged contention in 1856, when Douglas reported a bill approved by the Pierce administration providing for subsequent admission of Kansas into the Union and authorizing its people to prepare a constitution. The slavery issue in Kansas had reached the stage of bloodshed, and statehood was advanced as a remedy. But antislavery Senators feared that Kansas as a state would be dominated by proslavery interests; consequently the measure was futilely considered from March 20 till June 25, when it was again referred to committee. Many of the

[17] *Cong. Globe,* 31st Cong., 1st Sess., Appendix, p. 861.

long speeches had served merely to prove that the bill could not be brought to a vote because of unyielding opposition. Not until 1861, when several Southern states had already seceded and when Northerners could push through a free-state bill, was Kansas to be admitted to the Union.

Perhaps no obstruction has been attended with greater violence and passion than that which marked the scenes of 1856. For it was during the period of heated debate on that controversy that there occurred the famous assault upon Senator Charles Sumner. In May the Massachusetts Senator planned to hurl forth the most thorough philippic ever pronounced in a legislative body. In his startling speech, entitled "The Crime against Kansas," he denounced with almost unparalleled bitterness the forces and the advocates of slavery. Sumner's characterization of Senator Andrew P. Butler led directly, within three days, to the violence which fell on his own head.

"The Senator from South Carolina," Sumner thundered, "has read many books of chivalry, and believes himself a chivalrous knight, with sentiments of honor and courage. Of course he has chosen a mistress to whom he has made his vows, and who, though ugly to others, is always lovely to him; though polluted in the sight of the world, is chaste in his sight—I mean the harlot, Slavery. For her, his tongue is always profuse in words. Let her be impeached in character, or any proposition made to shut her out from the extension of her wantonness, and no extravagance of manner or hardihood of assertion is then too great for this Senator. The frenzy of Don Quixote, in behalf of his wench, Dulcinea del Toboso, is all surpassed. The asserted rights of slavery, which shock equality of all kinds, are cloaked by a fantastic claim of equality. If the slave states cannot enjoy what, in mockery of the great fathers of the Republic, he misnames equality under the Constitution—in other words, the full power in the National Territories to compel fellow-men to unpaid toil, to separate husband and wife, and to sell little children at the auction block—then, sir, the chivalric Senator will conduct the

State of South Carolina out of the Union! Heroic knight! Exalted Senator! A second Moses come for a second exodus!"[18]

After that outburst Preston S. Brooks, a Representative from South Carolina and a kinsman of Senator Butler, came upon Sumner in the Senate chamber, busily writing letters after an adjournment. Without offering an opportunity for defense, Brooks swung blow after blow from a gutta-percha walking stick upon the Senator's head and shoulders. The cane broke, but Brooks beat on with the butt till Sumner, rising desperately from his seat, staggered and fell in a pool of blood. From those blows the Senator from Massachusetts never fully recovered.

The year 1863 marked an important turn in the history of Senate obstruction. A little-heralded filibuster on the 2nd and 3rd of March, despite its small place upon the page of history as it has been written, looms large in interest and significance. A measure to "indemnify" the President of the United States for having suspended the writ of habeas corpus was the incentive for tactics unparalleled in the Senate even to this hour. The administration considered the legislation necessary for the most effective prosecution of the war against the Confederacy. The war must not be impeded. Without an indemnifying law, officers of the government who had placed citizens under arrest might under some circumstances be personally liable for their actions. Opponents of the proposition feared arbitrary arrests by executive officials and insisted upon a continuance of regular judicial protection.

The filibuster itself occurred on the question of adopting the report of a committee of conference appointed to reconcile conflicting positions of the House and Senate on the bill; but spectacular opposition had developed even during earlier consideration in the Senate. Pyrotechnics began in earnest on the 27th of January when Senator Willard Saulsbury of Delaware cast aspersions upon President Lincoln: "I have seen him and conversed with him, and I say here, in my place in the Senate of the United States, that I never did see or

---

[18] *ibid.*, 34th Cong., 1st Sess., Appendix, p. 530.

converse with so weak and imbecile a man as Abraham Lincoln, President of the United States." Now Senators may vituperate the President or most citizens in any way they please, short of profanity, without violating the rules; and a protest against the language of the Delaware Senator was unavailing. But when he referred in speaking of other Senators to "blackguardism that can be uttered on this floor" he transgressed the freedom of speech permissible under the rules by impugning the conduct of other Senators, and Vice President Hannibal Hamlin promptly ruled him out of order. Appealing from that decision, Saulsbury launched forth in mad fury: "Sir . . . if I wanted to paint a despot, a man perfectly regardless of every constitutional right of the people, whose sworn servant, not ruler, he is, I would paint the hideous form of Abraham Lincoln. If that be treason—"

Here the Vice President ruled that the Senator was not speaking upon an appeal and ordered him to take his seat.

Shouted Saulsbury, "The voice of freedom is out of order in the councils of the nation!"

When the Vice President threatened to order the sergeant at arms to take the Senator in charge, Saulsbury muttered, "Let him take me."

The Vice President gave the order and after brief urging the sergeant at arms persuaded the Senator to leave the chamber. The decision of the chair to which Saulsbury had objected was then promptly sustained by the Senate, and debate continued. But in a short time Saulsbury was once more on the floor persisting in his recalcitrance, and the sergeant at arms was again ordered to take him in charge.

The yellowing pages of the *Congressional Globe* record mildly: "It was understood that Mr. Saulsbury refused to retire, but at a subsequent period he left the Chamber." This innocuous sentence must continue to stand as a notable example of official understatement, since actually the enraged Senator had levelled a gun at the sergeant at arms and threatened to shoot him on the spot. Only after a sweeping apology, offered by the Senator from Delaware two days later, did the Senate drop proceedings for expulsion.

The bill as the Senate preferred it was passed on the 27th of January, but not until the 2nd of March was it reported from conference. Immediately Senator James W. Wall of New Jersey suggested that it should go over "until tomorrow," Henry Wilson of Massachusetts suggested five o'clock that afternoon, and a general discussion developed. Lyman Trumbull of Illinois (then a Republican), who had submitted the report, wanted an assurance that factious opposition to delay the bill would not be attempted. Senator William A. Richardson, his Democratic colleague, replied, "We intend to express, at length, our opinions in reference to this whole measure, to which we are opposed." Lazarus W. Powell of Kentucky resented the charge of partisan opposition and added, "I looked upon that as an imputation that our object was to do what is commonly called fillibustering [sic]." It was finally agreed that the report should be considered at seven that evening, and at that hour it was laid before the Senate. Senator Wall took the floor for an extended opposing speech, and when he concluded at midnight Saulsbury of Delaware moved an adjournment. The yeas and nays were forced, but the motion was defeated 5 to 31. Senator Powell promptly took the floor for a long speech, being relieved for a time by Edgar Cowan of Pennsylvania and being interrupted occasionally by votes refusing to adjourn. Thus wore on the early morning hours of the 3rd of March. Powell was followed by James Asheton Bayard of Delaware, who yielded for an unsuccessful motion to adjourn; and at that point occurred an instance of high-handed parliamentary procedure till then altogether unprecedented in the Senate.

Republican Senator Samuel C. Pomeroy of Kansas sat in the chair; and in the momentary lull after the weary Senate had rejected the motion to adjourn, he said quickly in a low voice: "The question is on concurring in the report of the committee of conference. Those in favor of concurring in the report will say 'ay'; those opposed 'no.' The ayes have it. It is a vote. The report is concurred in."

So low had been the tone of the presiding officer that many Senators were unaware that action had been taken. When Trumbull moved immediately that the Senate consider another matter, Powell, evidently still unaware of the situation, insisted that consideration of the conference report be continued. In the ensuing discussion, the chair held that the report had already been passed. On that issue Bayard appealed from the decision of the chair; but, by a continuation of arbitrary procedure, no attention whatever was given the appeal. To the Delaware Senator's protest, "I appealed from the decision of the Chair a few moments ago, and I have a right to do that if there are any rights remaining," Wall replied dismally, "There are none." Adjournment was then voted at five o'clock in the morning.

When the Senate convened later in the day, reading of the journal was at first dispensed with by unanimous consent; but Preston King of New York soon protested and the journal was read. A great discussion at once arose over the proceedings of the night, and the minority denounced the procedure bitterly and at length. Argument was particularly hot over a doubt whether the chair had even put the "noes" in calling for a vote on the conference report; but a few Senators declared that the whole proceeding had been audible to them, and little progress was made. It developed that the House had already been informed of the Senate action in adopting the conference report; and a motion to ask the House to return it was defeated by 13 yeas to 25 nays. That was the test vote; and the minority found itself helpless beneath the ruthless weight of superior numbers. The filibuster had failed, but it had failed because of arbitrary action by the majority.

The defense for the action of Senator Pomeroy in calling for a vote, if there is any real parliamentary defense, rests in the fact that if no Senator is ready to speak it is time for the question. The burden of continuous talking must be upon those who wish to talk. But ignoring an appeal, despite the fact that it would probably be voted down, is altogether beyond the pale of parliamentary procedure. All things considered, the action of Senator Pomeroy in hastily calling a vote in the midst of obvious obstruction, coupled with refusal to entertain an appeal, is the most arbitrary proceeding in the history of Senate filibustering. Had it been continued as a regular policy, instead of being buried among almost forgotten Senate debates, there would have been little about which to write in these pages.

Moreover, the unsuccessful filibuster of 1863 is the first in Senate annals which can be said without shadow of doubt to have been truly intense. Earlier filibusters had been extended, but for the most part they were virtually uncontested; habitually the majority had abjectly even if impatiently waited for release by the minority. In 1863 the opponents of the filibuster employed strategy so forceful and effective that it has not to this day been outdone in the Senate. It is interesting, too, that this filibuster was staged near the end of a session when prospects for success might well have been brightest; it was organized with determination; and its participants utilized dilatory tactics as varied and as obstructive as the Senate had seen. Filibusterism as a potential champion of desperate causes had emerged full-panoplied into the Senate arena.

In 1865, as the 38th Congress neared its close, Charles Sumner and a few others contrived dilatory tactics to defeat a resolution recognizing a reconstructed state government in Louisiana. Military officers, under the direction of President Lincoln, had held an election and arranged the adoption of a constitution. But Sumner was determined that only Congress could authorize the erection of a state government, and he was also insistent upon more liberal terms of Negro franchise. When the resolution of approval became the business of the Senate on February 23, the Massachusetts Senator began a program of concerted opposition. He was not a solitary minority, however, and opponents of the proposition, both Democrats and Republicans, joined in obstruction by long speeches and dilatory motions. Lyman Trumbull of Illinois denounced the procedure as "a determination to browbeat the Senate"; but Sumner countered that he thought the measure "dangerous" and therefore that he was justified "in employing all the instruments . . . in the arsenal of parliamentary warfare."[19] The session would end on the 4th of March, and the remaining time for important business was growing brief; on the 27th of February, after hours of fruitless argument, the majority abandoned the resolution. The filibuster had been mild and unexciting, by the standards of a modern obstructionist, but it brought victory to its sponsors. Louisiana waited until 1868 for Congressional recognition of statehood.

As a matter of fact, sixteen years were to elapse after the stirring events of 1863 before the Senate witnessed a filibuster of equal magnitude. But the unprecedented episodes of 1879 marked still another development in Senate experience with obstruction. Without in any way encountering arbitrary action or sharp practice by the majority, a filibustering minority turned the Senate deliberations into a hopeless scene of inaction, confusion, and turmoil.

Democratic majorities in Congress proposed to repeal federal election laws, particularly statutes allowing the use of federal troops in state elections. They contended that soldiers could be used to coerce elections in the South, and they called upon lovers of liberty to unite in opposing military interference with free expression at the polls. Republicans pointed out that troops had not recently been employed at election places and probably would not be again, but they argued that armed intervention might sometime be necessary in any part of the country to preserve honest elections. Were not repeal efforts in actuality attempts to undo the humanitarian gains of the Civil War? Against such repeal all the perfervid oratory of the Republicans was called forth. James G. Blaine with clarion voice strove dramatically to accept the challenge in the Senate: "All the war measures of Abraham Lincoln are to be wiped out say leading Democrats! The Bourbons of France busied themselves, I believe, after the restoration in removing every trace of Napoleon's power and grandeur, even chiseling the 'N' from public monuments raised to perpetuate his glory; but the dead man's hand from Saint Helena reached out and destroyed them in their pride and in their folly. And I tell the Senators on the other side of this Chamber—I tell

19 *ibid.*, 38th Cong., 2nd Sess., p. 1108.

the Democratic party North and South—South in the lead and North following—that the slow, unmoving finger of scorn from the tomb of the martyred President on the prairies of Illinois will wither and destroy them. 'Though dead he speaketh.' "[20]

A Democratic rider to an army appropriation bill, providing that none of the money should be used to keep soldiers near polling places, caused President Hayes to veto the legislation; and the House failed to override the Presidential disapproval. But a new army appropriation bill passed by the House contained the rider in an ambiguous form, requiring that no money be used to maintain the army "as a police force to keep the peace at the polls"; and the measure became the unfinished business in the Senate on June 16, 1879. On the 17th the bill was debated, at times acrimoniously, and next day consideration was continued.

Republicans scathingly opposed even the mildly phrased rider preventing the use of the army in elections; and at about six in the evening of the 18th, organized filibustering was undertaken in earnest. Roscoe Conkling of New York, taking the lead in the fight, announced that the Republican minority would allow a vote the next day if they were given an opportunity to present their views on the bill, and moved an adjournment till the morrow. When that motion was defeated by 22 yeas to 25 nays, the session became and remained all night one of unprecedented parliamentary confusion. In reckless and undignified mood the minority relied, as never before, almost exclusively upon dilatory motions, roll-call votes, and quorum breaking to accomplish their purpose. On every roll-call vote (requiring a quorum) the Republicans sat silent in their seats, refusing to answer their names and forcing the Senate to direct the sergeant at arms to bring in absent Senators willing to be counted as present. By the Senate precedents, a quorum consisted of a majority of the membership answering to roll call; if Senators refused to answer, they were not present—however loudly they might be clamoring over some point of order within the next minute.

[20] 9 Cong. Record, p. 418.

Conkling, himself among the foremost of the Republican orators, pilloried the proposed legislation. "What is this Army bill?" he demanded. "It is a juggle, in my opinion a contemptible juggle and subterfuge. It is an attempt, by indirection, by stealth, by trick, by an act which is to operate as a fraud, to do that of which we had high-sounding proclamation at the end of the last session."

The withering answer of the Democrats was given by the scholarly Lucius Q. C. Lamar, Senator from Mississippi. Said he: "With reference to the charge of bad faith that the Senator from New York has intimated toward those of us who have been engaged in opposing these motions to adjourn, I have only to say that if I am not superior to such attacks from such a source, I have lived in vain. It is not my habit to indulge in personalities; but I desire to say here to the Senator that in intimating anything inconsistent, as he has done, with perfect good faith, I pronounce his statement a falsehood, which I repel with all the unmitigated contempt that I feel for the author of it."

Replied Conkling, after desultory bickering, "I understood the Senator from Mississippi to state in plain and unparliamentary language that the statement of mine to which he referred was a falsehood, if I caught his word aright. Mr. President, this not being the place to measure with any man the capacity to violate decency, to violate the rules of the Senate, or to commit any of the improprieties of life, I have only to say that if the Senator—the member, from Mississippi, did impute or intended to impute to me a falsehood, nothing except the fact that this is the Senate would prevent my denouncing him as a blackguard and a coward." [Applause in the galleries.]

The very title—"member," not "Senator"—which the New Yorker employed to describe his tormenter was a studied insult.

But Lamar would have the last word: "Mr. President, I have only to say that the Senator from New York understood me correctly. I did mean to say just precisely the words, and all that they imported. I beg pardon of the Senate for the unparliamentary language. It was very harsh; it was very severe; it was such as no good man would deserve and no brave man would wear." [Applause on the floor and in the galleries.]

It was a night of sleeplessness and commotion, of points of order and heated dissension over procedure, of bitter feelings and strong language. The President pro tempore, the venerable Allen G. Thurman of Ohio, said upon the floor: "This is a new idea which has been inaugurated tonight. . . . I have known bills talked to death . . . but the course of first a motion to adjourn and a call of the yeas and nays on that, and then a motion to dispense with the call of the Senate and then the yeas and nays on that, and then this dilatory motion and that dilatory motion, has never belonged to this end of the Capitol, according to my knowledge or information, until this night."

Under the leadership of Conkling, with the active cooperating generalship of James G. Blaine and others, the Republican filibuster continued unabated till an already exhausted Senate adjourned at 11:51 on the morning of June 19 to convene at noon, nine minutes later. Conkling immediately demanded that the journal be read, but obviously it had not been completed. The President pro tempore ruled that the Senate could not be prevented from transacting business because the journal had not been completed. Conkling appealed, Frank Hereford of West Virginia moved to lay the appeal on the table, and the yeas and nays revealed the Republicans silent and no quorum voting.

Roll calls were futile, and discussion arose whether the chair might not count a quorum if one were physically though silently present. The President pro tempore held that the chair could count the Senate to determine the actual presence of a quorum; but at the same time he believed that a quorum must actually vote to make effective a roll-call vote requiring the presence of a quorum. To decide that a quorum is present in the chamber would avoid the necessity of sending the sergeant at arms for more Senators, and would slightly ameliorate the paralyzing effects of the filibuster; but under the ruling of the chair, the necessity remained that a quorum of Senators actually vote if the body were to legislate.

To count a quorum present to allow the Senate to proceed to business, and to count a quorum on a vote in order to declare a motion carried, are different things. The President pro tempore (Senator Thurman) was willing to uphold the former but not the latter. That his view would nearly thirty years thereafter be enlarged to include the second step, on the basis of his own ruling, he could not foresee; that was to be the work of another generation.

Routine matters having been disposed of after the reconvening on June 19, the chair laid before the Senate the unfinished business, the army appropriation bill with its rider. Conkling's appeal upon the issue of reading the journal resulted in no further action. The exhausted Senate adjourned within two hours. But on the 20th the Republicans resumed their dilatory tactics, this time by long speeches. Finally, however, they surrendered and the bill with its rider was passed 32 to 19 in the early hours of the 21st; at two o'clock in the morning the Senate adjourned. Many Republican Senators were doubtless glad that the bill had passed, particularly since its rider was really innocuous and virtually meaningless; and President Hayes evidently considered the rider a Democratic retreat from the earlier demand of absolute prohibition of the use of troops at the polls, for he promptly approved the measure. The filibuster, as a device to prevent passage of the rider, despite the intense stage which it reached and the elaborate tactics employed, was unsuccessful.

It is both striking and singular that thus far in the Senate history the filibuster had been used, with increasing boisterousness, primarily to prevent the passage of legislation. But, on the whole, it had been a device remarkably unsuccessful; almost every obstructed measure was eventually passed despite filibustering opposition. The day of ruthless prostration of the Senate still belonged to the future.

CHAPTER III

FILIBUSTERING UNRESTRAINED

CHAPTER III

FILIBUSTERING UNRESTRAINED

IF dilatory tactics upon the Senate floor, increasing in turbulence and boldness for more than fifty years, had largely been fruitless expenditures of energy in a parliamentary sense, the closing decades of the nineteenth century reveal another story. Tactics remained essentially the same, but boldness gave way to ruthlessness, and obstruction began to be bounded only by the daring ingenuity of its designers. If courtesy required restraint, it was forgotten; if dignity demanded moderation, it was sacrificed to political or sectional advantage. With the determination never to surrender short of sheer physical exhaustion came success for the devotees of filibustering. So intensive became the use of dilatory tactics in a body of increasing membership, so determined were Senators never to yield principles to politeness, that for decades the concerted filibuster held, and to some extent still holds, its place as a well-nigh invincible recourse.

That the filibuster could be a weapon of success even with relatively little exertion the Republican minority demonstrated in the closing days of the 46th Congress, early in March 1881. Democrats moved again and again to go into executive session to take action upon appointments of retiring President Hayes. Republicans for reasons of their own refused to consider those appointments, forced roll-call votes upon motions, and sat silent in their seats upon the votes. It was a factional fight; obstructionists knew that delay would permit the newly elected Republican President, James A. Garfield, to fill the vacant offices. The Democrats were never able to muster a quorum from their own ranks, and as a result nominations went unconsidered.

On March 4 the Senate was convened in special session to consider the Garfield appointments; and for more than two months the body was racked with filibusters which succeeded—and for weeks succeeded to the exclusion of virtually everything else. Both Republicans and Democrats, in their respective ventures in obstruction, demonstrated that they could and would block business until the *sine qua non* of their demands should be met.

Control of the Senate organization in the preceding 46th Congress had been in the hands of the Democrats; but prospects for Republican control in the 47th Congress were bright. A full membership at that time consisted of 76 Senators: 37 were regular Democrats, David Davis of Illinois was known as an independent, and General William Mahone of Virginia called himself a Readjuster. In local politics the Virginia Readjusters, who demanded reduction of the state debt, had broken with the regular or "Bourbon" Democrats, but it was supposed that on national issues, having supported Hancock for President, they would follow the Democratic standard. If all these votes could be counted for the Democratic cause, Senate control would belong to them by a majority of one. If, in a full Senate, either Davis or Mahone should vote with the Republicans, a tie would result, with the Republican Vice President, Chester A. Arthur, rendering up the victory to his own party. As a matter of fact it soon became apparent that General Mahone was at least likely to follow such a course. However, the Republican ranks had been reduced by the death of Matt Carpenter of Wisconsin and the appointment of three Senators, James G. Blaine of Maine, William Windom of Minnesota, and Samuel J. Kirkwood of Iowa, to the Cabinet of President Garfield. In order that the party might achieve victory, action must be prevented until four Republican states should fill vacancies and the new Senators be sworn.

From the 4th through the 9th of March no action was pressed, but on the 10th Senator George H. Pendleton of Ohio proposed the election of committees controlled by the Democrats. Under the rules, the matter went over till the following day (Friday), when it was debated at length. The Republicans refused to accede to organization in such fashion when victory for them was merely a question of convenient delay. The independent Senator Davis announced that he would adhere to the Democratic position on the question of organization, but no progress was made and the Senate adjourned till Monday. When the body reconvened two Republican Senators were sworn, but the Democrats still had the votes to win if the question could be brought to a head.

The famous Southern orator and former Senator in the Confederate Congress, Benjamin H. Hill of Georgia, determined to force the insurgent Virginian, Mahone, into an open statement of his position. Hill vehemently contended that a full half of the Senate had been elected as Democrats and that with the vote of the independent Senator Davis only Democrats could organize the chamber unless some Senator should be guilty of treachery. "Who can he be? Do you receive him with affection? Do you receive him with respect? Is such a man worthy of your association? Such a man is not worthy to be a Democrat. Is he worthy to be a Republican?"

The clever and biting speech of the Georgian brought General Mahone to his feet in fierce resentment. "I do not intend," he snapped, "that any Senator on this floor shall undertake to criticize my conduct by innuendoes, a method not becoming this body. . . . You have been notified that I was supremely indifferent to what you did; that I had no wish to prefer, and was indifferent to your performances; that I should stand on this floor representing in part the people of the State of Virginia, for whom I have the right to speak. . . . The gentleman may not be advised that the Legislature which elected me did not require that I should state either that I was a Democrat or anything else. I suppose he could not get here from Georgia unless he was to say that he was a Democrat, anyhow. . . . Now, I want the gentleman to know henceforth and forever here is a man, sir, that dares stand up and speak for himself without regard to caucus in all matters."

After long continued applause in the galleries and on the floor had greeted the bold defiance of the Virginia Senator, Hill retorted: "Mr. President, I hope nobody imagines that I rise to make any particular reply to the remarkable exhibition we have just seen. . . . I say to the Senator from Virginia that neither Jefferson, nor Madison, nor Henry, nor Washington, nor Leigh, nor Tucker, nor any of the long list of great men that Virginia has produced ever accepted a commission to represent one party and came here and represented another."

That imputation Mahone promptly branded as "unwarranted and untrue," but Hill passed on to pose a query. "I should like to ask the gentleman a question: Was he not acting with the Democratic party, and was he not elected as a Democrat to this body? Answer that question."

"Quickly, sir," came the reply. "I was elected as a Readjuster. Do you not know what they are?"

Vice President Arthur rapped with his gavel to restore order before the Georgia Senator could be heard. "I understand," Hill declared, "that there are in Virginia what are called Readjuster Democrats and debt-paying Democrats, or something of that kind, but as I understand they are all Democrats. We have nothing to do with that issue. We are not to settle the debt of Virginia in the Senate Chamber; but I ask the Senator again, was he not elected to this body as a member of the national Democratic party?"

General Mahone, though diminutive in size, was never lacking in boldness. "I will answer you, sir," he said. "No. You have got the answer now."

The die was cast. With the aid of Mahone the Republicans were sure of success merely by resorting to obstruction in order to gain a few more days. The filibuster was for the most part uncontested, and by Friday, the 18th of March, the Republican contingent had regained its full strength. Thereupon Henry B. Anthony of Rhode Island moved as an amendment to the resolution for committee organization a personnel favorable to the Republicans. The vote was taken: 37 yeas, 37 nays, 2 absent. Vice President Arthur voted in the affirmative, and his party received the fruits of its filibuster. But the bargain was clear. William Mahone, a Confederate major general and new to the Senate, had been made through Republican support chairman of the Committee on Agriculture.

Five days later, on the 23rd of March, the Republicans again undertook to exploit their alliance with Senator Mahone. Henry L. Dawes of Massachusetts moved to elect officers for the Senate—in effect to turn out the existing Democratic incumbents. Among the nominees of the Republicans were George C. Gorham for secretary and Harrison H. Riddleberger for sergeant at arms. The bestowal of that office upon Riddleberger, himself a leading Virginia Readjuster and actually a Presidential elector for the Democratic Hancock, was to be another concession to Senator Mahone. But this bargain was more than the Democrats could brook; they rose in defiance, relentless and unquenchable.

Joseph E. Brown, governor of Georgia during the days of the Confederacy, propounded the major Democratic strategy: simply the alternation of dilatory motions, as Conkling had maneuvered in 1879, for the purpose of so involving the Senate that it should be bound helpless in the intricate skein of its own rules. "Old Joe," known from his sanctimonious air as "the Mormon Elder," proclaimed in his precise and solemn fashion: "We are ready at every moment to go into executive session and do the proper business of the session. . . . If you are not ready to do that, then we will invite you to adjourn, and if you will not adjourn, we will invite you to go back to the business for which you were called together by your President, and we will continue that operation until we see justice done. . . . We may be here to June; we have till December."

Conscientious Senator George F. Hoar, Republican of Massachusetts, shocked at the implications of the bold threat and minimizing the recent performance of his own party, replied: "There have been instances very numerous elsewhere, some instances here, of what is called filibustering in order to obtain what the minority deemed a reasonable and proper delay in regard to the action of the Senate or the House upon pending measures by motions of this class; but this has been the first time in the history of this country that any gentleman sustaining the character of a Senator of the

United States has declared that the will which should finally and to the end govern the Senate of the United States should be the will of a minority and not of a majority of its members. . . . I say that the honorable Senator from Georgia has in my judgment affirmed the most unconstitutional doctrine, full of treason in substance, ever uttered within the walls of this Chamber by the lips of any Senator. . . ."

The Republicans two days later met in caucus to consider policy in the face of a determined filibuster. It was decided that they should stand firm and keep the resolution before the Senate. But the Democrats could not be shaken in their position; hours upon hours were consumed by long speeches and by motion after motion voted upon by the yeas and nays. The more votes taken, the more constantly the Republicans would be tortured by attendance to defeat the motions. Republican attendance was likewise compelled in order to keep a quorum and permit Senate procedure to continue.

Persistent and extended as were the Democratic filibustering tactics, they were at no time contested with every potential resource of the majority. Adjournments for three days at week ends were permitted; all-night or continuous sessions were not undertaken; no one attempted to be harsh with the minority. Some Republicans had little liking for an alliance of votes which smacked so loudly of a partisan bargain. Privately, some of them sympathized with the Democratic point of view. Of the two candidates, Riddleberger was no Republican; and Gorham had been on the "repudiation" side of financial issues.[1]

But in another caucus, on the 4th of April, the Republicans once more decided to continue their resistance and to insist upon the election of their candidates to Senate offices. They agreed that no motion to consider executive business, for which the session had been called, should be allowed to break the deadlock. Two major reasons influenced the decision: (1) the Republicans contended that the majority should rule and that the minority should not be allowed

[1] *New York Herald*, March 29, 1881.

to thwart them; (2) the Virginia alliance, offering an opportunity for enhancing the Republican cause in the South, appealed to many as a sound policy which should not be abandoned.[2]

Still Democratic resourcefulness gave no sign of abating. For a month longer the session was deadlocked through resentment and its vigorous expression. The minority would not yield; they were obviously inflexible; short of majority surrender, the situation seemed hopeless.

At times the debates grew acrimonious and bitter. No one, Democrat or Republican, could forget that potential Republican control of the chamber sprang solely from alliance with a man whom most people called a Democrat, the Readjuster Senator from Virginia. In a warm debate Republican Edward H. Rollins of New Hampshire taunted the Democrats with their inability to make any arrangement which would bring them the vote of General Mahone. Instantly Hill of Georgia interposed with the caustic comment, "But we would not have bought it."[3]

That remark, called to Mahone's attention, aroused his intense resentment, and on April 13 he rose in the Senate to say: "I come to ask the Senator from Georgia now, as this language in one aspect to my mind implies either that my vote had been or could be bought, whether in this language he intended to convey any such impression?"

Hill insisted upon having the Senate floor in his own right before he would answer; he would run no risk of being cut off in his reply. "I deny," he said to the Senator from Virginia, "that we buy your vote, I deny that we wanted to buy your vote, and we deny that we would have bought your vote; we would not have given you a fig for your vote. That is what I intended to deny. I did not charge that the Senator had sold his vote. I would not charge, unless I knew the fact to be a fact, that any Senator on this floor had sold his vote. If the Senator wants me to go further and say what I believe, that is a different question; and I wish to say to

[2] *ibid.*, April 5, 1881.
[3] 12 *Cong. Record*, p. 235.

the Senator now that if he proposes to call everybody in this country to account who has a belief on that subject, he has a heavy task upon his hands."

Mahone was not satisfied to let the matter rest here: "As the Senator from Georgia fails here to answer directly a direct question, I give him a problem to solve; he shall have a conundrum. I say to him if he did mean to imply that my vote had been or could be bought, he states that or undertakes to convey that which is foul, untruthful, false, and that no man less than a coward will make such a statement."

Senate deliberations were momentarily interrupted when the galleries burst out in applause. But Hill closed the incident upon a note of defiance: "If the Senator thinks that he can suppress gentlemen in discussion in this Senate by assuming to play the bully, he has made a mistake."

On the 3rd of May the majority recognized in caucus that the minority could never be subdued. They agreed that on the morrow they would vote for an executive session to consider business which had now been long and unavailingly before the Senate.[4] The next day Senator Dawes, implying that the resolution to elect new officers would be brought up later, explained on the floor that the consideration of executive business was imperatively necessary. His motion for that purpose was at once unanimously approved.

But after only two days of executive sessions, Dawes tried once again to press forward the resolution for Senate officers. Filibustering was immediately renewed, and the Republicans at last became convinced that the Democrats had forgotten neither their tactics nor their determination. The Senate went once more into executive session, and the resolution so offensive to the minority was dead. The filibuster had flourished in full vigor from the 24th of March through the 3rd of May—a period of forty-one calendar days, during twenty-six of which the Senate sat in helpless and inglorious session. On May 16 Roscoe Conkling and Thomas C. Platt, Republican Senators from New York, resigned because of a patronage quarrel

4 *New York Herald*, May 4, 1881.

with President Garfield. With their departure disappeared all hope of a Republican majority. Further consideration of the long-fought resolution, had it been desired, would have been impossible.

Early in 1890 the Senate was treated to a filibuster of different pattern, an instance of positive rather than of negative purpose, and conducted for an extended period of time primarily by a single Senator. Never intense, it was none the less a remarkable demonstration, and for sustained personal obstruction it was then perhaps unique.

Witty and suave Henry W. Blair, New Hampshire Republican, had, with the nominal support of his party, brought forward an education bill, which bore his name in popular title, for the federal aid of schooling. For years he had advocated distribution of federal money to the states on the basis of illiteracy. Southern states would receive the largest sums. Advocates pointed to the social importance of an educated electorate and to the need for helping every state to fit its citizens for intelligent participation in a democracy. Opponents, however, saw chiefly the dangers of centralization, of federal encroachment upon the states, and of governmental paternalism which would sap from local communities the initiative to do for themselves.

The education bill had on several occasions been before Congress, and on February 5, 1890, it again became the business of the Senate. But the Senator from New Hampshire found that he lacked the requisite votes to pass it. Thereupon he adopted, as he himself later confessed, "the tactics of getting time." From the 5th of February till the 20th of March, when in session, the Senate considered for the most part the measure of the New Hampshire Senator. For two weeks, almost every working day, Senator Blair talked upon the subject himself; later he encouraged others to speak, whether they favored or opposed the legislation. In the meantime the Senator labored and argued with his colleagues till he believed that, with the casting vote of the Vice President, the bill would pass; and he therefore allowed it to come to a vote on the 20th of March. But at the last minute two Senators decided to vote in the negative instead

of the affirmative, and the day was lost. Voting himself in the negative in order to be eligible to move reconsideration, Senator Blair
saw the bill for which he had filibustered defeated 31 to 37. He
moved reconsideration, but at that stage the bill rested,[5] never to be
revived. Technically, the filibuster was lost almost by accident when
success was apparently within reach; but the episode bore unmistakable witness not only to the power of one man to tie up the
business of the Senate but also to his potential ability to force by
sheer persistence reluctant acquiescence in his own terms lest,
through long delay, legislation of every kind be defeated. Not in
the result but in the example of the obstruction lies its importance.

The Blair obstruction, as it happened, was little more than a
skirmish in the interlude between two momentous Democratic filibusters. The Democrats had been successful in an extended and
spectacular, even if relatively uncontested, parliamentary encounter
in 1881; and within ten years they were to be equally successful
in one not only truly intense but even more extended and far more
spectacular.

The celebrated "Force Bill" filibuster of 1890-1891 is even to this
day one of the most famous of them all; it shook not only the Senate
but also the country as few parliamentary battles have done.

It was the Republican plan to enact legislation, already passed
by the House, for federal supervision of Congressional elections, a
measure aimed especially against Negro disqualification and in-
timidation in the South. Friends of the proposal called it the Federal Elections Bill; its enemies termed it the Force Bill. Many Republicans believed that it would encourage genuine expression of popular sentiment and improve the chances of their party in the South.
Democrats regarded it as an attack upon self government and an
invitation for conflict between the races. Designated to steer the
measure through the shoals of Senate procedure was George F. Hoar
of Massachusetts, who moved on December 2, 1890, to consider the
bill. The motion to consider was carried by 41 yeas against 30 nays,

5 cf. Blair's remarks, 22 Cong. Record, pp. 322-3, Dec. 11, 1890.

and it was plain that enough votes were available for enactment if a final vote could be reached.

The next day the Democrats met in caucus for an hour and a half to discuss the perturbing situation. From their conference came the solidifying decision to resist the bill at every point; but—as if the minority were fearful of a none too respectable term—word went out that they would not filibuster![6]

Full debate was the program, and Democratic Senators spoke at tremendous length to galleries crowded with spectators eager to witness the struggle for delay. Whether or not the name comported with dignity, a determined filibuster was actually in progress.

Republican Senators in caucus decided upon long sessions to tire out the Democrats; and already there was talk, if that should not be found sufficient, of a movement for cloture, or a rule for closing debate.[7] Indeed, Senator Nelson W. Aldrich of Rhode Island two days before Christmas served notice that he would later move an amendment to the rules to close debate by majority vote. But not all was harmonious within the Republican ranks. Preston B. Plumb of Kansas, for one, was heard to say that if the disputed measure were not soon disposed of, he would move to displace it with a coinage bill. The silver men were growing restive. It was apparent that Republicans were close to a split: some favored consideration of the elections bill, some demanded a chance for a silver bill, and others were inclined to shelve both.[8] Plainly the Democrats were of no disposition to yield; the talk went on despite what amounted to a respite of only four days for Christmas and a similar period for New Year's. But with the brief holidays over, the impatient silverites would wait no longer. On January 5, 1891, Republican William M. Stewart of Nevada moved consideration of currency legislation; and, through a coalition of Democrats and silver Republicans, his motion prevailed by 34 yeas to 29 nays.

[6] *New York Herald,* Dec. 4, 1890.
[7] *ibid.,* Dec. 11, 1890.
[8] *ibid.,* Dec. 10, 21, 1890.

Democrats breathed easily once more, believing that a Force Bill had now only the faintest of prospects. But on January 14 consideration of the currency bill was ended by its passage, with provisions for the free coinage of silver. Advocates of the cause of silver had gained a victory, but one which was soon to be lost in an unsympathetic House. Senator Hoar immediately moved that the Elections Bill be once more the business of the Senate. The vote stood 33 to 33; Vice President Levi P. Morton voted "yea" and the motion was carried.

The Democrats were seriously alarmed; they resolved at once to talk if necessary till the session ended on the 4th of March. But the Republicans were determined to overcome the minority in a test of sheer physical endurance by holding the Senate in continuous session, and on the evening of January 16 a motion to adjourn was defeated 27 to 32. The Senate remained in session throughout the night and all the next day till six o'clock in the evening. Through the weary night of January 16-17, Senator Charles J. Faulkner of West Virginia held the floor, occupying it nominally for eleven and one-half hours and establishing a record which set the nation agog. Actually, the exhausted Senate was unable to muster a quorum for approximately eight hours of that time; and under the rule that the work of the Senate must stop in the absence of a quorum, when a point of order to that effect has been made, the Senator was happily enabled to refrain from talking.

It was 1:20 o'clock in the morning when a formal call of the roll first revealed the absence of a quorum. Only motions to request or require the attendance of absent Senators, or a motion to adjourn, could be in order without a quorum present; and the crippled Senate proceeded to direct the sergeant at arms to request Senators to appear.

After almost an hour of "requesting" had resulted in no arrivals, the sergeant at arms was instructed to compel attendance of Senators, excusing only those who were ill. The hours dragged on, and at ten minutes before three o'clock in the morning enough Senators had been mustered to account for a quorum. But before the hands of the clock had reached the hour of three a quorum was no longer in the hall; Senators had quietly but effectively disappeared. Once more the sergeant at arms undertook his searches, continuing intermittently for the remainder of the night; but the Democrats had no intention of assisting him in his labors. They congregated even in the Capitol itself, lounging here and there and whiling away the time, but they refused to be induced into the session of the Senate. Why should they assist Republicans to break the filibuster? The sergeant at arms solemnly reported that James H. Berry of Arkansas, found in the cloakroom, had suggested that the Senate be informed "that he would come when he got ready," and that Matthew C. Butler of South Carolina had joined him in the defiance. Doubtless the sergeant at arms, impressed by the importance of his superiors, was of no mind, in obeying his instructions to produce attendance, to take literally the word "compel." Meanwhile the Senate continued to murder sleep, although not till 9:30 in the morning could a quorum be maintained. But there came no pause in the wearisome proceedings. By the end of the day the rigors of continuous session proved to be beyond the endurance of the majority, and that strategy was abandoned.

A scheme for cloture then became the program of the Republicans, and on January 20 Senator Aldrich moved consideration of his resolution. Democratic oratory was promptly turned against the cloture proposition; the Force Bill would never be passed by means of a change in the Senate rules if talk could prevent it.

A resolution for cloture, itself debatable, would have a real opportunity for passage only if the presiding officer should be willing to rule upon points of order in a firm fashion favorable to action. Much depended upon Republican Vice President Morton; and the leaders, none too sure of his cooperation in questionable parliamentary maneuvering, suggested that he go to Florida for his health. The plan was obviously to place in the chair some Senator more subservient to party dictation. However, the Vice President insisted that he would preside, and the hope of the Republicans to break the filibuster remained with him.[9]

The plan of Senator Aldrich was to allow debate to proceed for a time on the cloture resolution, then to make a point of order that debate had gone far enough and that an immediate vote should be had. It was admitted that the Vice President would overrule such a point. No Senate parliamentarian could respectably do otherwise. But, when the point had been overruled, an appeal would be taken; and Aldrich hoped that the Vice President would cooperate to the extent of ruling (though against precedent) that the appeal itself could not be debated. Aldrich evidently believed that if a vote could be taken on the appeal the Republicans would reverse the decision of the chair, on the basis of a distinction between dilatory and legitimate debate, and thus make possible an immediate vote on cloture.[10] One embarrassing difficulty remained: Would the Vice President cooperate even to the indispensable extent of ruling undebatable an appeal from a decision of the chair? Such a ruling would unquestionably endanger the reputation for parliamentary fairness of the man who made it.

There were the strongest indications, as a matter of fact, that Vice President Morton would not enter into the understanding. On the 22nd of January, for instance, Blair of New Hampshire, when an appeal was pending upon an entirely different matter, insisted that debate was not in order. The Vice President replied, "The Chair is of opinion that debate is in order." Blair attempted to cover or weaken the reply by saying, "At the election of the Chair"; but debate proceeded, and it was plain that the Vice President must reverse himself if he were later to rule otherwise. But Aldrich and others evidently held hopes that they could still force or persuade the Vice President to rule in their favor;[11] and there was always the possibility that some Senator of more favorable mind could be got in the chair if the Vice President were temporarily absent.

[9] Robert McElroy, *Levi Parsons Morton* (New York, 1930), p. 189.
[10] *New York Herald*, Jan. 24, 1891.
[11] *ibid.*, Jan. 27, 1891.

The Democrats were more than ever alarmed at the turn of events. Fearful that a way would be found to close debate and thereby pass the hated measure, they worked desperately to win by some compromise or stratagem enough votes to displace the bill. At last they secured the pledged support of Senator James Donald Cameron of Pennsylvania,[12] and with silverites as allies they were ready to accomplish their purpose. On the 26th of January Republican silverite Edward O. Wolcott of Colorado moved to consider an apportionment bill. The vote would be close, it was seen at once, and there was a sharp skirmish in which Aldrich fought bitterly, even desperately, to count pairs in such a way that the Elections Bill would be saved; but when the final vote was taken Wolcott's motion, supported by half a dozen Republicans, prevailed by 35 yeas to 34 nays.

The filibusterers had won after a battle fought intermittently from December 2 to January 26, in which the Senate had been subjected to thirty-three calendar days of actual obstruction against the "Force Bill" and the cloture resolution. Senator Hoar, impressed by the vehemence of the opposition to the measure which he had unsuccessfully piloted, wrote in his memoirs: "The Election Bill deeply excited the whole country. Its supporters were denounced by the Democratic papers everywhere, North and South, with a bitterness which I hardly knew before that the English language was capable of expressing."[13] John T. Morgan of Alabama marked the end of the long, fierce struggle with its cherished victory by crying out in the Senate, "Mr. President, have I leave to hang up my 'bruised arms for monuments?'"

Filibustering against the Federal Elections Bill had supplied the most remarkable spectacle of obstruction then known to the Senate, and the country was amazed. When, in 1893, a still longer if perhaps less bitter struggle paralyzed the august assemblage, there was real national concern over the conduct and future of the Senate.

---

[12] ibid.

[13] George F. Hoar, *Autobiography of Seventy Years* (New York, 1903), Vol. II, p. 156.

Such leaders of thought as Professors H. von Holst and John Bach McMaster, eminent historians, and Senator Henry Cabot Lodge wrote earnest articles discussing the problem.[14] Henry Jones Ford in 1898 remembered with apprehension the 1893 proceedings as an endeavor "to extort a compromise . . . an exhibition of the degradation of the Senate, which made a profound impression upon public opinion."[15] So genuine and so enduring was public perturbation over the lack of dignity and gravity in the Senate that even in 1897 the venerated George F. Hoar, Senator from Massachusetts, felt called upon to write a defense.[16] But like most outbursts of popular opinion, the clamor over Senate disturbances was allayed by the healing touch of time.

The occasion for a major outbreak of filibustering in 1893 was the avowed intent of President Cleveland and his followers to repeal the silver purchase provisions of existing law. The country was in the grip of financial stringency which historians have called the Panic of 1893. Banks failed, railroads and other important enterprises went into receivership, factories and shops closed their doors, men were thrown out of employment, and public confidence in business and even in the government was shaken to its foundations. Many financiers advised as a remedy the immediate repeal of the so-called Sherman Silver Purchase Law enacted as a compromise in 1890 and requiring the monthly purchase of 4,500,000 ounces of silver.

President Cleveland himself believed in such repeal and resolved to call a special session of Congress for that purpose. In the late spring, however, he and his physicians discovered that an ulcer in the roof of his mouth presented symptoms of malignancy and made urgent an immediate operation. The President was faced with both

[14] Von Holst, "Shall the Senate Rule the Republic?" *The Forum*, Vol. XVI (Nov. 1893), p. 263; McMaster, "How to Deal with a Filibustering Minority," *ibid*. (Dec. 1893), p. 470; Lodge, "Obstruction in the Senate," *The North American Review*, Vol. CLVII (Nov. 1893), p. 523.

[15] *The Rise and Growth of American Politics* (New York, 1898), pp. 270-1. See Robert Luce, *Legislative Procedure* (Boston, 1922), pp. 292-3.

[16] "Has the Senate Degenerated?" *The Forum*, Vol. XXIII (April 1897), p. 129.

a personal and a political crisis. In the midst of a national panic important business elements demanded repeal of the silver law. The Vice President was a staunch supporter of silver, and even a rumor of the dangerous malady, with the possibility of a change in the Chief Magistracy, would raise new perils of economic uncertainty. Firm action must be taken, and Congress was called into session for August 7. By that date, it was hoped, the President would be well.

Insistent upon secrecy, Cleveland submitted to an operation performed while the Presidential party cruised slowly on a yacht in the New York harbor. The upper left jaw was removed and later replaced with vulcanized rubber, the country being left in ignorance of the surgery and the convalescence.

When Congress convened, the President recommended repeal. Lines of battle were drawn; against the financial East stood the Far West and most of the South. Silverites from the latter sections demanded more silver, not less. Free and unlimited coinage was their goal, their panacea for the financial ills of the country.

Senate cleavage on the portentous issue was not primarily along party lines; it was a sectional rather than a partisan battle. Technically the filibuster began on the 29th of August when a House measure was reported in the Senate by Daniel W. Voorhees of Indiana, known as the "Tall Sycamore of the Wabash," who was administration leader for the financial fight. Silver Republicans with silver and "farmer" Democrats, under the generalship of Republican Fred T. Dubois of Idaho and others, formed the alliance which was to break all records for extended Senate obstruction. The genuine opponents of the filibuster were of course the administration Democrats. Repeal elements among the Republicans were too conscious of the political benefits resulting from the Democratic split to wish for immediate harmony. That staunch Republican, Senator Henry Cabot Lodge, expressed himself as wishing fervently that the dissension might continue unabated, at least until after the Massachusetts election.[17]

[17] Jeannette Paddock Nichols, "The Politics and Personalities of Silver Repeal in the United States Senate," *American Historical Review*, Vol. XLI (Oct. 1935), p. 33.

Every effort made by Voorhees to obtain an agreement for a vote was repulsed. He himself believed it futile to propose a cloture rule; for, as he admitted on the 19th of September, the discussion of it "would occupy the limit of the present session, the next session, or the entire Congress." It was his plan to force long though not yet continuous sessions, hoping to wear down the minority. The opponents of repeal talked and talked, one after another, in diffuse and turgid speeches. Among the most verbose were Senators John P. Jones and William M. Stewart of Nevada, William A. Peffer of Kansas, William V. Allen of Nebraska, and Henry M. Teller of Colorado. One stupendous speech by Jones of Nevada, requiring large parts of seven days for delivery, occupies one hundred of the great double-columned pages in the Appendix of the *Congressional Record*. Senator Stewart boasts in his *Reminiscences* that his own speeches fill between 200 and 250 pages of the *Record*.[18]

Some Senators, among them Orville H. Platt of Connecticut, George F. Hoar of Massachusetts, David B. Hill of New York, and later Jacob H. Gallinger of New Hampshire, introduced resolutions for cloture. Proposals for closing debate through majority action evoked stormy discussions. Henry Cabot Lodge contended on September 21 that "there is another right more sacred in a legislative body than the right of debate, and that is the right to vote"; but on the next day Henry M. Teller of Colorado retorted: "I have not learned in anything I have read in the teachings of the fathers that the right to vote exceeds in sacredness the right to speak; and I want to say, with all deference to the Senator from Massachusetts, that the rule he has indicated is the rule that Napoleon III laid down for the French Assembly, that the right to vote was of more importance than the right to speak." Teller went even further: "It is useless for anyone to say that the majority are capable of conducting things properly, and will always conduct things properly. There is nothing in the world more wicked and cruel than the majority; and govern-

[18] *Reminiscences of Senator William M. Stewart of Nevada* (New York, 1908), p. 315.

ments are instituted and preserved to protect minorities against majorities. Majorities protect themselves."

David Turpie of Indiana, although in favor of silver repeal and opposed to the purposes of the filibuster, nevertheless took the floor for a sweeping defense of unlimited debate. The framers of the Constitution, he contended, in requiring the yeas and nays upon any question to be recorded in the journal at the desire of one-fifth of those present, had meant to compel deliberation, to place in the hands of a minority a weapon to force delay.

Turpie looked beyond the scenes of parliamentary action and saw the threat of violence: "It is the fortune, sir, of free parliamentary government to be subject to the sleepless vigil of dissent, of resistance, and of that sort of resistance which may end in revolution. The shadows of agitation and of revolution are constantly following the feet of those who are engaged in free parliamentary discussion and legislation. Behind obstruction at a greater or less distance is always agitation, and at some distance and at some time may be revolution.

"We have been frequently entertained here [he continued] with a description of the hardships, and I do not wish to disparage them, of continuous session, of night sittings. They are very feeble antetypes, they are very frail mimic representations of the campfire and bivouac, but they do foreshadow them. I very much doubt whether the establishment of cloture in this body would tend to increase the chances of public order, of public security, of wholesome agitation, and of legitimate resistance."[19]

Said Matthew C. Butler of South Carolina on October 4: "I am asked, and the question has been asked over and over again, what, then, is to be done if we are not to reach a vote? I reply, compromise." Mr. Calhoun, he declared, had pointed out that the conservative principle in constitutional government is compromise, and that the conservative principle in absolute government is force.

At last, in mid-October, John M. Palmer of Illinois burst out in disgust: "I have been kept here night after night listening to

[19] 25 *Cong. Record*, pp. 1703-4.

speeches, not debate, listening to speeches that it is asserted in the public prints were intended to consume time, not to inform the Senate, but to consume time. I submit that except in the methods employed, in the instruments employed, there is no difference between that and revolution, that and armed resistance. There was a time in the history of this country when men chose to take up arms to resist the will of a majority."

In the meantime, however, the Senate continued to be subjected to speech after speech of tedious length and excruciating boredom. Voorhees determined that he would resort to continuous session to break the obstruction. After the Senate convened at eleven o'clock on the morning of Wednesday, October 11, it remained in unbroken but troubled session till 1:45 in the morning of Friday the 13th. The minority utilized the most strenuous dilatory tactics to harass the majority. Talk of the most prolonged variety was of course the major stratagem. Allen of Nebraska, for instance, occupied the floor with interruptions for fourteen hours.

The minority unhesitatingly, even gleefully, also employed frequent dilatory motions, roll-call votes, and quorum calls to torture the unhappy majority. Indeed, members of the majority were in far more desperate straits than the minority; for minority leaders, sitting calmly in their seats, refused to answer their names on roll-call votes and thus broke a technical quorum of the august but helpless Senate. If a quorum was to be maintained, majority Senators found it necessary to stay in the chamber; if they slipped away for rest, a quorum disappeared and the business of the body, such as it was, came to a halt. And that, they believed, was no way to stop a filibuster.

At best the Senate found itself in a predicament, depending upon the point of view, either ludicrous or humiliating. A Senator would rise solemnly to make a trivial motion and demand the yeas and nays. Duly seconded, the request would result in calling the roll for a vote, when obstructionists, including perhaps the Senator who made the motion, would remain silent when their names were called. Less than half the Senate answering to the roll call, the presiding officer would announce that no quorum was present, though a quorum sat within plain sight of everyone. But, as no quorum had responded upon a roll-call vote, the roll would be called again merely to determine whether Senators were present. This time Senators would answer; a quorum. Once more a roll-call vote would elicit only a few responses; no quorum. Another call for those present; a quorum. But no quorum answered upon a vote. And so on, hour after hour, ending only when the vexed majority could bring in enough of their own forces to produce a quorum upon a vote and thus break the deadlock.

Infuriated, Joseph N. Dolph of Oregon once rose to voice his exasperation: "Mr. President, that is disorderly conduct. It is a violation of the spirit of the rules of the Senate. That course is bringing the Senate into disrepute in the country and bringing scandal upon the Senate. I am myself getting very tired of this sort of thing."

Imperturbably Senator Isham G. Harris of Tennessee, sometimes known from his long mustaches as "the Mandarin," replied: "I am sorry the Senator from Oregon is tired, and being tired I think the best remedy would be to sit down and rest. It would be a relief to him and to the Senate."

Retorted Dolph, after further rebuke from the Tennesseean: "Mr. President, I have often wondered what would become of the Senate and the country if the Senator from Tennessee should happen to die. He supposes that he embodies all knowledge on parliamentary subjects and almost everything in the Senate."

"That," said the Southerner, "will largely depend upon whether the Senator from Oregon will survive."[20]

It was urged on the Senate floor that the body ought to have "backbone" enough to deal adequately with Senators present but refusing to vote. But what discipline could be employed against a Senator in such a case? As Charles F. Manderson of Nebraska asked, "How would you open his mouth if he sees fit to stand mute?" A test of sorts was undertaken in the case of one of the leading filibusterers, Dubois of Idaho. Parliamentarians pointed to the

[20] ibid., p. 2576.

requirement in the rules that Senators must vote unless excused. But Dubois flatly refused to cast his vote even after the Senate had formally and by roll call declined to excuse him,[21] thereby presenting an example, perhaps unique, of obstruction clearly in defiance of the rules. What could be done? For the time, nothing. The burden of doing the voting fell upon the majority. Not until 1908, a decade and a half in the future, did the Senate adopt the expedient of simply counting a silent Senator as one of the members making a quorum and listing him as present but not voting.

Continuous session was too much for many men, aged and in health far from robust. Voorhees was forced to surrender, with the filibuster still in full vigor. A few among the filibuster opponents held hope of high-handed parliamentary assistance from Vice President Adlai E. Stevenson; but he remained faithful to the silver sympathies which had been responsible for his elevation and gave the administration repealists no favor. Senator Hill of New York sought to obtain a petition signed by a majority of Senators asking that the Vice President rule out dilatory motions, but even that failed because of Republican reluctance to lose the political capital bestowed upon them by the filibuster.[22]

The distinguished John Sherman of Ohio lent the weight of his support to a movement to close debate. "The rules of the Senate are made to expedite the public business in an orderly and proper manner," he said. "We are not here for any other purpose except to legislate, to make laws. . . . All the rules ought to aim for the accomplishment of that purpose and no other. . . . The right to debate a question broadly has been recognized by the Senate of the United States from the beginning of our Government; but when the rules of this body, intended to expedite legislation, are used as an obstruction by the minority in order to defeat the will of the majority, those rules should as soon as possible be corrected, changed, and altered."

The size of the Senate membership had increased, he pointed out, and with that increase came the necessity for a means to limit dis-

21 *ibid.*, pp. 2399-400.
22 Nichols, *op. cit.*, pp. 38-9, 43.

cussion. Moreover, he argued, the example of the House of Representatives and of foreign legislative bodies should be followed. "In my own judgment, the better way would be at the next session of Congress—not now, in the midst of this heated debate—to have the Committee on Rules strengthened and enlarged, and have them take up and reëxamine all these various rules and provide for carefully limiting debate, giving to the minority the full power and proper opportunity to express their opinions, and prescribe some reasonable method by which the majority, after that limit has been reached, may prescribe the time when the final vote shall be taken."

He chided the Senate for its slowness: "The House of Representatives has performed its duty, while this body, which has been here staggering under this long, long debate, has as yet been unable to have a single vote on any question presented upon which any difference of opinion exists.

"Sir, if this continues, the Senate of the United States will be a marked body; it will no longer command the respect of an intelligent and active people like ours. Our people are people of action in every department of industry in this country, and the Senate of the United States ought not to be the great log which weighs down and obstructs legislation."[23]

But Teller of Colorado expressed the view of those who would never consent to such action. "It is perfectly proper," he insisted, "that the majority of legislative bodies shall be compelled to wait until public opinion may indicate that public opinion is back of them.

"What is the majority in this Chamber? What account is that if there is not a majority of the people of the United States back of the majority? It is not the majority of this Chamber that controls; it is the majority of the American people."

Later he contended: "The minority have a right to say, 'You shall not do it at this time; you do not come here representing the public;

[23] 25 *Cong. Record*, pp. 2595-6.

the people are not behind you; wait.' The minority have a right to do that."[24]

By the time the filibuster had reached its height, it was plain that there were three elements among advocates of repeal: a faction led by Senator Hill who insisted upon cloture to bring a vote, an element quietly led by Arthur P. Gorman of Maryland who hoped to compromise for a bill involving less than complete repeal, and administration followers led by Senator Voorhees who proposed to crush the filibuster without cloture and without compromise. Cloture being impossible and the efforts of those who sought compromise having failed, the chief hopes for repeal then centered in the plan and the influence of the administration.[25]

Finally on the 24th of October, while Stewart, "the Nevada windmill," stirred the air in the Senate, a group of the Democratic "farmer" allies of silver, Isham G. Harris and William B. Bate of Tennessee, Matthew C. Butler of South Carolina, Francis M. Cockrell and George G. Vest of Missouri, James L. Pugh of Alabama, and others, met with administration forces in the room of the Appropriations Committee. These Democrats, feeling the pressure from the administration, agreed to surrender; and Harris conveyed the information to Dubois. Senator Dubois, hearing the news at one o'clock in the afternoon of the 24th, announced to the newspapers that "the jig is up"; the silver Senators would not fight without the aid of their farmer friends. Perhaps even the irreconcilable champions of the silver cause believed that there are limits set by popular tolerance to the extent of filibustering in which a small minority may indulge. Perhaps they counted their numbers, almost too few to force constant roll calls, as too weak to warrant further struggle. Indeed, it has been suggested that the silverites preferred to go before the country with an approximate count of 30 votes against repeal instead of a showing of perhaps a dozen against some compromise which might be evolved. At any rate, the filibusterers suddenly surrendered; events in politics are frequently unexpected.

[24] ibid., pp. 2640, 2647.
[25] Nichols, op. cit., pp. 36, 43-9.

Even that very morning Pugh had vowed that he would filibuster "until the cows come home" and Harris, who had declared that the bill would not pass in the form proposed until hell had frozen over, within a few hours "had his skates on ready to take advantage of the freshly formed sheet of ice."[26]

With the battle virtually lost, Jones of Nevada, a pathetic figure in his long black coat and flowing white beard, announced that no more time would be consumed than that necessary to present views to the Senate and the country. The tension was over; Voorhees marched jauntily to his seat, looking years younger. But days were necessary for Senators to complete their fulminations and allow the bill to pass. Pugh said in a passionate protest, "I am still willing, if I had sufficient support, to resort to any and all means left to defeat this iniquitous bill," and declared that he would rather be called a filibusterer "by the conspirators and lick-spittles of the gold kings than to be called a traitor or a faithless representative" by the State and the people who had honored him with trust and confidence.[27] Stewart, declaiming his sentiments, asserted, "Mr. President, the die is cast. . . . The gold kings are victorious." But, he announced, "the betrayal and capture of the White House and the two Houses of Congress is not the end of the war. There are other cities and other people in this country besides those who rule in Wall Street and at the capital of the nation. The honeyed words, the false promises, and the glittering banners of the gold aristocracy have lost their power of deception. . . . The next campaign will be fought in the open field, with no traitors in the army that will do battle for justice and equal rights. . . . Let the vote be taken; let the deed be done; let the object lesson be given. We will abide the result."[28]

Not until seven o'clock on the evening of October 30 was the last speech concluded; and then the bill was passed, 43 yeas against 32 nays. Properly the Silver Repeal filibuster itself may be said to have lasted from August 29 through October 24. During that period of

[26] *ibid.*, p. 50; *New York Times*, Oct. 25, 1893.
[27] 25 *Cong. Record*, p. 2821.
[28] *ibid.*, p. 2957.

fifty-seven calendar days the Senate was in session forty-nine, of which three were spent on other matters. For forty-six days, then, the filibusterers had performed upon the Senate stage; and the endeavor failed only because some of its participants deserted the enterprise.

Another filibuster, so mild, in comparison, that it was little more than incipient, was lost in 1897 by that intrepid political adventurer, Matthew S. Quay of Pennsylvania. The circumstances of his failure were unusual and certainly are not to be attributed to restraint upon the practice of filibustering.

The incentive for the Senator's tactics was the politically profitable wish to include in a naval appropriation bill a provision for a maximum purchase price of $400 per long ton for armor plate rather than the less attractive maximum of $300. On March 1 Quay lost a motion to lay on the table (or kill) a proposed Senate amendment to fix the maximum price at $300. But all was not yet lost to the Senator and the steel industry, even if a majority of the Senate preferred to specify the lower maximum. Quay resolved to filibuster against the report of the committee of conference on disagreements between the two Houses, in order to force the Senate to approve a figure higher than $300.

On the night of March 3-4, even before the conference report could be made ready, the Senator showed his disposition to obstruct the business before the chamber: Senators must be convinced that they must yield the issue or lose their own favorite measures. Particularly did he force repeated quorum calls, and in one instance reiterated a demand for a roll call when not even debate had taken place since the last one. That was too much for the chair, and it was ruled that quorum calls could not be ordered unless business had intervened. While there was no implication in this ruling that debate was not to be considered business, it was clear that at least something must be said or done between consecutive quorum calls. The precedent thus innocently established, certainly no real restraint upon filibustering, was destined to be the basis, slightly more than a decade thereafter, of a radical change in Senate interpretation of its rules.

Untroubled by the future, immediate or distant, the Senator continued his filibuster, admitting frankly that he obstructed business but insisting that he did so "in the interest of millions of Pennsylvania capital and the wages of thousands of Pennsylvania workingmen." But the House of Representatives, sitting at the other end of the Capitol, then did a surprising thing; it receded from its former preference for a $400 maximum and concurred in the Senate's lower figure. The Senator from Pennsylvania was defeated, since further filibustering on his part would have been purposeless. Ruefully he confessed as much and contented himself with inserting in the *Record* more than 275 pages of materials which he had intended to read to his unfortunate colleagues.

A far more famous filibuster, altogether successful in its purpose, closed the short session of Congress just four years later. Thomas H. Carter, Republican of Montana, retiring from the Senate within a few hours, neatly obstructed business in order to defeat a river and harbor bill. The chief factor assuring his success was the automatic adjournment of Congress, under the terms of the Constitution, at noon on March 4; whatever business might be transacted must be completed before that final hour. Some matters in disagreement between the two Houses had been settled by an adopted conference report, but a few others remained to be disposed of when the Senator from Montana rose, on the night of March 3, 1901, to ridicule the bill and its exorbitant appropriations for small improvements.

The bill, he declared, was a raid upon the Treasury; appropriations were included in many instances for no other purpose than to get enough votes for the final passage of the measure. And most Senators willing to vote for the bill demanded their share of the "public improvements" in order to make a good showing before their constituents. "I feel now," said the Senator from Montana, "that a public service will be performed in preventing this bill from becoming a law."

Would the Senate like specific illustrations? "For instance," he said, "we have the sum of $5,000 appropriated to take care of Mattituck Harbor, New York. Who ever heard of Mattituck Harbor before tonight? . . . If you will turn to page 40 of the report [of the committee], you will find where Mattituck Harbor is. . . . 'This harbor is a tidal inlet extending about 2 miles south from Long Island Sound to the village of Mattituck, on Long Island, about 70 miles east from New York City. . . . The natural depth of water at the entrance is from 1 to 2 feet.'

"We are to start in with from 1 to 2 feet of water to dig out a harbor to get up to the village of Mattituck, unknown to anybody outside of the postal authorities of the United States and the persons living in the immediate vicinity."

"What is the depth of water we are to get?" asked William E. Chandler of New Hampshire.

"They want 30 feet of water at Mattituck Harbor," Carter replied. "The Senator from West Virginia very aptly suggests to me at this point that the turkeys are required as towboats to tow the catfish out of that place when the water gets low. The Senator from Maryland says to me we had better sink a well up there and pump the water out in order to get a harbor."

Appropriation items for small improvements brought back interesting memories to the Senator: "I recall a survey demanded by a member from Texas, during my brief service in the House of Representatives, of a river in that State, with a view to having some improvements made upon the river in the interest of navigation. When the engineer of the United States Army went down there to examine the river, with a view to having deep water for a hundred miles up through the channel, the member met him at the mouth of the river and said: 'Do you think we would be more comfortable going up the river in a buckboard than on horseback?'"

Rivers to be provided for in the present bill also received the attention of the Senator from Montana. Of South Carolina he commented, "We have the Santee River, $20,000. Then the Wateree River. Here we are getting down to the genuine article—'water.'"

But Benjamin R. Tillman, known to the nation as "Pitchfork Ben," interrupted to suggest that the Senator, a Westerner and unfamiliar with the natural benefits of water, should let South Carolina alone. "I sympathize with the Senator," said Tillman, "for I have been out through . . . [his] country, and I never could see what it was made for except to hold the world together."

Still Carter insisted, "We may go to the West coast, to the South coast, to the East coast, and through the interior of the country, and by critical analysis of this bill we will find that a majority of the items constitute a useless waste of public money." So far as he was concerned, the legislation would never be enacted.

It was patently not the intention of the Senator to kill all other measures before the Senate, as he might have done; for he yielded willingly for other business when he was sure of holding his right to the floor on the river and harbor bill. In the final rush of the session it was not a difficult task for the Senator to block the bill he opposed; but whenever necessary, through the whole of the night, he continued his remarks against it, persisting in item-by-item denunciation. Republican George L. Wellington of Maryland, who spoke of the "iniquitous measure—to use the vulgar term, a steal," helped him by reading a pamphlet. The final hours of the session found the Montana Senator once more on his feet talking against time. Actually little or no effort was made to contest the obstruction, and the majority for the bill surrendered completely when they allowed Carter to yield shortly before noon on the 4th for the formal courtesy resolutions with which the session closed sine die.

The successful obstruction was certainly not displeasing at the White House. It was understood widely that President McKinley would seriously consider a veto of the bill if it passed; and it was even rumored that the Montana Senator had blocked the legislation at the request of the President, to shift the responsibility from the executive to Congress.[29] True, Senators from arid Western states had reasons of their own for desiring to block the bill, since the House of Representatives had been adamant in refusing appropriation items for three Western reservoirs. Indeed, Francis E. Warren of Wyoming had said flatly on the floor of the Senate, "I want to predict that before another river and harbor bill passes and becomes

[29] *New York Herald*, March 5, 1901.

law there will be reservoirs built or provided for by this nation, either in the river and harbor bill or on some other appropriation bill or in an independent measure."[30] About the whole situation current reports cast an air of grim humor. It was said that the Republicans, in return for Democratic promise to allow unobstructed passage of an army bill, had assured the Democrats of succulent appropriations for "pork barrel" projects in the river and harbor bill. To that deal Senator Carter was presumably not a party, and his carefully timed obstruction deprived the Democrats of their compensation.[31] The Senate had evidence enough, if it were needed, of the effectiveness of a "veto" by even one of its members.

Indeed, so thoroughly had Senators become aware of the possibilities of last-minute obstruction that at the close of the next Congress occurred one of the most recounted "hold-ups" of the Senate, effected without a single maneuver of actual obstruction. The tactics, which "Uncle Joe" Cannon of Illinois branded in a speech in the House as "legislative blackmail,"[32] were simple. On the night of March 3, 1903, during the consideration of a deficiency bill, "Pitchfork Ben" Tillman of South Carolina demanded that a claim of some $47,000 for expenses incurred during the War of 1812 be included for his state. Piled on the floor was a stack of books almost as high as his desk, and open for use was a volume of Byron's poems. Mr. Tillman privately offered to defeat all legislation before the Senate by reading and talking till adjournment the next day. But Senators had no wish to test the endurance of the South Carolinian, and the item became a part of the bill.[33]

For that session of Congress, however, such a threatened filibuster was mild. Overshadowing that and other obstructive incidents was a major filibuster against an omnibus statehood bill, deadlocking much of the whole session. Under the leadership of Albert J. Beveridge of Indiana, chairman of the Committee on Territories, a Sen-

[30] 34 Cong. Record, p. 3545.
[31] New York Herald, March 5, 1901.
[32] 36 Cong. Record, p. 3058.
[33] Indianapolis News, March 4, 1903; New York Herald, same date.

ate minority fought desperately though intermittently for weeks against the strategy of Quay of Pennsylvania and a majority of their colleagues.

The House had passed a bill admitting into the Union Oklahoma, Arizona, and New Mexico, with the further provision that Indian Territory should not be included within the boundaries of Oklahoma. This bill the Senate Committee on Territories revised completely, striking out the admission of Arizona and New Mexico and providing that Indian Territory should be an integral part of Oklahoma. Beveridge contended that Arizona and New Mexico were not sufficiently populous for statehood. He suspected that railroads and other corporations were interested in ending territorial status in order that the new states might be induced to grant subsidies. Upon the Oklahoma question, he demanded that development of the Indian Territory should not be retarded and that it should be incorporated in the area given the political advantages of statehood. But Quay and a majority of the members of the Senate, actually a coalition of Democrats and a few Republicans, favored the House proposal.

Both political parties in the campaign of 1900 had made platform declarations in favor of statehood for the three territories. Democratic and Republican politicians, with characteristic opportunism, hoped for additional party strength in Congress and in the electoral college. Yet Beveridge and his cohorts, unyielding in their convictions, pitted their strength against the famous Pennsylvania strategist and his majority, to defeat the omnibus bill and if possible to arouse enough public sentiment to pass the Oklahoma measure.

On December 10, 1902, Quay, a minority member (in respect to this bill) of the Committee on Territories, submitted his views to the Senate. Immediately thereafter Knute Nelson of Minnesota presented the committee report with an amendment to strike out the House bill and insert the modified proposal. Evidently becoming fearful that an undebatable motion to table the proposed amendment would be made by the opposing majority, Nelson thereupon withdrew the amendment for the time being.

The parliamentary question therefore became the House bill. That measure Quay was determined to pass with his supporting votes, and the committee majority intended to defeat it. Talk had begun before the Christmas recess, but the real contest came after the holidays. The Senate convened again on January 5, 1903, and Nelson obliged his companions in the battle by speaking for days to elucidate the finest points of the issue. Quay tried again and again to obtain unanimous consent for a vote on any day before final adjournment, but always he was rebuffed.

"We have the votes to pass the bill," said Quay. "The majority of the Senate are in favor of it, and it is being willfully . . . obstructed."

Beveridge chose to deny, a favorite resort with obstructionists, that he and his friends were filibustering. "No person has a greater admiration for the political skill and management of the Senator from Pennsylvania than I have. I recognize my inefficiency even to express my appreciation of his surpassing cleverness as a political tactician. . . . But the burden is not upon us, Mr. President, nor shall it be permitted to rest upon our shoulders, that we obstruct because we debate a needful measure needfully.

" 'Let the galled jade wince, our withers are unwrung.'

"Let the Senate and the country understand what they do understand now, that the real obstructors of this legislation, if obstruction occurs, as it has not yet, are not those Senators who stand here in good faith and debate this measure . . . but the Senator who, day by day, announces that he has got the votes and will pass this bill, or the country will not be permitted to have any other needful legislation at present."[34]

Despairing of securing consent for a vote, Quay on the 16th of February introduced a resolution setting forth: "That it is the sense of the Senate that a date and hour prior to the 2nd of March next should be fixed for a final vote upon the bill and all amendments that are pending or may be offered thereto." James K. Jones of Arkansas and John C. Spooner of Wisconsin, fearful of the wily

[34] 36 *Cong. Record*, pp. 991-2.

Quay, objected that such a resolution if adopted might be construed to fix a time for a vote without need for unanimous consent. In the face of opposition to his wording, Quay presented a modified resolution reading, ". . . it is the sense of the Senate that by unanimous consent a date and hour . . . should be fixed. . . ." It might be possible at least, he thought, to put the Senate on record in favor of the bill. But even from that effort there came no result.

As the filibuster continued, Beveridge found himself near the limit of his resources to keep the talk going and relied upon a desperate expedient. A customary courtesy of the Senate required that no vote be had on a measure unless the chairman of the committee which had considered it should be present. Beveridge, as the chairman of the committee, resolved to take advantage of that courtesy and disappear. For days he hid in a den at the Washington home of Gifford Pinchot, later escaping unnoticed to Atlantic City.[35] Time was gained by that stratagem, and the filibuster went on.

As the session drew to a close, however, obstruction of the omnibus statehood bill was less difficult; for Quay was compelled to consent that other important legislation be considered. Still, whenever attention returned to the statehood question, Beveridge and his allies were prepared with something to say. The long fight of the minority was bearing the certain fruits of success.

Near the closing hours of the session Quay himself decided upon filibuster tactics, hoping thereby to force adoption of the omnibus statehood bill, with some modifications by way of compromise, as a rider to an administration measure to reduce the Philippine tariff. Clearly his attitude revealed to Senators that, if the Philippine bill were to pass at all, the statehood rider should be attached; and, to give teeth to his argument, he began obstruction by starting the clerks reading an amendment to the Philippine bill (the statehood rider) forty-six printed pages in length. His amendment he withdrew, however, when the reason for his filibuster effort, as in the

[35] Claude G. Bowers, *Beveridge and the Progressive Era* (New York, 1932), pp. 200-1.

case of his former effort with naval appropriations, collapsed.[36] For it became clear that, with or without the statehood rider, the Philippine bill could not pass. If that bill came up, said Senator Teller of Colorado, he for one would filibuster against it.[37]

Hope of passing the statehood bill vanished. As Quay said of it, "The cerements of the grave have been wrapped around it . . . it has been carried into the gloomy cavern of death, and laid away there for resurrection."

Moreover, it was necessary to abandon banking legislation proposed by the arch-conservative, Senator Aldrich. Democratic Senators left no doubt that they would defeat that measure by filibuster.[38] They regarded as class legislation in favor of the plutocracy the proposal allowing the Secretary of the Treasury to accept bonds other than those of the federal government as security for public funds. The Democrats would fight without stint to prevent enactment. The session was expiring with the Senate helpless before conflicting elements of obstructionists.

The Senate adjourned after a brief but crowning filibuster on the 4th of March by William E. Mason of Illinois, then retiring from service, a man who proved that he would and could defeat changes, requested by Senator Joseph W. Bailey of Texas, in the 1902 river and harbor act. Sardonically Senator Mason used the last precious minutes for a denunciation of Senate filibusters and for suggestions that the rules be altered to avert them.

"When any bill touches a thing that we think is not quite right," said Senator Mason, "we arise and, as some one has said before, we enjoy the physical exercise of the use of tongue, teeth, and vocal organs without the least impairment or exertion of the brain.

"My final appeal, then, to my colleagues is: Amend your rules so that the majority can transact your business. This is a Government of majorities."

[36] 36 *Cong. Record*, pp. 3005-8.
[37] *New York Herald*, March 3, 1903.
[38] *ibid.*

Fiercely Senator Bailey strove to force Mason from the floor in order to secure a vote on the bill. Overruled in his efforts, Bailey roared to the presiding officer, "Then I will at least force him to speak this session out."

"Well," said Mason, "the Senator from Texas can force me to no more pleasing duty. Like the distinguished Senator, I love to hear the sound of my own voice."

The legislative hours of the short session of the 57th Congress were thus consumed chiefly by the use of dilatory tactics. As if the Senate had not suffered enough, John T. Morgan of Alabama in the secrecy of executive sessions read large sections of the history of the world in order to defeat the Colombian Treaty for the Panama Canal.[39] The veteran legislator, having seen twenty-six years of service in the Senate and now nearing eighty years of age, doggedly held the floor and poured out hundreds of thousands of words. Convinced that a canal through Nicaragua would be preferable, he fought without retreat. Since he was almost unsupported in his position, Senators thought that he could soon be tired out. Instead he tired out the whole Senate. In order to secure ratification of the treaty, President Roosevelt was compelled to convene the Senate in special session on March 5, 1903. The hard-won Senatorial approval did not end the President's troubles, for the Colombian Senate rejected the treaty. Only after a revolution had brought independence to Panama could the administration negotiate effectively for a right of way for the Panama Canal.

A final fling at filibustering, before Senators should be engaged in a prodigious and in a sense long-continued effort to curtail it, came in 1907. For ten years Republicans had sought to increase the subsidy to American merchant shipping. They argued that exports could thereby be increased and that national defense, particularly through adequate communications with territorial possessions, could be promoted. The merchant fleet should be enlarged, said Republican spokesmen, and construction could be stimulated by voting a bounty for shipping. Democrats were not willing to accept the

[39] *ibid.*, March 1, 1903.

thesis of their political opponents. They replied that American ships could meet foreign competition if steel were sold to shipbuilders at a reasonable price. A subsidy, they held, would be a gift to the steel industry, an enforced but unnecessary contribution from the tax-payer without real benefits to the national interest.

In spite of opposition President Roosevelt and other leaders of the administration favored subsidy legislation and hoped to obtain Congressional approval. As the 59th Congress drew to a close, on March 2, 1907, Senator Jacob H. Gallinger of New Hampshire, in charge of the subsidy bill, undertook to expedite action by moving to concur in a House amendment. To save the subsidy principle, he would accept modifications. But filibustering against Senate consideration of the amended measure immediately broke out; and after a number of roll-call votes had been forced to delay proceedings, it was finally arranged to take up the question the next day.

On Sunday, March 3, the measure was duly considered, but Democratic Edward W. Carmack of Tennessee (retiring from the Senate) got the floor, in high good humor, for a long speech patently intended to obstruct the bill. The Senator opened his extended remarks with feigned horror that he had been called a filibusterer; and he pointed out, with easy loquacity and mock indignation, that Webster's dictionary defined such a person as a freebooter and therefore a pillager or buccaneer. "Mr. President, in my career in politics I have been accused of almost everything except appendicitis, I believe, but it remained for the Senator from New Hampshire to take me from my inland home and launch me as a buccaneer and a pirate upon the sea."

But Gallinger of New Hampshire insisted that he had referred to filibustering in its legislative sense, and read from the Century dictionary the following quotation to illustrate the use of the word:

" 'The Democrats filibustered and postponed the vote till a day when strength could be fairly measured on it.' "

"Mr. President," retorted Carmack, "the last quotation the Senator read with reference to Democrats impeaches the authority he brings before the Senate. It shows very plainly that it is a Republican dictionary."

As the debate continued in flippant style, Senators grew impatient and the venerable William P. Frye of Maine offered a reprimand. "It occurs to me," he said, "that even a filibuster may be conducted in a dignified manner; that the Sabbath day might be remembered in the United States Senate, and that to amuse the galleries and excite their laughter does not assist at all in defeating the ship-subsidy bill."

Losing his temper in a manner for which he later apologized, the Tennesseean snapped, "If any part of those remarks were intended for me, I want to say to the Senator from Maine that I am not responsible to him for my conduct, and that I shall conduct myself according to my own ideas of propriety. If the Senator from Maine wants to leave the Senate Chamber here on Sunday and attend church, he has my permission to do so."

Obviously the obstruction was a Democratic filibuster against a Republican measure. At times Carmack was assisted by Lee S. Overman of North Carolina, but for the most part he bore the brunt of the battle himself. But the Democrats had no intention of needlessly defeating other legislation if it could be avoided, and Senator Carmack yielded frequently for other business. With such interruptions, his obstructive remarks consumed the day and evening of the 3rd; and when the Senate met early on the 4th he was ready to speak again. Senator Gallinger, acknowledging defeat, abandoned the bill and allowed the Senate to consider other last-minute business in the brief remaining time.[40] Senators had learned well the futility of opposing a determined filibuster in a short session immediately before the automatic 4th of March adjournment.

Filibustering had now quite clearly assumed astounding proportions in the Senate. In the last two decades of the nineteenth century storms of obstruction had swept the chamber; and, while filibuster-

[40] See Paul Maxwell Zeis, *American Shipping Policy* (Princeton, 1938), *passim,* for discussion of many legislative battles over merchant marine proposals.

ing early in the twentieth century was hardly so spectacular as that in the years immediately preceding, the practice continued without parliamentary restraint. And with the more daring use of filibuster techniques that practice became essentially successful. If filibusters failed, the reasons lay in the surrender of participants or in developments not arising from the rules of the Senate. Parliamentary tactics to overcome obstruction proved to be hopeless and ineffectual; it was the heyday of brazen and unblushing aggressors. The power of the Senate lay not in votes but in sturdy tongues and iron wills. The premium rested not upon ability and statesmanship but upon effrontery and audacity.

CHAPTER IV

THE MODERN FILIBUSTER

CHAPTER IV

THE MODERN FILIBUSTER

IN 1908 came the historic obstruction of the Aldrich-Vreeland Currency Bill, and with it efforts of major importance to make more difficult the practice of filibustering. The formal rules of the Senate remained unaltered, but their interpretation, in an acutely significant aspect, was turned in a new direction. That turn pointed toward opposing strategy most inconvenient for obstructionists, particularly when they are few in number. Developments indicated curtailment of hitherto almost untrammelled power and, however slow and uncertain in progress, opened a new period in the story of Senate filibustering.

The filibuster against the financial measure which bore the names of Senator Nelson W. Aldrich of Rhode Island and of Representative Edward B. Vreeland of New York was relatively brief (only two days, May 29-30, 1908) but bitter and intense. It was timed against the conference report on the bill, and that fact in itself, since the measure was not then subject to amendment, operated to the parliamentary disadvantage of the obstructionists.

Framers of the legislation hoped for immediate action in order to provide a more elastic currency and to stabilize the values of many securities. If banks could issue currency secured by commercial paper or by bonds of various types, they decided, a pressing problem would be solved. Bankruptcies and other financial difficulties during the year 1907 had alarmed conservative Republicans. Emergency currency measures must be taken to preserve business and keep the country Republican. Opposing forces denounced the whole plan as one designed to enhance beyond reason the values of securities and to stuff the wallets of the rich. They saw in it only another scheme of the money power, an attempt of the privileged few to tighten their grip upon the capital and credit of the country.

Most determined of the embattled opponents of the Currency Bill was their leader, Robert M. La Follette of Wisconsin, whose distrust of Senator Aldrich was profound. From the governorship of his state La Follette had come to the Senate two years earlier as a champion of reform and as an enemy of special privilege. He was a Republican but an avowed foe of the conservative leaders of his party.

When Aldrich obtained consideration of the conference report about noon on the 29th of May, La Follette took the floor in extended opposition—a speech of more than eighteen hours which remains a record for continuous occupancy of the Senate floor. However, the Senator was not compelled to occupy all of that time in talking, but was relieved not only by occasional interruptions but also by frequent quorum calls. Many of the quorum calls were upon his own demand, with the patently twofold purpose of securing brief respites from speaking and of forcing members of the majority in favor of the bill to feel the strain of constant attendance in the Senate.

Senator Aldrich personally led the majority forces and that influential Rhode Islander was no mean parliamentary antagonist. Of all men who have designed and employed strategy opposing the progress of filibusterism he was perhaps the most resourceful. The majority leadership therefore spared no parliamentary maneuver. Even before La Follette began his celebrated speech there were plain evidences that the majority would go far to win their victory and that little hesitation would be shown in enlarging the precedents of the Senate.

During brief remarks by Charles A. Culberson of Texas, La Follette forced two quorum calls; on his third attempt Culberson refused to yield the floor for the purpose. A point of order that La Follette had not the floor to call for a quorum was sustained by Vice President Charles W. Fairbanks, and on appeal the chair was sustained by a division.

Thomas P. Gore of Oklahoma immediately raised the point that the division had revealed one short of a quorum. How had the issue been settled in the absence of a quorum? The Vice President replied that one Senator not voting had been present to make a quorum; and to sustain his position he read a precedent on June 19, 1879, when Allen G. Thurman of Ohio was in the chair. But the Vice President had now taken an important step beyond the Thurman ruling. The latter had merely counted a quorum to determine whether enough Senators were present to do business; Fairbanks had counted a quorum, as had Speaker Thomas B. Reed in the House in 1890, to declare that action on a vote had been taken.

Under such a ruling the regular practice of breaking a quorum on roll-call votes by sitting silent in the chamber was ended. Filibusterism had received the first significant blow.

When La Follette himself assumed the floor, maneuvers to end the filibuster became all the more furious. After sharp words directed toward Aldrich by La Follette, Joseph B. Foraker of Ohio called the latter to order in an effort to deprive him of the floor; and under the rules the Senate must vote whether the speaker should proceed in order. On a viva voce vote the "noes" seemed to have it; but on a yea-and-nay vote Senators were not willing to be recorded as preventing a colleague from speaking, and only Foraker voted against the right of La Follette to continue. Ere long Gallinger of New Hampshire was on his feet to object to assistance given La Follette by a secretary who counted attendance and informed the speaking Senator when another quorum demand should be made. While secretaries discharging official duties are entitled to presence on the floor, Vice President Fairbanks promptly ruled against performance of the objected service. Clearly the sympathies of the chair were with the majority.

It was soon manifest, too, that the rule that no Senator should speak more than twice on the same subject in the same day (without leave of the Senate) would if necessary be strictly applied. That rule was not new to the Senate, but heretofore it had not been made an effective weapon of filibuster opponents. Intense filibusters in the past had usually been conducted by many Senators acting together, and on parliamentary issues subject to amendment; even if a Senator had exhausted his technical opportunities to speak, a convenient amendment could be proposed to allow him a fresh start on a new subject. But the filibuster facing Aldrich and his majority was conducted by few Senators and, more important, it was aimed at an unamendable conference report. When Senators had spoken twice, under strict enforcement of the rule and with the Senate technically held (through recesses) in one legislative day, the filibuster could be throttled with relative ease. Senator La Follette later charged that the official reporter's notes for the *Congressional Record* had been "doctored" to make it appear that, even in his first speech, he had held the floor twice.[1] If he had asked for the floor a second time an effort would have been made to debar him.

As La Follette talked on and on, it became apparent that the Senate would be held in continuous session. Aldrich was determined not to be thwarted, and already by his opposing strategy he had forced the filibuster to a degree of intensity never before known in that body. But still other maneuvers were at his command, and his next victorious procedure was to set a precedent of prime importance in the trend toward curtailment of filibusters.

After La Follette had held the floor for hours, when the Senate had suffered thirty-two quorum calls or roll-call votes since the filibuster began (thirty since La Follette had begun to speak), Aldrich acted to relieve the majority from the strain of persistent attendance. "If repeated suggestions of the want of a quorum can be made without intervening business," he said in disgust, "the whole business of the Senate is put in the hands of one man. . . ." And Gallinger grumblingly added, "If the entire business of the Senate can be put in the hands of one man, that one man could destroy the Government; he could prevent appropriations being made to carry on the governmental machinery, and it is absurd to suppose that it was ever so intended."

[1] *Autobiography,* 4th ed. (Madison, 1920), pp. 471-3.

When the Wisconsin filibusterer next suggested the absence of a quorum, Aldrich rose to a point of order. He contended that without intervening business a quorum call is not in order, and he cited the precedent of March 3, 1897, when Senator Quay had attempted to force a roll call immediately after one had been concluded. To La Follette's objection that debate had intervened since the last roll call, Aldrich replied that debate is not business. The issue was clearly drawn: Aldrich and his majority once more proposed to expand the Senate precedents. In 1897 there had been no suggestion that debate is not business. What actually happened was that Quay had demanded a quorum call when not even debate had taken place since the last one. In 1908 Aldrich simply intended to draw the net tighter against the practice of filibustering. Vice President Fairbanks, however, declined to participate directly in the new maneuver. Without decision he submitted the question to the Senate. The majority, obedient to its leadership, supported the point of order; and when the last straggling vote was counted the yeas and nays stood 35 to 8 for the new interpretation.

The importance of the ruling thus made by formal vote of the Senate was tremendous. No longer could a single Senator under all circumstances torture his colleagues by keeping a majority in almost continuous attendance. True, a Senator could call for a quorum if business had been transacted since the last call; but with the transaction of business the speaking Senator would lose the floor, and he could regain it only once more on the same subject. During the consideration of an unamendable conference report, frequent demands for a quorum are virtually impossible. As a matter of fact, since 1908 the Senate has seen few solitary obstructionists with sufficient mastery of parliamentary technique to force call after call even when legislation is in a stage subject to amendment. Occasionally such obstruction is attempted by a series of dilatory propositions; but a parliamentary blunder might turn the most elaborate scheme into a fiasco, and most filibustering Senators not expert in procedure prefer simply to talk. But talk, however long continued, does not subject the Senate to the merciless inconvenience of oft-repeated quorum calls.

Having been deprived of an opportunity to demand again and again that the roll be called to ascertain the presence of a quorum, Senator La Follette was forced to rely upon extended speech to delay the conference report. He boldly accepted the challenge; and through the night he read and talked, interrupted only by another roll-call vote on procedure at 2:25 in the morning, and by occasional questions. He held the floor till seven o'clock in the morning; and the feat is doubly remarkable inasmuch as he had just recovered from illness, and in view of an event on the floor which nearly resulted in his death.

During his long speech he sustained himself by drinking glasses of milk and egg, but when he tasted one portion (brought from the Senate restaurant) he rejected it as doped. Later analysis actually revealed enough ptomaine in the glass to have resulted in certain death, although no charge of a deliberate attempt at poisoning was ever made. When the exciting filibuster had closed, for several days the Senator was ill at his home because of the deadly potion which he had tasted.[2]

When La Follette surrendered the floor, Senator Aldrich proved once more his command of strategy. He rose and asked that the yeas and nays be ordered on the conference report. Such a demand must be seconded by one-fifth of the Senators present, and it is usual that the request be made and that seconding Senators rise to be counted just prior to an actual vote. But Aldrich asked and obtained an order for the yeas and nays before debate had been concluded. Speeches were not thereby precluded, but the Senate was primed for quick action. If there should come a lull in the filibuster, a call of the yeas and nays had merely to begin and the possibility of further obstruction would end.

<hr />

[2] Letter to author from Col. John J. Hannan, former secretary to Senator La Follette, April 1, 1938. Cf. Lynn Haines, *The Senate from 1907 to 1912* (Bethesda, Md., 1912), p. 18.

William J. Stone of Missouri, known among politicians as "Gumshoe Bill," followed La Follette as a filibuster speaker, continuing his remarks until Aldrich at 1:30 in the afternoon permitted the Senate to recess for thirty minutes. At the outset of the Missouri Senator's contribution to the delay, the filibusterers failed once more to force quorum calls. Thomas P. Gore of Oklahoma made the attempt but Senator George Sutherland of Utah, presiding at the time, held a call not in order; business had not intervened. To test the issue once more, in the sober hours of daylight, Gore appealed from the decision of the chair. Sutherland, who was later to sit upon the Supreme Bench of the country, brazenly ruled that even an appeal was not in order. Rarely had the Senate seen more arbitrary practice from the chair; but the majority were in no mood for the niceties of parliamentary procedure.

Indeed, there were threats of an arbitrary ending even of the dilatory talk. Shortly before the brief recess at 1:30, Stone, in his monotonous reading of a pamphlet, had reached a description of the monetary system of Portugal. Aldrich and Foraker, goaded to indignation by the irrelevant delay, interrupted to quote from Jefferson's authoritative *Manual* statements which could be used by the chair, they argued, arbitrarily to shut off tedious reading and debate. Foraker went so far as to submit a point of order in an effort to take the reading Senator from the floor. But recess, brief though it was, cleared the ominous situation somewhat. At the urgent request of Augustus O. Bacon of Georgia, Henry M. Teller of Colorado, and others, after the Senate had reconvened, Foraker withheld his point of order. Closing debate by action of the chair, even supported on appeal by a strong majority, would have been revolution indeed for a Senate proud of its privilege of unlimited speech.

Stone held the floor when the Senate met after its recess, but totally blind Senator Gore of Oklahoma soon took up the cudgels of filibuster. It had been arranged privately that Senator Gore should talk for a time, be relieved by Stone for another speech, and after that La Follette, rested a bit from his long vigil of the night, would hold the floor again. Senator Stone returned in due time to keep his appointment, and Gore, apprised of the fact, yielded the floor. But after his return, Stone had been called for a moment to a cloakroom; and Gore, unable to see and therefore not knowing that Stone had left, surrendered the floor when no one was ready to claim it. It was a costly error, and many have been the speculative suggestions that trickery was involved. A popular report that Senator Gore was forced to sit down by pulling his coat tails has been repudiated.[3]

Aldrich, grasping the situation, demanded that the roll be called for the already ordered yeas and nays. But to forestall a vote when Senators still desired to speak, Weldon B. Heyburn of Idaho shouted for recognition. Aldrich, wildly excited, dashed to the well of the Senate chamber, shook his finger at the Vice President, and literally yelled for a roll call. Heyburn was still clamoring; the Vice President hesitated in the confusion; and the secretary began to call the roll. Aldrich, first on the list, had barely time to respond to his name, when the Vice President declared that he thought it only fair to recognize the Senator from Idaho inasmuch as the attention of the chair had been distracted for a moment. But Aldrich insisted that the roll call had begun and that it could not be interrupted, under the rules, after a Senator had responded. Upon such insistence, technically correct, the roll call was continued. La Follette, dashing in when he learned of the turn of affairs, desperately tried to save the day by voting in the affirmative in order to move reconsideration and then debate that; but he was defeated when Aldrich made the motion to reconsider. Hale of Maine and Foraker immediately moved to lay the reconsideration motion on the table, which was done, and the conference report was irrevocably passed.

In view of the fact that Heyburn had certainly asked recognition prior to the beginning of the roll call, it must be said that the filibuster was overcome by doubtful practice. The hope of the obstructionists had been to talk until general Congressional demands for adjournment sine die forced the abandonment of the legislation. The

---

[3] Nathaniel Wright Stephenson, *Nelson W. Aldrich* (New York, 1930), p. 477, n. 24; letter from former Senator T. P. Gore to author, Aug. 18, 1939.

majority had guarded their position in that respect, however, by cleverly holding back favorite bills which would also fail if the Currency Bill failed. Still, the filibuster had little chance of success even against parliamentary strategy fully within the rules. Since Senators could actually speak only twice, their opportunities would soon have been exhausted. The session need have been prolonged only a few days at most. Consequently sharp practice could scarcely be justified even by necessity.

For the first time since the practice had risen to great prominence in the Senate, a majority ruthlessly confronted filibusterism with restraints. Two new interpretations of procedure were introduced to curtail the liberty of filibusterers, and a third weapon, a provision in the rules, was thrown into the light of new significance: (1) the chair might count a quorum, if one were physically present, even on a vote, whether or not Senators would answer to their names; (2) mere debate would not be considered business, and therefore more than debate must take place between quorum calls; (3) Senators could by enforcement of the rules be restrained from speaking on the same subject more than twice in the same day.

However embarrassing to the Currency Bill filibusterers, in the large view these efforts at curtailment were a mere beginning. Dilatory tactics, though hemmed in by new precedents, remained a policy of tremendous effectiveness. And with the next spectacular obstruction, in 1911, Senator Robert L. Owen of Oklahoma demonstrated that the resources of a determined filibusterer may well be ample to brush aside, as it were, the relatively meager weapons of a majority. It must be remembered that the Senate can do almost anything by unanimous consent, and an artful maneuverer may take advantage of that convenient procedure.

On the 3rd of March, 1911, Senator Joseph W. Bailey of Texas obtained consideration of a resolution to admit New Mexico to the Union. Arizona had been eliminated because of provisions in her proposed state constitution for popular initiative, referendum, and recall, political devices distasteful to many conservative Senators. President Taft strongly opposed such a movement for direct government and threw his influence against it. Especially did he recoil from the proposed constitutional arrangement in Arizona for the recall of judges. But Senator Owen was determined that both New Mexico and Arizona should be admitted. He therefore rose to filibuster against the New Mexico resolution until the majority known to be favorable to the measure might accede to the inclusion of Arizona. Moreover, he would not consent to the abandonment of the resolution altogether, as might have been suggested. Both prospective states should be admitted or he would end the session in filibuster. Such obstruction would involve failure of important appropriation bills, and the Senator was therefore in a splendid position for extortion.

Aside from his wish to delay passage of the appropriation bills in order that he might use them for leverage in possible bargaining, the Oklahoma Senator had no objection to the consideration of matters other than the statehood proposal—provided he did not lose the floor. Technically, if other business should be considered, the Senator could not keep the floor for his first speech but would end one of his opportunities for talking. That difficulty was avoided simply by obtaining *unanimous consent* to regard his remarks, though much interrupted, as one speech. By the pressure of the situation, through the desire of Senators to salvage pet measures, the rule limiting a Senator to two speeches on the same question in one legislative day was as effectively nullified as though it had not existed. In addition, the filibustering Senator blandly relieved himself of the necessity for uninterrupted personal obstruction by shifting the attention of the Senate to other matters comparatively harmless.

Through the night of March 3-4 the filibuster was continued when necessary. Owen was deliberately attempting to coerce his colleagues. He would have his way, or others should pay the price. "I wish to say in extenuation of my conduct," he declaimed grandiloquently, "that I do it because I feel honor bound as a soldier of the common good to stand faithfully and firmly, in spite of all opposition, in support of what I believe to be essential to the integrity and welfare of our glorious Republic. . . ."

The Senate adjourned for eight minutes at 7:52 in the morning and at 9:00 recessed for an hour. Two hours remained until the session should adjourn sine die, but no one could persuade the Oklahoma Senator to yield his determination. Compromise was the only remaining resort of the majority. It was finally agreed that, if Owen would refrain from further obstruction which might despoil the majority of important legislation, a vote would be permitted by unanimous consent on the combined question of admitting both New Mexico and Arizona. When the roll was called the combined proposition was defeated by 39 yeas to 45 nays. Statehood legislation in any form was dead for the session. But if the filibuster had not won a complete victory, it had forced a major parliamentary compromise which at least smacked of success.

Indeed, Senator Bailey of Texas, absent from the chamber when unanimous consent was granted for voting on the admission of two states instead of one, flew into a fury upon learning that Owen had been permitted to gain even a partial victory. And in a fit of pique that so many of his colleagues had actually voted for the admission of Arizona, to which he was bitterly opposed, Bailey telegraphed his resignation to the governor of Texas and handed a copy to Vice President James S. Sherman. The Vice President purposely neglected to present it, and friends of the irate Senator persuaded him to withdraw the resignation.[4]

The short session of the next Congress, at the close of Taft's administration, witnessed a series of filibusters, none of them glaringly spectacular but all in a degree effective.

Democrats determined to block the retiring President's appointments by dilatory speeches in executive session. Republicans in caucus decided upon forceful strategy to put an end to the obstruction. They would compel the Senate to devote all its time to executive business, and nothing else would be done until the nominations were confirmed. Difficulties began in January 1913, and on the 28th

[4] *New York Herald,* March 5, 1911.

the Senate was held all day in executive session. Next day, however, Republican Senators Bristow, La Follette, and Poindexter joined the Democrats in opposing further executive sessions to consider nominations. Republican leaders being unable to secure enough votes to enforce the caucus decision, their program was lost.[5] For a time filibuster had existed, but increased voting strength soon made it unnecessary.

Shortly thereafter a few disgruntled Republicans engaged in a filibuster of their own against features of the bill creating the Department of Labor. Senators Simon Guggenheim of Colorado and Asle J. Gronna of North Dakota, particularly opposed to some of the labor provisions and to relocation of bureaus, actively engaged in filibustering on the night of February 25 when tired Senators were reluctant to remain in the chamber to form a quorum. Roll-call votes were forced, accompanied by quorum calls; and so wearisome did the situation become that the Senate adjourned. The next day, after Senator William E. Borah, in charge of the measure, had used his influence with the obstructionists and after two conciliatory amendments had been adopted, the bill was passed.[6] Obstructing Senators had been few in number, and the incipient filibuster ended in compromise.

On that very day, February 26, Senator Stone of Missouri demonstrated, by tactics similar to those of Senator Tillman ten years before, that the Senate could be made to capitulate at critical moments by the mere threat of filibuster. The Missourian, during consideration of an omnibus public buildings bill, sent to the desk an amendment for $47,550 for improvements in the Saint Louis post office. Openly he proclaimed, "I will agree not to make a speech if it is agreed to"; and the Senate surrendered.[7] Before its final passage, the bill underwent more troubled history, for later threats of filibuster by the distinguished Senators Henry Cabot Lodge and Elihu

---

[5] *New York Times,* Jan. 29, 30, 1913.
[6] 49 *Cong. Record,* pp. 3922-5, 4004-7; *New York Times,* Feb. 27, 1913.
[7] 49 *Cong. Record,* p. 4063.

Root forced the Senate to reject a conference report and to insist upon another conference.[8]

After Woodrow Wilson had come into the Presidency he convened Congress in special session on April 7, 1913. Filibustering against major issues was not the program of the Republican minority in the Senate, but there were occasions when obstruction was conveniently practiced. For instance, Republicans determined that the President's appointee to the position of director of the census should not take office till the end of the fiscal year. In the secrecy of executive sessions they persistently blocked the confirmation of W. J. Harris of Georgia, a man later to represent his state in the Senate. On the afternoon of May 20, when the issue came to a head, Charles E. Townsend of Michigan piled his desk with periodicals dating from before the Civil War, threatening to read them all. Theodore E. Burton of Ohio declared that he could and would present vital statistics from the time of King David to the present day. Democrats, facing filibuster and alarming threats of prolonged delay, yielded the point and agreed to vote on the nomination near the end of the fiscal year.[9]

Later in the session, during the consideration of tariff legislation, Republicans made long dilatory speeches as a warning against a program for immediate currency adjustments. Their belligerent attitude was duly respected and majority leaders withheld suggestions for currency alteration.[10]

The next session of the same Congress was notable for long legislative fights and protracted debates, some of which may well have been (as was claimed) merely extended expressions of opposition by many Senators. The Panama Canal Tolls debate ran intermittently from May 2 till June 11, 1914. The Hay-Pauncefote Treaty with Great Britain stipulated that the canal should be open to vessels of all nations without discrimination, but Congress had enacted legislation exempting from toll payments American vessels in coastwise

[8] New York Times, March 4, 1913.
[9] ibid., May 21, 1913.
[10] ibid., July 29, 1913.

trade. Britain protested that treaty guaranties had been violated, and American railroads objected to the competition. President Wilson recommended that the toll exemption be repealed, and after prolonged discussion Congress followed his advice. Contention over the Federal Trade Commission Bill extended from June 25 until August 5. Finally, as the President wished, the new Commission was created with investigatory and regulatory powers applicable to many types of business engaged in interstate commerce. Arguments over antitrust legislation consumed most of the time from August 12 until September 2 and, after a conference report, from September 28 until October 5. But the Clayton Antitrust Act at last emerged as a law.

An incipient filibuster was openly and successfully waged by two Democratic Senators, Willard Saulsbury of Delaware and Atlee Pomerene of Ohio, in order to force the Senate to adjourn on Saturday, August 8, 1914, before passing a ship registry bill. Such legislation was sought by the administration to allow freer transfer of merchant vessels from foreign to American ownership. After the outbreak of war on the European continent American exporters experienced difficulty in finding ships ready to carry cargoes across the Atlantic, for owners of vessels sailing under the flags of belligerent nations feared to risk voyages on the high seas. Existing laws of the United States permitted only those foreign ships not more than five years of age to be registered under the American flag. Exporters hoped that removal of the age limit would result in transfer of many ships to the American merchant marine and a consequent increase in tonnage available for trans-Atlantic shipping. Americans who had invested in foreign ships, now endangered by the war, anxiously sought protection under a neutral flag. Great Britain and France objected. They feared that Americans would purchase German ships and also take advantage of the war to acquire a monopoly of world trade. In the Senate there was hesitation. A few opponents of the proposed legislation were fearful that changes of registry would involve the United States in international disputes. In the midst of Senatorial deliberation Saulsbury and Pomerene staged their brief filibuster. Their colleagues believed that the filibustering Senators talked and demanded a quorum when none was present merely as a strategic move to delay action in the hope of compromise or a deal, or until their forces were better consolidated. President Wilson insisted that the bill was desirable and that any danger could be avoided by "wise and prudent administration."[11] The Senate yielded and the measure was passed.

Early in September 1914 a filibuster conducted by a group of Republicans became genuinely intense and, in one stage of the parliamentary battle, promised to become of real importance in further developing a gradual trend toward curtailment of Senate filibustering.

On the 9th of September a river and harbor bill carrying large appropriations became the business of the Senate, and a small coterie of Republicans began to talk. They asserted that funds allotted for numerous projects were unconscionably exorbitant and that obstruction would be justified to prevent so unreasonable a drain upon the Treasury. The bill as drafted appropriated more than $50,000,000, and Republican objectors fought to reduce the amount. From the 15th to the 17th William S. Kenyon of Iowa alone consumed most of the time, and Democratic leaders became so disgusted that they undertook to do something about it. Accordingly, by a new interpretation of the rules, a parliamentary effort was made to inconvenience as much as possible the course of the obstruction.

Even under the strictest enforcement of the rules it had hitherto been considered altogether in order for a speaking Senator to yield to another for a question, but only for a question. No Senator had the right to farm out the floor to others for statements and long interruptions; the power of recognizing Senators to speak rests and always has rested with the presiding officer. Even questions, however, might relieve and rest a tiring filibusterer. The possibility of such relief the Democratic leaders determined to avert.

[11] Ray Stannard Baker, *Woodrow Wilson: Life and Letters* (New York, 1927-39), Vol. V, p. 111.

After one of the numerous interruptions which Kenyon allowed, Senator Nathan P. Bryan of Florida on September 17 sought by means of a point of order to prevent yielding to other Senators for any purpose except by unanimous consent. Joseph T. Robinson of Arkansas sat in the chair as presiding officer and promptly sustained the point. Reed Smoot of Utah appealed from the ruling, but by a vote of 28 yeas to 24 nays the Senate rejected the appeal by laying it on the table. The dignified body had formally decreed that filibusters seeking to delay business by talk must undergo the strain of occupying the time without interruption.

Kenyon accepted the challenge. "It is a most amazing thing," he said, "that . . . a gag rule is to be applied to the Senate to pass a 'pork-barrel' bill. If the Senators who have so nicely arranged this drama think that they will gain anything by that kind of performance, they will be very much mistaken."

So stern a ruling, which might also cut off much of the important cross-fire of debate, troubled the conservative Senate. When the issue rose again later in the day, Senator Pomerene occupied the chair. Unsympathetic toward efforts to curtail Senate debate under the terms of the new interpretation of the rules, he refused to render a decision and submitted the question once more to the Senate. Lengthy debate ensued, lasting so long that the second vote could not be taken till the following day.

Gallinger of New Hampshire branded the ruling as "revolutionary and unjust," a procedure amounting to an amendment of the rules—which could be accomplished only after due notice. Senator Bryan argued at length that a speaking Senator had no right to the floor except to occupy it himself. If there were interruptions, he thought, they took place with common consent; a single objection could prevent a Senator from interrupting or questioning another. Frank B. Brandegee of Connecticut openly called such a suggestion ridiculous. "Such a rule," he declared, "would absolutely bring to a standstill the business of the Senate, and if enforced it would reduce the whole procedure to a series of soliloquies delivered here by individual Senators. If nobody could take part in the debate there would never be any Senators here to listen to them; it would be a funereal proceeding, and would result in a farce; but it is utterly idle to think that the enforcement of that rule would stop any filibuster."

William J. Stone of Missouri announced that he had been converted by the arguments of Senator Bryan. The need to stop the filibuster would justify action. "It has been astonishing to me," he submitted, "that three or four Senators should put themselves in this strange attitude of strenuous, persistent, and uncompromising opposition to this great measure of such wide national importance. . . . I can not escape the feeling that they are afflicted with a most exaggerated sense of egotism or else with some other mental abnormality or disease. . . . I can not believe that they alone of all Senators have a proper conception of public duty."

Kenyon's memory supplied him with a ready retort. "Mr. President," he began, "it is very delightful to listen to a lecture on filibustering from the distinguished Senator from Missouri." He then went on to recall that in 1908 the same Senator had been an important contributor to the stupendous filibuster against the Aldrich-Vreeland Currency Bill. Men were present who remembered that Stone had read about the Argentine Republic, Australia, New Zealand, China, and Japan. "There is not a smarter man in the world," Kenyon said, "than the Senator from Missouri, nor a more likable man. . . ." Then, turning directly to the Senator, he paid the final tribute. "Filibuster! Why, bless your dear old soul, you are the king filibuster of the United States!"

The second vote on the new ruling came after time for calm deliberation, when many Senators had become convinced that the value of debate would be seriously limited if a single objection could prohibit a speaker from yielding even for a question. Consequently the august body reversed itself, 15 voting for the new interpretation and 35 against it. Rules governing the Senate and making possible the practice of filibustering remained as they had been.

Already John Sharp Williams of Mississippi had pungently suggested that the majority wear down the filibustering coterie. "There are still some Senators who think they are the Senate," he had said, "but the Senate can teach them better if the Senate will. . . . The only way under the sun to do it is to pass a resolution in this body to stay in permanent and perpetual session until this bill is passed. Do not give the filibustering Senators from eleven o'clock at night until eleven o'clock the next morning to hunt up new pegs whereupon to hang verbiage. . . . Let them talk until they drop upon their seats. Let them talk until their mouths are so dry that they can not utter another word."[12]

As persistent obstruction of the river and harbor bill continued, the majority agreed that they could at least force a continuous session in an endeavor to crush the opposition. Through the night of the 18th-19th of September, in response to necessity, Theodore E. Burton of Ohio talked against the bill. It was an exhausting experience for speaker and listeners, but Burton talked on and on against time. He was relieved by occasional interruptions and at last, at 6:30 in the morning, by the inability of the sergeant at arms to muster a quorum for an hour. Senators had gone home for rest, and they were reluctant to be brought back to boredom and inaction. A dryly humorous announcement by Coe I. Crawford of South Dakota brought a flicker of amusement to the grimness of the occasion. Shortly before seven o'clock he entered the chamber to remark, "I desire to say to the Senate that I did not have very much rest, but I enjoyed what little I did have."

But the ranks of the Democratic majority had already begun to yield to the prolonged resistance of a few Republicans. It was understood that members of the Committee on Commerce had agreed to reduce appropriations in the bill to less than half their original level.[13] At 5:30 on the afternoon of the 19th the majority abandoned the idea of further continuous session and permitted a recess. When the Senate reconvened after a week-end, Republicans demonstrated once more that they would filibuster. The majority readily capitulated and allowed the bill to be sent back to committee with instruc-

[12] 51 *Cong. Record*, p. 15319.
[13] *New York Times*, Sept. 19, 1914.

tions to reduce the appropriations. Another filibuster had ended in victory for its organizers.

A month later, in the same session, the final business of Congress was thrown into discord by another sharp filibuster. A few Southern Democrats, led by the noted Hoke Smith of Georgia, strenuously attempted to force consideration of legislation for the benefit of cotton growers. The economic outlook for cotton interests was serious. With the outbreak of the war abroad many foreign markets had been closed, but the Southern crop was large and the consequent surplus appalling. The price of cotton stood several cents below the cost of production, planters were in debt for fertilizer and other supplies, and the entire credit structure dependent upon cotton was in danger of collapse. Although the fall Congressional campaign was in full swing and the election near at hand, cotton producers and their friends demanded remedial legislation before adjournment.

Congress had been in session throughout the summer of 1914 and many members were eager to get home. Since neither House can adjourn for more than three days without the consent of the other, the House of Representatives passed a concurrent resolution that the Congress adjourn sine die at six p.m. on the 22nd of October. Leaders in the House had made up their minds and pushed through the resolution only at the last minute, and it was conveyed to the Senate an hour and a half before the time it was presumably to be effective. But the leaders of the Democratic majority in the Senate had agreed to adjournment, and it was supposed that the resolution would be approved promptly and formally by the assembled Senators. Representatives in the House made hasty preparations to leave, packing bags and purchasing railway tickets. For them the important things now were home and the approaching elections.

News of the impending adjournment reached President Wilson on the golf links. Prior to 1920 it was generally thought that bills passed by Congress must be signed by the President before final adjournment or lapse without becoming law. President Wilson therefore conceived it to be his duty to rush to the Capitol to be ready to sign last-minute measures. So great was his haste that he arrived at the Capitol dressed in golfing clothes and without his reading glasses. As bills began to arrive for his attention, the discomfited President, believing Congress about to adjourn and the necessity for signatures therefore urgent, borrowed from his Irish-born friend, Senator William Hughes of New Jersey, a pair of glasses through which he could peer at the documents.[14]

But Senators who demanded legislation for the welfare of cotton had no intention of permitting final adjournment. Only an hour and a half need be killed to render ineffectual the proposal for adjournment at six o'clock. And despite the fact that the House adjournment resolution was held undebatable, Smith of Georgia and his supporters forced so many yea-and-nay votes on motions to adjourn for the day, to recess, and to proceed to executive business that the hour of six passed without a Senate vote upon the House proposition. The concurrent resolution was dead. The President's haste in leaving his game of golf went unrewarded.

Southern Senators ardently favoring a cotton bill believed that by preventing adjournment sine die they could hold members of Congress in Washington for action or, failing that, they could pass legislation for cotton without an actual quorum. As Congressional rules are interpreted, a quorum is presumed to be present unless the point is raised or its absence is revealed by a vote. If legislation could be passed by unanimous consent instead of by formal vote the embarrassing question of a quorum might be avoided altogether.

The next day, however, it was found that a quorum could not be convened in either House till after the fall elections, since impatient members had gone home without waiting for final adjournment. And it was soon apparent that no compromise measure framed in favor of cotton could be passed by unanimous consent without a quorum.

James P. Clarke of Arkansas, President pro tempore of the Senate, waxed indignant that Congress should be held helplessly in session without a quorum in either House. "The whole proceeding

[14] *ibid.*, Oct. 23, 1914.

with which we are confronted today assumes to me the proportions of a farce," he announced. No chance remained, he argued, for legislation favorable to cotton growers. To him the maneuvers were a "sham battle" with "all the elements of a deliberate deception." He would leave the scene of struggle that very evening, he declared. "I think this vaudeville ought to stop, and I think this Congress ought to get away from here."

Morris Sheppard of Texas resented the remarks disparaging to Senators filibustering for aid to cotton. "I want to denounce," he replied to the Senator from Arkansas, "the insinuation by him or by anybody else that we are engaged in any grandstand play or sham battle or in any insincere movement, as unjust and as unworthy of a Senator of the United States. . . . I want to say further," he continued, "that, so far as I am concerned, I will never vote to adjourn this session of Congress as long as any hope of relief for the cotton growers of the South remains."

The filibustering Southerners held Congress in session through the 23rd of October, but on the 24th they abandoned all hope of passing a cotton bill. Sheppard himself admitted "that the events of yesterday demonstrated that there is no hope for any kind of relief from Congress at the present session." And said Smith of Georgia, "I have no apology and no regret for the action which I have taken. . . . My own personal judgment would be to stay here, but I am almost alone in that opinion." Adjournment sine die was then duly voted by both Houses.

The filibuster to delay adjournment had succeeded, even though its ultimate purpose was lost through inability to agree upon an acceptable legislative compromise. The episode demonstrated once more that filibustering, even within a single session, may be a weapon for members of every party and of every group.

That dilatory tactics might be used by both political parties even in the same extended filibuster was indicated in the prolonged contest over the Ship Purchase Bill in 1915. The administration proposed that, at least during the world crisis of war in Europe, the government should purchase merchant ships. War conditions which

had resulted in a shortage of vessels and in high shipping charges
had not been fully alleviated despite valiant governmental efforts
If the government should go into the shipping business charges to
exporters could be reduced and goods could be moved more rapidly.
Private shipping interests, however, had no wish for such competition. Naturally they preferred the huge profits to be made under
existing circumstances. Conservative Republicans and even many
Democrats lost no time in defending the position of the shipping interests. Government entry into business was socialistic, they argued.
The plan would involve the nation in difficulties with belligerent
powers; it was not sound economically; it was an attempt by the
President to dominate Congress and the country. Such bitter attacks
were immediately forthcoming.

In the Senate the struggle began on January 4 when the bill came
before the body on motion of Duncan U. Fletcher of Florida. Gallinger of New Hampshire promptly spoke for the Republican minority. "It has come to our ears on this side of the Chamber," he
announced, "that there is to be undue haste in the consideration of
this bill, that it is to be pressed in season and out of season, at season-
able hours and unseasonable hours." Therefore he served notice of
filibuster; to the Republicans the measure was unacceptable at any
season. They would, the Senator warned, "be compelled to resist it
in every proper and parliamentary way." Democratic annoyance
over delaying the bill found expression in the words of Stone of
Missouri who asserted on the floor, "We have the votes to put it
through if ever we can get a chance to vote. Unless Senators on the
other side adopt some plan or scheme of inexcusable and unpardon-
able obstruction we will get to a vote. . . ."

Elihu Root of New York, about to retire from the Senate, rose to
defend delay. "The discussion of measures in this body," he insisted,
"does not consist alone in the making of speeches. We discuss measures with but very few Senators here. There are not twenty in the
room at this moment. I counted them a few minutes ago, and there
were fourteen. What, then, is the use of discussion? The use is this,
that every speech is going to the country, that every hour passed is

calling the attention of the country to the measure. The people of the United States begin to consider, begin to read, begin to discuss, and gradually week by week they form their opinions, and their opinions find their way back here. The process of discussion results ultimately in the reaching of conclusions which are conformable to the will and judgment of the people of the United States. That, sir, is why the long, patient, and sometimes tedious discussion of questions in the Senate of the United States is of vast utility, although we would suppose that it was useless from counting the men who are listening to the speeches which are made."[15]

Republican orators, believing at the same time that a special session would be a political asset if it could be forced by delay, dragged out the discussion for weeks. Democrats in conference agreed that they would hold the bill before the Senate for a vote even to the detriment of appropriation bills. Republicans in turn voted in conference that they would fight the bill to a finish.[16] On and on they talked, day after day, sometimes giving up the floor only when practically exhausted. Gallinger, nearing eighty years of age, held the floor continuously for more than seven hours and professed himself "about as fresh" as when he began.

Regular session hours had been prolonged by the Democrats until late in the evening; and by the 29th of January, after more than three weeks of filibuster, the majority determined to resort to continuous session. The proceedings during that evening, when it was clear that the Senate would sit through the night, were for hours a pandemonium of tangled motions, points of order, appeals from decisions of the chair, votes, demands to be excused from voting, and consequent votes on the demands. In the welter of motions, amid heated and disconnected argument over every detail of procedure, not even the presiding officer could always tell what question was before the Senate.

[15] 52 *Cong. Record*, p. 909. See Philip C. Jessup, *Elihu Root* (New York, 1938), Vol. II, pp. 278-84.
[16] *New York Times*, Jan. 17, 22, 1915.

When the Senate became calmer as the hour grew late, Smoot of Utah rose to begin a speech celebrated in the annals of filibustering. "As a servant of the American people," he commenced, "I feel it my duty to do everything in my power to defeat the pending bill. It is undemocratic, unrepublican, un-American, vicious in its provisions, and will be dangerous and mischievous if it ever becomes a law." Suiting his action to the word, he talked relevantly and fervently for more than eleven hours and a half with few interruptions and without a roll call. Not even the privilege of resting upon the arm of his chair was allowed him, for a point of order against that effort for relief brought a prompt ruling from the presiding officer that the Senator "will either take his feet or take his seat." The performance is justly ranked among the great feats of physical endurance in the history of the Senate.

Yielding the floor at 9:35 in the morning, Smoot was followed by his colleague from Utah, George Sutherland, who spoke at length in a very low tone. Impatiently Owen of Oklahoma demanded that the chair compel the filibustering Senator to speak audibly. "No Senator," he objected, "has a right to occupy the floor mumbling to himself. . . ."

"The Senator's language," Sutherland retorted angrily—and this time loud enough to be heard—"may be parliamentary, but it is offensive." He would challenge Owen's demand and his power to carry it out. "Perhaps the Senator from Oklahoma," he said in an acid tone, "knows of some way by which he could compel the Senator from Utah to raise his voice."

Owen declared that the Senate ought nevertheless to compel it; but Vice President Thomas R. Marshall could reply only that "the Chair has no power to decide in what tone of voice a Senator shall discuss a question."

Continuous session, as in other instances in Senate experience, soon became as wearisome to the majority as to the minority. Doggedly the Republicans talked until at last at 11:15 p.m. on Saturday the 30th, after more than thirty-six hours of oratory, the Democrats consented to a recess till Monday.

When the Senate reassembled, on the 1st of February, an amazing situation presented itself. Democratic James P. Clarke of Arkansas, President pro tempore of the Senate and a trusted leader of the party, moved that the bill be sent back to committee. The Vice President ruled the motion out of order, but the Senate promptly refused to sustain the chair by 37 yeas to 46 nays. A revolt of seven Democrats had thrown control of the chamber into the hands of the Republicans. In the opinion of Clarke of Arkansas, Bankhead of Alabama, Camden of Kentucky, Hardwick of Georgia, Hitchcock of Nebraska, O'Gorman of New York, and Vardaman of Mississippi, all Democrats, the filibuster and the efforts to restrain it had lasted long enough;[17] they believed that other important legislation should now take precedence over the shipping bill.

Vainly Stone of Missouri, on behalf of the regular Democrats, moved to adjourn. The Republicans and their new-found allies were determined to force a vote to recommit and virtually kill the bill. The scene had changed; no longer could Stone boast, "We have the votes." Desperately the Democrats, having denounced obstruction for days, themselves resorted to filibuster.

James A. Reed of Missouri rose and talked for the day. Like other Democrats loyal to the caucus decision he was furious at the turn of events. No better bill had been proposed, he reminded his opponents. "If you have a better proposition, why have you not submitted it? You have put orators upon the floor who have sung their wearisome songs and filled in their dry platitudes and maunderings with long extracts from newspapers that had nothing whatever to do with the case.

"We listened to a speech that was concluded this afternoon presumptively upon this bill. . . . It originated in a burst of poetry, which was some kind of eulogy upon old age. It ran and ranted up and down the scale, through the falsetto, the orotund, the guttural, and all intermediate noises, natural and supernatural, human ears can endure. It continued to run on, like the stream, almost forever,

17 *ibid.*, Feb. 2, 1915.

and it ended, so far as I know, without for a single moment touching this bill. . . ."

Stone on the next day castigated the Democrats in alliance with Republicans as "seven conspirators." "I did not believe," he lamented, "there were seven such Democrats in the world, and certainly not in the Senate." It was an outrageous breach of party fealty, he thought, a departure from the leadership of the Democratic President. "And I want to say right here," he roared, "that I prefer the leadership of Woodrow Wilson to that of Elihu Root, Henry Cabot Lodge, Theodore Burton, William Edgar Borah, Jacob H. Gallinger, or that of any recreant alleged Democrat who goes about with a murderous dagger in his sleeve."

For five days the Democrats filibustered, in the meantime seeking to compose their differences and urging Democratic Senators absent in distance parts of the country to return posthaste. J. Hamilton Lewis of Illinois, sick in Asheville, agreed to return; Francis G. Newlands of Nevada undertook a swift journey from the West; Ellison D. Smith of South Carolina reluctantly made plans to leave an ill family. A recess from Friday to Monday gave the Senate a respite; and on Monday the 8th, with every Senator in Washington, the Democratic organization was once more in control.[18]

The Republican filibuster was promptly revived. Wesley L. Jones of Washington took the floor for a lengthy speech in which he admitted freely his purpose to filibuster. That practice, moreover, he boldly defended. "No important legislation," he asserted, "no legislation of great benefit to the people of this country has ever been defeated by filibustering." Rather, he thought, only legislation which a great section of the country and perhaps a great number of Senators have believed "most injurious and most dangerous has been defeated by filibustering."

Moses E. Clapp of Minnesota implied that the attitude of a filibustering minority might be as nearly representative of majority sentiment in the Senate as the professed attitude of an actual majority of Senators. He developed his remarks from the fact that

[18] *ibid.*, Feb. 4-9, 1915.

legislation is reported to the Senate from one of its committees. "Beginning with a committee of the Senate, say, of seventeen," the Minnesotan pointed out, "nine constitute a majority. The nine are of the majority side. Five constitute a majority of the nine. Any power that can coalesce five makes it a party measure of a majority, to which the other four must subscribe or be charged with want of loyalty to party." In such a situation, as the Senator said, "instead of a majority framing the bill a small minority frames it"; and at times "it is utterly impossible to put most desirable and meritorious amendments upon the bill unless the little coterie of five, the beginning of the power, consent to it."

Charles S. Thomas of Colorado, himself a Democratic filibusterer a few days earlier, considered obstruction a bad practice which ought to be ended. "I am not concerned . . . with the results of a filibuster," he said. "There is no question but that some of them have resulted in better conditions. That is true of every bad situation; but I believe such results would have sooner or later followed without them. . . . The vice of the situation is that where the filibuster is permissible you can place no limit upon its use."

The Republican position upon the bill was summed up by the eminent Elihu Root. "A Senator said to me a few days ago, 'You can not afford to be engaged in a filibuster.' Mr. President, I can not afford to flinch from the duty which upon my oath and my conscience seems to lie before me."

In the meantime the exasperated Democratic majority had resorted again to continuous sitting of the Senate. The session which assembled at noon on the 8th of February adjourned at 6:10 on the evening of the 10th after fifty-four hours and ten minutes of uninterrupted debate and contention. It was a weary and bedraggled group of men who withstood the strain of those hours. Senators slept where they could, or dozed in the chamber. Some were still dressed in evening clothes in broad daylight. One Senator, awakened suddenly to rush into the chamber for a roll call, appeared to his noticeable embarrassment without a collar.[19] Not then could the Senate be called

[19] *ibid.*, Feb. 9, 1915.

a deliberative body. It was rather the stage for a physical contest, a battle in which the majority suffered even more than the opposing minority whom they sought to punish. The public, apprised of the unbelievable confusion resulting from the actions of Democrats and Republicans alike, might well have been pardoned for exclaiming with Mercutio, "A plague o' both your houses!"

On the 11th the Republican filibuster continued unabated; and on the 12th Senator Reed of Missouri, on behalf of the regular Democrats, brought up for consideration a resolution for cloture. As a means of paying respects to that proposal, La Follette immediately discussed international peace and William P. Dillingham of Vermont followed with a speech on immigration.

Discussing the resolution for cloture, Burton of Ohio expressed his conviction that "there are three cases in which a filibuster is not only justifiable but salutary." The first would arise, he thought, "when a vital question of constitutional right is involved"; the second, "when the measure is evidently the result of crude or inconsiderate action"; and the third, "when the Senate is convinced that because of some compulsion" a vote "will not express the honest conviction of the Members."[20]

Robert L. Owen of Oklahoma disagreed. "No one man," he declared, "no matter how sincere he may be or how patriotic his purpose, should be permitted to take the floor of the Senate and keep the floor against the will of every man in the Senate except himself, and coerce and intimidate the Senate. To do so is to destroy the most important principle of self-government—the right of majority rule." The Oklahoma Senator, noted as a filibusterer since his 1911 attempt to coerce the admission of New Mexico to statehood, recognized that his position might be criticized on the score of inconsistency and shrewdly pointed out the fact instead of leaving that pleasure to his opponents. "My use of this bad practice to serve the people," he argued, "does not in any wise change my opinion about the badness of the practice of permitting a filibuster. I acted within the practice, but I think the practice is indefensible, and I illustrated its

[20] 52 Cong. Record, p. 3708.

vicious character by coercing the Senate and compelling it to yield
to my individual will."

To Owen's mind the Constitution itself affords adequate protection against the practice of filibustering. The very provision, he contended, that "the Yeas and Nays of the Members of either House on
any question shall, at the Desire of one fifth of those Present, be
entered on the Journal"[21] guarantees to one-fifth of the Senate the
right "to demand the *immediate taking of the yeas and nays on any
question pending and the record of that vote in the journal of the
Senate.*"[22] Nor could true debate, he thought, be conducted in a body
where members could speak without limit and without relevancy.
"This practice of the Senate in having no cloture, in having no time
fixed for voting, has destroyed debate in the Senate and has driven
the debate into a conference room, where colleagues can get together
and express their minds and hearts to each other and arrive at some
measure of solidarity."[23] If the Constitution were rightly interpreted,
he felt, the Senate practice of allowing unlimited debate would be
broken.

William J. Stone of Missouri, called by Boies Penrose of Pennsylvania "the most notorious filibusterer in the United States Senate,"[24]
announced his conversion to the principle of cloture. "Debate,"
Stone admonished his colleagues, "is one thing; a defiant filibuster,
without pretense of legitimate discussion intended to enlighten the
Senate or the country, is quite another thing." He asserted, moreover, that if cloture could not be adopted by votes it ought to be
made effective by force. "In face of the situation as we have it today,
the presiding officer ought to be—and I hope is—brave and strong
enough, despite any outburst of yells and whoops, to direct the secretary to call the ayes and noes when they have been ordered and thus
force the issue to a decision. If he should do that, he would receive
the plaudits of the American people. . . ."[25]

21 Art. I, Sec. 5.
22 52 *Cong. Record,* p. 3718. Italics in the source.
23 *ibid.,* p. 3732.
24 *ibid.,* p. 3376.
25 *ibid.,* pp. 3736-7.

The Senator from Missouri was not alone in that view. Ollie M. James of Kentucky declared that if he were in the chair a motion to close debate would promptly be put to a vote; the technical rules of the Senate should not stand in the way of a larger parliamentary right. "No Senator here and no citizen of America," he averred, "can take the position that a majority is not entitled to rule, even in the Senate of the United States, which has been so long the bulwark of greed and special privilege."

Elihu Root two days later voiced the opinion that such action would be "revolution." "I use the term advisedly," he said. "If the Senate of the United States does not proceed in accordance with its rules, then there is no deliberative body to consider and make the laws. You may consider a rule inexpedient and unwise; if so, you can change it; but so long as rules stand there is no protection for liberty, there is no protection for representative government, unless they are obeyed. . . . If a rule is broken after debate has continued for a month it can be broken when debate has continued for a week, or for an hour, or when it has not begun. . . . You can not have your rules and ignore them. You can not break them today and have their protection tomorrow."

Senator James then suggested a more subtle and technical procedure for accomplishing the purpose. If a Senator seeking to move the previous question (to close debate at once) should be ruled out of order by the chair, he asked, could not that Senator appeal from the chair to the Senate? And if a majority of the Senate should vote that the motion ought to be considered in order, would it not be the duty of the chair to put to a vote the question of closing debate? That proposal Root regarded as simply "an ingenious method of violating the rules of the Senate." He preferred to stand upon the ground that it would be no less revolutionary even for a majority to break the rules of the Senate. "The purpose of rules," he insisted, "is to establish a course of conduct which shall be a protection to the minority and preserve them . . . against arbitrary repression on the part of the majority."

The proposal offered by Reed of Missouri that the Senate adopt cloture brought a barrage of opposition, particularly from the Republicans. Henry Cabot Lodge, who in 1893 had favored a rule to end debate and had written and spoken in support of that position, declared that he had long ago changed his mind.[26] Gallinger of New Hampshire announced that, although he too had once favored limiting debate and had introduced a resolution to that end, service in the Senate had convinced him years earlier that no arrangement for cloture should be adopted.[27]

Democratic Senator James P. Clarke of Arkansas asserted that George F. Hoar, shortly before his death in 1904, had in a private conversation retracted his endorsement of cloture. " 'There was a time in my legislative career,' " the Arkansas Senator quoted Hoar as saying, " 'when I believed that the absence of a cloture rule in the Senate was criminal neglect, and that we should adopt a system of rules by which business could be conducted; but the logic of my long service and observation has now convinced me that I was wrong in that contention. There is a virtue in unlimited debate, the philosophy of which can not be detected upon a surface consideration.' "[28] Had Clarke known it, Hoar's change of mind—authority for which historians have based upon the statement of the Arkansas Senator—had been confirmed even in the Senate debates. On February 18, 1903, in a colloquy with John C. Spooner of Wisconsin, Hoar had announced his agreement with that Senator's contention against the principle of cloture. The elderly Senator from Massachusetts recalled his own experience when in charge of the famous "Force Bill" of 1890-1891. The prolonged discussion of that measure—constituting one of the most noted of organized filibusters—had, he thought, actually altered the opinion of the majority.[29]

The question was simply this: Should unlimited debate in the Senate be ended, in the face of tradition and against the advice of

[26] *ibid.*, p. 3786.
[27] *ibid.*, pp. 3724-5.
[28] *ibid.*, p. 3942.
[29] 36 *Cong. Record*, p. 2337.

distinguished statesmen? Opinions differed both upon the value of tradition and upon the weight of advice given. Not even upon the functions of the Senate could there be a unanimous judgment. Moreover it seemed that, should a movement for limitation be undertaken, there might immediately ensue a filibuster against this attempt to end filibusters which would be more rigorous and more spectacular than any yet seen.

Like Burton of Ohio, Republican Albert B. Cummins of Iowa argued that there are occasions upon which a filibuster "is not only justified but . . . imperatively demanded." Two conditions, he thought, could make a filibuster necessary. The first would result from an attempt by the executive, the President of the United States, "to impose his will upon the Senate"; the second, from a party effort by means of a caucus to bind the members of the Senate majority to action against "the judgment and the conscience" of some of their number. The weight of the argument upon cloture rested, to his mind, upon the side of a rule for eventual limitation of debate; but no such rule should operate in situations which would justify a filibuster.[30]

Whatever the merit of abstract arguments, the practical advantage for the regular Democratic majority upon this occasion lay in bringing debate to an end. If the Ship Purchase Bill were to pass, the filibuster must be broken. But the Republicans talked so persistently against cloture that upon the 17th of February the majority decided upon new strategy by way of compromise. House amendments, in the nature of a modified Ship Purchase Bill (attached to another measure which had already passed the Senate) were presented for consideration. Whatever hope for the bill remained, as the session drew near its automatic close, rested in the chance that a compromise proposal could induce the minority to yield. But the Republicans held their ground and on the 18th the majority gave up the fight. In order to find time for other legislation the issue was shelved by disagreeing to the House amendments and sending the

[30] 52 *Cong. Record*, p. 3840.

whole matter to a committee of conference. A determined and sizable minority had once more proved itself unconquerable.

The filibuster had continued thirty-three calendar days, twenty-seven of them devoted to actual obstruction. Of the latter number the Republicans had consumed twenty-two and the Democrats five. On March 3 the issue flickered again when Fletcher of Florida proposed that a further conference be ordered on disagreements between the two Houses. But John W. Weeks of Massachusetts promptly produced a list of twenty-three Senators who would speak at length on the subject, and Fletcher acknowledged defeat for the session. A year was to pass before the administration could obtain Congressional approval, given with qualifications, for government purchase of merchant ships.

Two years later another great filibuster, one of the most famous in the history of the chamber, deluged the Senate with a tide of popular disfavor which resulted in that dignified body's most drastic rule against filibustering. The short session of the 64th Congress came to an end on March 4, 1917, after fierce filibustering by Senators to whom Woodrow Wilson affixed the soon-popularized brand of infamy, "a little group of willful men." With the end of the session died the President's prewar measure to arm merchant vessels, the Armed Ship Bill.

Actually, this famous—or infamous—filibuster by "willful men" had been immediately preceded by Republican obstruction designed to delay business and force a special session of Congress, thus embarrassing the administration. Republicans on February 23 agreed in conference to precipitate a filibuster,[31] and they followed their plan. From the 23rd to the 28th of February, whenever it served their purpose, Republican orators repeatedly delayed proceedings.

Boies Penrose, celebrated political boss from Pennsylvania, opened the Republican offensive. A Treasury loan had been proposed "on account of the Mexican situation." Penrose solemnly denounced the use of such language in legislation. The word "situation" he regarded as extraordinary. He had known, he barked in ridicule, that

[31] *New York Times,* Feb. 24, 1917.

loans were "incurred for a war, or an epidemic, or a flood, or for starvation, or for an invasion, but here it is proposed to make a loan of $200,000,000 for a 'situation.' "

Democratic John Sharp Williams of Mississippi lamented that such a scene should be made by the Senator from Pennsylvania. "Why," he asked, "should he come here and try to create discord about nothing, about a word, a difference between 'a situation' and 'a mess'?" Williams continued, speaking in semiserious vein: "My friend from Pennsylvania is one of the most genial men who ever lived. He is all right in every respect except when his partisanship is aroused. It makes a man like me, who is really patriotic, sigh with grief when I view his partisanship."

The next day Republican Miles Poindexter of Washington consumed so many hours of Senate time that Williams was once more constrained to express his irritation. "The amount of latitude," he remarked, "permitted to himself by the Senator from Washington . . . was only equaled by the longitude of his observations, and the latitude and longitude were only equaled by the absolute futility of his argument."

Republicans were not now attempting to defeat specific legislation. Their program was to pile up such a congestion of business that Congress could not complete its work before the automatic adjournment on the 4th of March. After Republican Lawrence Y. Sherman of Illinois had harangued the Senate for two hours and a half on Saturday night, the 24th of February, Furnifold McL. Simmons of North Carolina sought on behalf of the Democrats to obtain unanimous consent for a vote on a pending revenue measure. Republicans were willing for the agreement, but objection came from Democratic ranks. Henry F. Ashurst of Arizona announced that there would be no agreement upon the revenue measure unless there should also be an agreement to vote upon an Indian appropriation bill. "You are going to pass that Indian bill," he threatened, "or you will not have any legislation."

The belligerence of the Senator from Arizona disrupted the program of his colleagues; he was urged to wait for suggestions. His reply was an ultimatum: "No; you sang me that kind of a song two years ago—'Wait, wait, wait'—and we waited forever. Now, the iron hand: You will pass the Indian bill, or you will get nothing." The threat was effective; Ashurst obtained his coveted agreement.

When the Senate met the next Monday, Warren G. Harding of Ohio, within four years to be elected to the Presidency of the United States, took the floor to continue the filibuster for portions of two days. In his desire to consume time the Senator resorted to reminiscences. "I had heard, in my rural way," he admitted in one of many personal confessions, "of the gay character of the French capital; and having been brought up along pretty restricted lines, and having that inevitable human tendency to break the confines just a little bit, on one of the trips that I had the fortune to make to the great French capital I said to Mrs. Harding, 'Now, I want a night off. I want to see the lights of this city, and if you will enter into a contract with me that I shall have a night off without any inquiries afterwards, I will buy you any Parisian bonnet you may elect to choose.' The compact was made, and I had my night. It was not worth it."

Nor was talk the only expedient of the Republican minority. On the night of the 28th of February, in an agonizing performance of nearly five hours, they forced thirty-three consecutive roll-call votes. Plainly the minority, if they wished, could continue utterly to disrupt the business of the Senate. But on the 1st of March, after Penrose had insisted on a prolonged reading of the journal, the Republican obstruction was suddenly abandoned. In public it was asserted that patriotic motives had prevailed to bring an end to dilatory tactics;[32] but a skeptic in politics may wonder whether the regular Republicans had not simply realized that their filibuster would be conveniently assumed by other tongues.

Almost forgotten were the Republican efforts after the spectacular prostration of business by less than a dozen "radicals" who called down upon themselves and the Senate rules an almost unparalleled storm of popular indignation and fury. The notable filibuster against

[32] *ibid.,* March 2, 1917.

the Armed Ship Bill began when that measure came before the Senate on March 2. Congress had been asked by President Wilson to authorize him to arm American merchant vessels as a protection against ever increasing dangers at sea. Germany had announced unrestricted submarine warfare in a great zone effective on February 1, and Wilson had severed diplomatic relations. Yet he still hoped to defend American lives and property without inevitably plunging the country into war.

The day before the Senate began consideration of the bill for arming ships, the famous Zimmermann note was released to the public. It was a message from the German foreign office, sent through the German ambassador at Washington, suggesting that in the event of war with the United States Mexico should be invited to form an alliance and should be offered assistance in seizing Texas, New Mexico, and Arizona. Moreover, the Mexican government should be asked to urge Japan to join the war against the United States. This amazing message aroused the country to a tempest of indignation against Germany, and popular support for drastic measures was assured.

Floor leadership for the Armed Ship Bill was placed in the hands of Gilbert M. Hitchcock of Nebraska because William J. Stone of Missouri, chairman of the Committee on Foreign Relations, would not support it. Such influential opposition added to the open threat of prolonged discussion guaranteed a tense situation from the outset. The bill must pass in less than forty-eight hours or die with the ending of the session. Opponents feared that such a law could lead the country only into war. They were determined not to support it but to fight to the end to defeat it. Excitement ran high among both the majority and the minority. William F. Kirby of Arkansas, fiercely denouncing the bill and its supporters, reached an impassioned peroration which he began with, "My fellow-citizens." Greeted with a roar of laughter from the galleries he changed his appeal to, "Gentlemen of the convention."[33] "The public mind," he

[33] *ibid.*, March 3, 1917.

cried, "has been inflamed by a hireling sensational press—that ought to be in hell—to a point where we are not able to deliberate about matters as we should."

Debate continued furiously through the 2nd of March, but after midnight Hitchcock and his majority permitted a recess until ten o'clock in the morning in return for an agreement that a House bill of the same nature be substituted for the Senate measure. By the canons of parliamentary procedure that maneuver indicated progress toward passage of the bill.

When the Senate reassembled, speeches and debate were resumed. Senator Stone, in the one really long speech of the filibuster, talked for four hours against the measure. Hourly the situation grew more embittered as Hitchcock repeatedly asked in vain for unanimous consent to fix a time for a vote. George W. Norris of Nebraska, in objecting to any such arrangement, declared that he would kill the bill if he could but that actually most of the time thus far had been consumed by proponents of the issue and that he would never agree to a gag on those opposed.

The angered majority could at least require the Senate to remain in continuous session; there should be no recess for the night. Both administration Democrats and regular Republicans were eager to force the bill through, and by both persuasion and invective sought to silence the unsubmissive minority.

Through the last night on which the Congress could meet, the tiresome speeches went on. At one-thirty in the morning a privileged conference report on agricultural appropriations unexpectedly came before the Senate, and Asle J. Gronna of North Dakota insisted upon talking at length on the subject of wheat. At three o'clock in the morning nine Senators were in the chamber while Gronna read in a mournful voice seemingly endless statistics about grains. In the meantime Senators were shouting with laughter in the Democratic cloakroom over a page's imitations of Senatorial peculiarities.[34]

Indignation mounted, however, as the hope of voting on the measure grew ever slimmer. At 3:20 in the morning Joseph T. Robinson

[34] *ibid.*, March 4, 1917.

of Arkansas, on behalf of the frustrated majority, read a manifesto signed by seventy-five Senators declaring that if a vote could be had they would pass the bill. Opposing Senators declared that theirs was a right for full discussion of a measure which might plunge the country into war. Still early in the morning Norris spoke upon the necessity for full debate. Many bills, he asserted, "were hurled upon Congress during the last few days of the session; and when anybody objected, when anybody thought it was his duty to find out what was being done with the taxpayers' money, or what kind of statutes we were placing upon the books, the cry always came, 'You are filibustering.' " The Senator from Nebraska for one would stand alert in the face of war hysteria. He would seek to learn the full meaning of legislation and expose it in debate. "If it is filibustering," he proclaimed, "to try to find out about something, to do the best you can —when it all comes at once, you can not do much—then I am guilty of filibustering." To substantiate his point that discussion should be thorough, he read from the doctoral dissertation of Woodrow Wilson, arguments of the President himself. "It is the proper duty of a representative body," Wilson had written, "to look diligently into every affair of government and to talk much about what it sees."[35]

As the hours of the morning passed, the filibuster took a new form. Remarkable to relate, obstruction was undertaken by the administration majority. It was known that Robert M. La Follette of Wisconsin wished to speak against the bill, but angry Democrats determined to talk themselves rather than give him an opportunity to speak before crowded galleries in the final hours of the session. In that spirit Owen of Oklahoma talked for a time, then Hitchcock took the floor. Vehemently La Follette demanded of the chair "whether I am to have an opportunity on this floor which belongs to me." Robinson of Arkansas sought by a point of order to prevent the Wisconsin Senator from making such an inquiry. "I will continue on this floor," retorted La Follette, "until I complete my statement unless somebody carries me off, and I should like to see the

[35] cf. Woodrow Wilson, *Congressional Government* (Boston, 1885), p. 303.

man who will do it." But the Senate, in effect, by a vote of 52 to 15 sustained the chair in ruling the inquiry out of order. Vainly La Follette strove to be recognized; Hitchcock unconcernedly talked on. Frustrated in his efforts, the Wisconsin Senator fumed in his seat, drumming on his desk and chewing viciously at an unlit cigar.[36] Once again Hitchcock asked unanimous consent for a vote. La Follette objected and asserted that he would continue to do so "as often as the request is made until I have an opportunity to be heard." In the last moments of the session, after another request for unanimous consent had been rejected, La Follette rose to make a point of order that Hitchcock had now spoken twice on the same subject and was no longer entitled to the floor. But the Senate may grant permission for more than two speeches, and Hoke Smith of Georgia moved that Hitchcock be allowed to proceed. By an overwhelming vote the motion carried. By their affirmative voices the majority announced beyond cavil their cooperation with the counter-filibuster. Hitchcock talked till noon, when the session was declared adjourned sine die. Filibusterism, practiced both by a minority and by the majority, had been victorious.

President Wilson, indignant at the defeat of his measure by recusant Senators, issued to the country a heated statement. The Senate and the Congress had been unable to act, the President asserted, only "because a little group of eleven Senators had determined that it should not." His conclusion was both an indictment and a proposal.

"The Senate of the United States is the only legislative body in the world," he wrote, "which cannot act when its majority is ready for action. A little group of willful men, representing no opinion but their own, have rendered the great Government of the United States helpless and contemptible.

"The remedy? There is but one remedy. The only remedy is that the rules of the Senate shall be so altered that it can act. The country can be relied upon to draw the moral. I believe that the Senate can

[36] *New York Times*, March 5, 1917; 54 *Cong. Record*, pp. 5012-13.

be relied on to supply the means of action and save the country from disaster."[37]

Upon the heads of the filibustering Senators were poured vials of wrath not only from the President but also from their countrymen. Everywhere "rolls of dishonor" were inscribed with their names. Men who had not signed the Senatorial "round robin" in favor of the Armed Ship Bill, or who had not made a satisfactory explanation of their actions, were grouped together as an infamous band of traitors, whether or not they had participated in obstruction. And in all the furor was no breath of criticism against the bitter majority which had actually closed the session in filibuster to deny a fellow Senator the satisfaction of speaking. Against eleven Senators the force of popular fury was displayed: Clapp of Minnesota, Cummins of Iowa, Gronna of North Dakota, Kirby of Arkansas, La Follette of Wisconsin, Lane of Oregon, Norris of Nebraska, O'Gorman of New York, Stone of Missouri, Vardaman of Mississippi, and Works of California. Some press denunciations counted twelve in the group, including William S. Kenyon of Iowa, but he disclaimed any connection with the filibuster.

Although the President's advisers held that merchant ships could be armed under statutes already existing—a policy soon to be followed—public condemnation was not one whit restrained. "As for those wretches in the Senate," said the *New York World,* "envious, pusillanimous, or abandoned, who with doubts and quibbles have denied their country's conscience and courage in order to make a Prussian holiday, they may well be left to the judgment that good men and true men never fail to pass upon delinquents and dastards." Other papers referred to "names . . . bracketed with that of Benedict Arnold," "this nation's blacklist," and "a few political tramps."[38] In Oregon extralegal efforts were made to invoke the famous recall law to unseat Senator Harry Lane. Students at the University of Illinois hanged La Follette in effigy. Long-scheduled speeches to be given by Senators who had filibustered were cancelled by indignant

[37] *New York Times,* March 5, 1917.
[38] *ibid.,* for many press quotations.

organizations. Wheeling, West Virginia, businessmen telegraphed La Follette that he was not wanted because he had "disgraced himself and the nation." The Kentucky Senate voted a resolution referring to "un-American, disloyal, unpatriotic, traitorous, and cowardly Senators," condemning their "outrageous action" as "unmanly, unpatriotic, un-American, unparalleled, and unwarranted." The Tennessee House called the filibuster "contemptible and little short of treason." Legislatures in other states adopted stinging resolutions of censure. Citizens of Mississippi sent to Senator Vardaman a large iron cross weighing forty pounds and inscribed "Lest the Kaiser Forget." Residents of Jonesboro, Arkansas, sent to Kirby thirty pieces of silver, declaring that "if Judas Iscariot earned his so have you."[39]

Never had a filibuster so stirred the public mind. The consensus of popular judgment was in agreement with the President: the situation had become unbearable and the Senate should at last be brought to provide the remedy.

[39] *ibid.*, March 6-9, 1917.

CHAPTER V

CLOTURE AT LAST

CHAPTER V

CLOTURE AT LAST

THE adoption of the Senate rule for cloture, after scenes of high drama, was itself singularly undramatic. The Senate convened in special session on March 5, 1917, a day on which the press was ringing with denunciation of its rules, and popular indignation had burst out in full fury against obstruction and obstructionists. On the 8th a rule for cloture was proposed by the Democratic floor leader, Thomas S. Martin of Virginia, considered immediately, and passed by a vote of 76 to 3.[1] Only Gronna of North Dakota, La Follette of Wisconsin, and Sherman of Illinois voted in the negative.

The debate was unimpressive. Indeed, as La Follette remarked, it "hardly rose to the importance of the occasion." The stage was carefully set, the resolution to amend the rules was slated to be passed, and no oratorical battle was needed as a prelude. For the Senate, speeches were brief. The fire and the showmanship of a great fight were lacking.

But the Senators were cautious. Public outcry against the Armed Ship filibuster might change the precedents of more than a century, but it should not be allowed to sweep them altogether away. Free speech in the Senate should still be the rule and cloture the exception. Both Democrats and Republicans in party conferences decided to support a much-qualified rule for ending debate upon the demand of a two-thirds majority.[2] Senators who thought that discussion should end at the will of a simple majority were overridden. Even upon the floor, when Henry F. Hollis of New Hampshire suggested

[1] 55 *Cong. Record,* p. 45. See George H. Haynes, *The Senate of the United States* (Boston, 1938), Vol. I, pp. 402-4.
[2] *New York Times,* March 8, 1917.

an amendment to provide cloture through majority action, a cry of "bad faith" and the intercession of Senator Martin induced him to withdraw it. Leaders of the Senate proposed to curb filibustering, but drastic action they would not support.

The procedure for closing debate, as adopted in 1917, is that which stands today. Cloture may be moved at any time if the motion be signed by sixteen Senators. "One hour after the Senate meets on the following calendar day but one," after a quorum has been ascertained to be present, the motion is voted upon and is carried by the affirmative voice of two-thirds of those voting. If it is actually carried no Senator is thereafter entitled to speak in all more than one hour on the pending measure, its amendments, and motions affecting it; and further amendments may be offered only by unanimous consent.[3]

Few Senators believed that so mild an arrangement would end obstruction in the chamber, or even that it could often be applied. However it was a step—many thought in the right direction, others as earnestly believed it in the wrong—in the long, slow trend toward curtailment of filibusters. It afforded an implement which could in emergency be used to prevent Congressional paralysis because of the stubbornness of a few dissenting Senators. But if anyone supposed that a provision for cloture would bring an end to filibustering, even by a small minority, events in succeeding years have proved him a poor judge of Senatorial characteristics. Intense filibusters have been waged exactly as before, and fierce discussion of the need for new changes in the rules has alternately flared and flickered.

The first spectacular filibuster after the inclusion of cloture in the rules came in the short session which closed in 1919. During the whole session business was delayed by the Republican minority, conscious that by virtue of the election victory of 1918 their party would have control of the Senate after March 4. Few sessions have been more notable for extended speeches on public policy; if post-

[3] Senate Rule XXII, *Senate Manual* (Washington, 1938), p. 28.

war America needed a Congressional forum of discussion, it existed in the Senate. Republicans had little intention of allowing a Democratic chamber to pass legislation; and by February 19 filibustering became chronic and remained so until adjournment sine die.

In addition to the general Republican feeling that the people had given them a mandate, leaders of the party insisted that a special session of Congress should be forced in order to keep representatives of the people closely in touch with peace negotiations in Paris.[4] Rumblings of opposition to a League of Nations were already loud.[5] An ostensible reason for extended filibuster needed to be found; and for a time the conference report on a mineral leasing bill, brought up for consideration on February 19, served the purpose. Should the public lands be developed, and should the government impose strict regulations upon private enterprise? Republican Senators talked on issues far afield, and even Democratic Senators could not refrain from speeches on various phases of national policy.

One of the bitterest opponents of the leasing bill was Robert M. La Follette, who thought the legislation too generous a gift to private business, but he had ample assistance from other Republicans who proposed to block the business of the session. The Democratic leadership resorted to night sessions and finally to all-night sessions, but the intense filibuster could not be broken. The mineral leasing bill reached its legislative climax during a four-hour filibuster speech by La Follette on the 1st of March, a flow of words interrupted by pungent exchanges between the Wisconsin Senator and Robinson of Arkansas. Robinson objected to a whispered conversation between Boies Penrose and the filibustering Senator.

"I do not know of any rule of the Senate," La Follette replied, "that regulates exactly how fast a man shall talk here."

"Is the Senator from Wisconsin talking as slowly as he can?" asked Robinson.

[4] *New York Times,* Feb. 27, 1919.
[5] See Denna Frank Fleming, *The United States and the League of Nations, 1918-1920* (New York, 1932), esp. Chaps. III, V, VI, *passim.*

"No; he is not," came the answer. "He has been covering a good deal of ground, and I hope it will be beneficial to the Senator from Arkansas."

"There is no doubt about the Senator covering a good deal of ground," Robinson taunted, "but he is scattering it out rather thin."

La Follette, growing angry as the heckling of the Arkansas Senator continued, refused to yield further. But Robinson furiously persisted, until La Follette, shaking his fist at the Southern Senator, shouted, "No; I do not yield." The breathless galleries, expecting a physical encounter, watched the Senators glower at one another in silence. But the incident passed without actual violence.[6]

The Democratic majority in the meantime agreed to abandon the leasing bill. They could not pass it in the face of such opposition, and they believed that even more important legislation should be brought before the Senate. Accordingly, at an evening session a measure for a Victory Loan was considered, but the prospect for transacting business remained discouraging. At 12:30 in the morning, apparently fully recovered from his lengthy effort of the afternoon, La Follette walked into the chamber, weighted down "like a packhorse" with books and documents. At 12:50 he took the floor; clearly the Senate was doomed to a night of filibuster. Yet the measure passed, for La Follette unexpectedly spoke only till 4:15 in the morning; and after difficulty in securing a quorum the bill was finally approved in the gray dawn of the 2nd of March.[7]

For the remainder of that day, which was Sunday, weary members enjoyed a brief rest by grace of memorial services for deceased Senators and Representatives. But the session which began at ten o'clock Monday morning, March 3, ended with legislation still blocked at noon on the 4th. A general deficiency appropriation bill was the chief business of the chamber, but there were Senators grimly determined that it should never come to a vote. During the final night and morning of the session, La Follette, Joseph I. France of Maryland, and Lawrence Y. Sherman of Illinois assumed the task of talking

[6] *New York Times*, March 2, 1919; 57 *Cong. Record*, p. 4710.
[7] *New York Times*, March 2, 3, 1919.

away the remaining hours. Sherman boasted that the bill would never pass "unless I drop dead." Helplessly the majority leaders paced about the Senate chamber, or sat tight-lipped in their seats. But the filibusterers subsided only in the last minutes of the session, too late for action upon a mass of important legislation. Great appropriation bills necessary for government expenditures were lost in the parliamentary wreckage and it was plain that a special session would soon be imperative.

Among those disgusted that the Senate had once more been compelled to surrender to the strategy of filibuster was Vice President Thomas R. Marshall. The press of the country reported that he banged his gavel and declared the session adjourned "sine Deo"— not "without day," as runs the usual form, but "without God."[8]

The cumbersome rule for cloture, with the large majority necessary for its adoption, could not have been applied in the short session ending in 1919. But the burning controversy over ratification of the Treaty of Versailles brought the Senate at last to a limitation of debate. On the 13th of November, 1919, a petition signed by twenty-three Democratic Senators was presented by Gilbert M. Hitchcock to end debate on the Lodge reservations to the treaty of peace. That motion for cloture was declared out of order; the rule provided that debate might be ended upon a "pending measure," not upon reservations or upon parts of the proposition before the Senate. Democrats were not alone, however, in wishing to close debate. It was widely rumored that a small group of antitreaty "irreconcilables" intended to talk on and on till the session ended without action on the treaty.[9] Leaders of both parties wished to avoid that eventuality. Later on the same day a cloture petition signed by thirty Republicans, intended to apply to the treaty and all related questions, was presented by Henry Cabot Lodge. On the 15th of November the motion was adopted by a vote of 78 to 16.[10] For the first time an

---

[8] *ibid.*, March 5, 1919.

[9] *ibid.*, Nov. 13, 1919.

[10] George Wharton Pepper, *In the Senate* (Philadelphia, 1930), at p. 101, points out that in securing action on treaties (requiring a two-thirds majority for ratification) the present modified cloture rule is as effective as majority cloture, if two-thirds of the Senators are actually eager to vote.

overwhelming majority of the Senate had acted to end debate by rule. But not until the 19th of November, four days after the adoption of cloture, had the last talkative Senator availed himself of the privilege for limited discussion. On that day the Senate rejected the Treaty of Versailles, with or without reservations, and the Congress adjourned sine die.

Less than two years thereafter signs of Democratic obstruction were evident during the consideration of the Republican measure known as the Emergency Tariff Bill, legislation designed primarily to aid agriculture. Oscar W. Underwood of Alabama, Pat Harrison of Mississippi, and other Democrats denied that they were engaged in dilatory tactics but insisted that proper, legitimate, and full discussion must be permitted.[11] None the less, appropriation bills were imperilled by the long delay; and on the 31st of January, 1921, Boies Penrose of Pennsylvania submitted a cloture petition signed by thirty-four Republican Senators. Two days later a vote on ending debate resulted in 36 yeas as against 35 nays, but two-thirds having failed to vote in the affirmative the motion was lost. Yet the bill was finally allowed to pass on the 16th of February, only to be killed by the veto of President Wilson.

A similar filibuster situation arose with consideration of the Fordney-McCumber Tariff Bill in 1922. The Harding administration discovered that its program to raise duties was fraught with political difficulties. Republican James E. Watson of Indiana charged as early as May 5 that Democrats were obstructing the measure, and he announced himself in favor of longer sessions. "The sole object of all this talk day after day," he declared, "is to filibuster, to postpone, to procrastinate, to delay, to put off the passage of this bill just as near election day as is possible." Five days later Porter J. McCumber of North Dakota, in charge of the bill on the Senate floor, himself accused the Democratic minority of filibustering to defeat the tariff legislation. "We will accept that gage of battle," he remarked in defiance, and went on to declare that the Senate needed an effective rule to end debate and a rule to compel Senators to

11 *New York Times,* Jan. 27, 29, 1921.

speak only upon the subject before the body. "We have neither of those rules," he admitted with regret, "and there is nothing left to do but to labor during the long hours of the day and the long hours of the night until Senators will agree to vote. . . ."

Oscar W. Underwood of Alabama denied that the Democrats were obstructing. To make his point convincing the Senator declared that, if a filibuster were really in progress, it would be possible to call for some 8,000 roll calls which he thought could be made to account for 2,000 hours or 200 ten-hour days, without a word of debate![12] But Republicans believed that the spirit of filibuster stalked the Senate halls. In their conference on the 25th of May they talked of cloture, and on the 31st the Republicans voted party approval of a change in the rules which would allow cloture upon revenue and appropriation bills by majority vote. While the resolution was adopted by 32 votes against 1, it was significant that twenty-seven Republicans, most of them understood to be against the proposition, did not attend the conference. Although a committee of five Republican Senators had been designated by the party leadership to study the form of such a rule, no further action resulted. Underwood for one had let it be known that no such alteration of the rules could be adopted without "full debate."[13]

In the meantime efforts were made for cloture under the existing rule, and finally a petition with fifty-two Republican signatures was submitted by McCumber on the 5th of July. Two days later the motion for cloture was lost, having failed to receive the requisite two-thirds vote; 45 Senators voted in the affirmative and 35 in the negative. The debate went on for weeks. Despite Republican fears, however, the Democratic filibuster tactics were only incipient and the bill was eventually enacted into law.

Far more famous is the confessed obstruction conducted by Southern Democrats in the brief third session of the 67th Congress, called late in 1922 by President Harding. The first of a series of notable filibusters marred the program of majority leaders in the Senate:

[12] *ibid.*, May 26, 1922; cf. 62 *Cong. Record*, p. 7627.
[13] *New York Times*, May 26, June 1, 1922.

an organized minority resisted legislation intended to invoke federal law against the crime of lynching. Advocates of the measure proclaimed it a humanitarian effort to free Negroes in the South from mob terrorism. They declared it necessary that the power of the federal government should be used to protect citizens from lawless violence. Southerners branded the proposal as an unconstitutional contrivance to supplant the criminal law of the states and as an ill conceived scheme which would incite racial friction. Under the leadership of Oscar W. Underwood and Pat Harrison, Senators made no secret of their intention to obstruct. Indeed their course was popular in the South, and there was every reason to flaunt rather than to deny the filibuster.

Trouble with the Southern Democrats began on the 27th of November when Samuel M. Shortridge, Republican of California, moved that the Senate consider the Dyer federal antilynching legislation already passed by the House. That day, however, Southerners found it unnecessary to exert themselves unduly. Henry L. Myers of Montana and Robert L. Owen of Oklahoma, with characteristic Senatorial discursiveness, relieved the situation by talking about the visit in America of the French statesman, M. Georges Clemenceau. Upon the conclusion of their remarks, La Follette sought unanimous consent for consideration of a resolution regarding mergers of meat packers; but Nathaniel B. Dial of South Carolina promptly disrupted the plan of the Wisconsin Senator by staging a bit of personal obstruction. He made it plain that he would block the business of the Senate unless the body should pass a measure for the relief of a former collector of internal revenue in his state.

"I should like to have that bill passed," the South Carolinian insisted. "I have been trying all day to secure its consideration. . . . I expect to leave the city in a day or two, to be gone two or three days. I should like to have my little bill passed before that time. If I could get unanimous consent to do so I should be very glad to have it considered, but, if I can not, I am going to object to any measure coming up by unanimous consent so long as I am in town. . . ."

Simmons of North Carolina inquired whether Dial would be willing to allow consideration of La Follette's resolution on the activities of meat packers if the Wisconsin Senator should consent to action upon the South Carolina matter.

"I did not pay any attention to the reading of the resolution," said Dial, "and I do not know anything about it and do not care anything about it for the present, but I want to be assured that I can secure the passage of my uncontested bill reported unanimously by the Claims Committee."

Senator Reed Smoot, however, announced that there would be objection to considering the bill which Dial so ardently advocated. The South Carolinian thereupon objected to the consideration of the La Follette resolution. The Senate, having accomplished nothing beyond a display of conflicting wills, soon adjourned for the day. Yet it was clear to all observers that this skirmishing was but a prelude to the strenuous opposition which Southerners would undertake toward a federal antilynching law. The South would never approve such a measure, and it would never be passed if Southern Senators could prevent it.

When the Senate convened the next day a spectacular filibuster began with devastating thoroughness. Pat Harrison insisted that the journal, usually dispensed with by unanimous consent, be read in full. When the reading had been completed, the Senator from Mississippi began to find fault with the reporting. Did the journal merely record that a given number of Senators had answered "present" upon a quorum call, without stating the names of the Senators? Then he would move that the journal be corrected by listing the names. Moreover, such motions to make trivial corrections could be debated, and were debated. J. Thomas Heflin of Alabama, for instance, discussed the agricultural situation, told jokes, and denounced the Old Guard of the Republican party.

Underwood admitted openly on the floor that Democrats were filibustering, and declared that they were prepared to continue. "We are not disguising what is being done. . . . It must be apparent, not only to the Senate but to the country, that an effort is being made to prevent the consideration of a certain bill, and I want to be perfectly candid about it." It was a "force bill," he contended, and he insisted that if it were to become a law "it would be the beginning of tearing down the last fabric left in the Constitution to support the integrity of the State governments." But it would not become a law, he predicted. "I think all men here know that under the rules of the Senate when fifteen or twenty or twenty-five men say that you can not pass a certain bill, it can not be passed." Important business awaited attention, he acknowledged; but such business must stagnate if the majority should persist in pressing forward an antilynching measure. "We are going to transact no more business," said Underwood, in the manner of an ultimatum, "until we have an understanding about this bill."

The next day the farce continued. The journal was read in full upon the insistence of Kenneth D. McKellar of Tennessee. Harrison then professed astonishment that the journal failed to mention the prayer with which proceedings had been opened. Solemnly he moved that the prayer be recorded verbatim, and with mocking piety he urged Senators to support his proposal. "What if a hundred years from now your great-great-great-grandchildren should look over the journal of yesterday and discover that no mention is made of the fact that there was prayer yesterday in opening this body, and then they should take the proceedings of the following day, as they will appear in the journal tomorrow, and should read that their great-great-great-grandfathers voted against my motion to amend the journal so that the prayer might be incorporated in the journal? Why, those children of tomorrow would hang their heads in shame over the action of their ancestors."

The Senate obediently approved the correction, but the Democrats were not yet content. Harrison moved that the journal indicate the exact hour at which the Vice President had arrived to take the chair. Upon that question debate arose, several Senators undertaking to discuss the general merits of the antilynching bill and to deplore or defend the minority obstruction. Legislative progress proved impossible, however, and the Senate adjourned for a brief Thanksgiving vacation. Sessions for two days after the holiday were shortened because of the death and funeral of Representative James R. Mann of Illinois, but there were clear evidences of filibuster during the brief hours in which the Senate met. Democrats would not allow the journal to be approved, and for legislative business the Senate was helpless.

Lee S. Overman of North Carolina summed up the unyielding position of the Democratic minority. "When any considerable number of Senators are satisfied and conscientiously believe," he said, "that any proposed legislation is unconstitutional, that it involves the integrity of the States and the liberties of the people, and if passed would undermine the very foundation stones of this Republic, I think they are fully justified in filibustering to prevent, if possible, a militant majority from roughshodding over a strong minority."

On the same day, December 2, the disturbed Republicans met in conference and, faced with frank Democratic declarations that the filibuster would never end short of victory, voted to drop the disputed measure.[14] Four days of prostration of public business by Senators whose constituents applauded the fight convinced the majority that surrender was the only reasonable expedient. Underwood forced Lodge of Massachusetts, the Republican leader, to admit on the floor of the Senate that the bill would not be revived during the special or the coming regular session of Congress. In triumph the Senator from Alabama proclaimed, "We have no apologies to offer for our fight, and we have nothing to take back in reference to what we have done." Southern Democrats would renew the battle, he warned, should such a measure appear in the Senate again; and later years were to demonstrate that the threat was no idle one.

A longer Democratic filibuster greeted the efforts of President Harding and his Republican followers to enact a ship subsidy bill in 1922 and 1923. Leaders of their party in Congress, even before the close of the Wilson administration, had engineered the passage of legislation authorizing the sale of merchant ships owned by the government. Their aim was a prosperous but privately owned mer-

14 *ibid.*, Dec. 3, 1922.

chant marine. The Harding administration, eager to sell vessels, sought a way to induce investment of private capital. A generous subsidy for operating ships would offer a solution, and the President recommended the policy to Congress. The measure was considered in the Senate on December 11, 1922, little more than a week after the end of the uproarious antilynching obstruction. Wesley L. Jones of Washington, in charge of the subsidy bill, sought to push it forward for early passage. His efforts met with immediate Democratic opposition.

"Frankly speaking," said Joseph T. Robinson of Arkansas, "this is a bill that ought to be considered and discussed at length by the Senate." Such efforts as those of the Senator from Washington to hasten consideration "are calculated to provoke obstructive processes," he threatened. "The bill passed the House of Representatives by a majority of only 24. Sixty-nine Members of the House who voted for the bill and constituted more than that majority have been defeated, and their places in the body at the other end of the Capitol, after the 4th of March, will be occupied by other Representatives. This bill in the form that it passed the House, if submitted to that body today, could not be passed if the Members who voted for it, although they had been defeated, sought in a direct way to reflect the will of their constituents."

The proposal to subsidize a merchant marine, argued the Senator from Arkansas, was unpopular with the people and ought to be defeated. "The time has passed in American politics," he asserted, "when measures which tax and burden the people of this Nation can be imposed upon them in conflict with their expressed will; the time has come when in this representative government men who hold their positions by the approval of the public must seek to reflect in a fair degree the intelligent, well informed, and deliberate conclusions of their constituents."

A. Owsley Stanley of Kentucky satirized the Republican program. "The motion that this bill, palpably promoting the shipping interests of the country in behalf of a few men disposed to get rich operating ships, should take precedence over great supply bills, admittedly in the interest of all the people, is most instructive. . . . The purpose of this Government," he sneered, "is to give any organization, any clique, any combination that is strong enough, a good, wholesome graft on the federal Treasury, and it is the privilege of these poor, disorganized creatures who do not belong to any organization, who do not affiliate with any clique, who are simply citizens, to be plundered, to be plucked, to be forgotten, to be despised."

For two days thereafter Jones of Washington explained the bill in detail. At the conclusion of his remarks the proposed legislation was subjected to sharply worded denunciations and there were persistent efforts by opponents to displace it. Even before the Christmas holidays, the majority felt obliged to allow other urgent business to be considered; and after the holidays, until the 9th of February, 1923, other legislation occupied most of the Senate attention. Whenever the subsidy measure was presented for deliberation, however, long speeches delayed its progress. The Democrats agreed with Senator La Follette in saying that the bill was "not only unwise and impolitic" but also, because of the results of the election of 1922, that its introduction at this time was "indefensible," a procedure "contrary to the expressed will of the American people . . . and a violation of the trust reposed by the people in their delegated representatives."[15]

On the 9th of February Senator Jones announced that the measure would be pressed. "We have been twitted on this floor because we have laid the bill aside from time to time," he admitted. However, he argued, "the only sure way to avoid an extra session was to pass the appropriation bills. . . . These bills have passed the Senate. . . . We are now ready to proceed with the shipping bill. It will not be laid aside for other measures except by a vote of the Senate."

Still the filibuster continued, and the majority in favor of the subsidy legislation was hardly large enough to keep the measure without interruption before the Senate. By the 17th, however, Jones was able to hold his bill steadily before the chamber, and the filibusterers settled down to a monotonous grind of opposition speeches. Morris

[15] 64 *Cong. Record*, p. 508.

Sheppard of Texas talked almost two days on the work of the League of Nations; James A. Reed of Missouri grew eloquent over the desirability of possessions in the West Indies; Atlee Pomerene of Ohio spoke upon the need for a residence for the Vice President; Pat Harrison discussed rural credits; Thaddeus H. Caraway of Arkansas and Kenneth D. McKellar of Tennessee debated removals in the Bureau of Printing and Engraving. Speech followed speech for days, and even some of the more liberal Republicans joined in the festivity of loquacity.

Administration Republicans were disgusted at the lengthy obstruction. They grumbled at the speeches and denounced the filibuster. Frank B. Willis of Ohio, in a colloquy with McKellar, challenged the latter to deny "that there is a filibuster." The Senator from Tennessee jovially reminded his Republican inquisitor that for practical purposes "the definition of a filibuster is rather problematical." He had observed that filibustering usually does not exist for those who choose to delay business but does for those who oppose delay. However he would make to the Senator from Ohio one definite statement: *"The ship subsidy bill is not going to pass at this session of Congress."*[16]

John Sharp Williams frankly found reasons to justify a filibuster. He agreed that the majority ought to rule, but he held that those who refer "to a majority of the two legislative bodies" use "what logicians call an ambiguous middle." He pointed out that "the maxim refers to a majority of the people and their representatives." Truly "a majority of the representatives of the people must be heard . . . but not a majority of the misrepresentatives of the people. . . ."

"Undoubtedly," he continued, "a man who has been defeated is a misrepresentative of his constituency in the opinion of that constituency. Whether properly or improperly, wisely or foolishly, that is their opinion." As a result of the election many of those who advocated a ship subsidy had become "misrepresentatives." To the Senator from Mississippi filibustering could be justified in only two situations. The first instance arose from the status of Senators "as

16 *ibid.*, pp. 4226-7. Italics in the source.

ambassadors of the States in a Congress" with a duty to protect the rights of the States, particularly "wherever a great, vital, fundamental constitutional question is presented and a majority is trying to override the organic law of the United States." "But there is another class of cases," he suggested, "and that is when an accidental and incidental temporary majority in a legislative body tries to forestall the future and defeat the will of the majority of the people as expressed at an election, and as will be expressed by a majority of their recently elected representatives."

The Senator contended that the present situation came well within the second category. "I dare say," he challenged, "there is not a man in this body who will have the hardihood to say that the ship subsidy bill can pass through the next Congress. If there be one who has that amount of hardihood, who is capable of that degree of recklessness of assertion, I should like to hear him now tell me that he thinks I am mistaken about it. Ah, Mr. President, the very reason why this bill is being pushed along to a conclusion at this tail end of an expiring Congress, where the 'left overs' hold the balance of power, is because every man, from the President in the White House down to the pages upon the floor of the legislative halls, knows that it can not be passed in the next and recently elected Congress of the United States fresh from the people."[17]

By the 23rd of February Republican leaders admitted that the bill was dead.[18] Robinson of Arkansas on the following day moved to recommit the bill, but still the majority forced the talk to go on. George Wharton Pepper of Pennsylvania rose on the 27th to deplore the failure of the bill "because a minority of Senators feel justified in making such a use of unlimited debate in this body as makes a vote impossible." He did not think highly of the attempt to justify obstruction. "Why not be honest with ourselves in dealing with such a subject as the filibuster?" asked the Senator from Pennsylvania. "Why not honestly admit, one with another, that as long as a filibuster is permissible under our rules there will be a filibuster on

[17] ibid., pp. 4093-4.
[18] New York Times, Feb. 24, 1923.

any and every conceivable subject whenever circumstances are such as to give it a chance of success? It is inevitable that this shall be so, because Senators will never agree as to the circumstances under which a filibuster is justifiable or unjustifiable." Until the Senate should be willing to enable the majority to function by setting a limit to debate, he warned, "just so long must we be content to incur the censure and something like contempt of those who speak in the name of common sense."

All hope for the subsidy had been abandoned; obviously the opposition could talk till adjournment on the 4th of March. Heflin of Alabama commented that the Senator from Washington, in charge of the bill, at last wore a black tie, "mourning for this miserable measure that has gone to its long, last sleep. Still, he does not want the corpse dismissed; he does not want it to be referred back to the committee. Why not take it out of the Senate Chamber? It is already dead." But Jones of Washington hoped to arrange for a more dignified surrender. He preferred that the motion to recommit should be rejected and that the subsidy measure should soon thereafter be displaced by common consent.

Accordingly Robinson's motion to recommit was rejected, on the 28th of February, by 36 yeas to 48 nays. Then Jones, true to a gentleman's agreement, allowed the subsidy bill to be displaced. The reluctant majority had found a face-saving retreat; Jones had won a test vote but lost the legislation. The measure was dead for the session, and with the known attitude of the next Congress there was no chance of revival.

Within a week the chamber was once more the scene of obstruction. J. Thomas Heflin of Alabama and a few other Southern Senators hoped to force action in the House of Representatives upon a Senate joint resolution to purchase nitrates for the aid of farmers. Republican leaders in the House refused to allow passage of the measure. Though the Senate had approved it, not even a vote could be had in the House of Representatives. Heflin and his cohorts thereupon determined to kill House bills and other legislation pend-

ing in the Senate; perhaps the House could be coerced into acquiescence. Filibustering began in the afternoon of March 3, with final
adjournment less than a day in the future. If the Senators should
continue their talking, dozens of bills must fail as a direct result.
Could the House be persuaded to pass the Senate proposal?

"I have several documents on my desk that would make very interesting reading between now and four o'clock tomorrow morning,"
said the Senator from Alabama. "I took about half of these breast-
works down today, hoping I would not have to resort to them again.
I am afraid I shall have to have them brought back."

When Heflin yielded the floor early in the evening, other Senators
were ready to take his place. "In my opinion," said William J. Harris of Georgia, "this bill would have passed the House long ago
except for the fertilizer and calcium arsenate trusts." But the Republican majority could help the situation, he thought. "The leaders on
the other side of the Chamber are perfectly able to bring about an
agreement with the Republican House leaders for a vote on this
measure." Let them do it if they would save the final business of the
session.

A handful of Senators might indeed tie up business in the legislative halls; but if results were not speedily forthcoming could they
themselves afford the price? The Southern Senators realized that
significant legislation, bills important to them as well as to others,
would be defeated in the final parliamentary tangle of the session if
the obstruction were continued. Still, Heflin of Alabama, Harris of
Georgia, and Ellison D. Smith of South Carolina were determined
to win relief for their cotton-growing constituents if they could. Till
near midnight the dilatory talk continued; but finally, under the
persuasion of many leaders, including prominent Democrats from
the South, the filibustering Senators gave way. The price was too
high. The farm credits bill and others must be passed; the rebellious
Southerners would not take the onus of crushing all legislation
pending in the expiring hours of the Congress. Regretting the necessity, they accepted defeat.

As the years passed, filibustering went on in the Senate. New men might come to the celebrated body, but the old tactics were still employed to dominate business.

The 68th Congress ended in 1925 in a legislative jam induced by a coalition of a dozen garrulous Democratic and Republican Senators. Discontent with many pending measures provoked the obstruction, spasmodic and almost clandestine in nature, and it succeeded.[19]

Again in the special session of the Senate in March 1925, the body was subjected to filibuster, on that occasion primarily a one-man demonstration. The crusade of Vice President Charles G. Dawes for a rule to limit debate, begun immediately after his inauguration on March 4, was having little effect. Administration leaders decided to ratify the Isle of Pines Treaty with Cuba, a document which amounted to a quitclaim from the United States for a small island off the southern coast of Cuba. In a treaty with Cuba signed in 1903 title to the Isle of Pines had been left for future adjustment, and the administration of Theodore Roosevelt had negotiated first one and then another treaty recognizing Cuban ownership. A number of Americans had invested in land, however, and the Senate delayed ratification. Admittedly, since the second treaty had been pending in the Senate for twenty-one years, reawakening of interest was unexpected.[20] Royal S. Copeland of New York was determined to obstruct consideration; he believed that, because of a general desire to end the session, filibuster tactics would induce the leadership to turn to other business and abandon the treaty. "Senators," he argued, "there are American citizens who, in good faith, relying upon the statements of Government officials . . . purchased property in the Isle of Pines, believing it to be American territory." Title should not be released in favor of Cuba, he declared, and the Senate ought not to vote upon the treaty until its importance should be thoroughly understood.

[19] cf. *New York Times*, Feb. 15, 16, 28, 1925.
[20] See Royden J. Dangerfield, *In Defense of the Senate* (Norman, 1933), pp. 135-42.

"If the importance of the treaty can not be understood after twenty-one years' deliberation, how many more years," asked M. M. Neely of West Virginia, "does the Senator think ought to be devoted to its consideration?"

The New York Senator, however, proposed to block ratification. On the 11th of March he talked at length; and on the next day he held the floor for eight hours, marching up and down the chamber with a tremendous flow of time-taking words. "Senators," he cried, "I can not believe it possible, I can not believe it possible that the men chosen by the various States of the Union should so disregard the property rights and the moral rights and the legal rights of those citizens who have gone to the Isle of Pines. To me it is an amazing thing. I feel humiliated almost beyond words to think that it should be necessary, as I believe it is or I would not be here, to go forward in this manner in order to defer action. . . . There is a tremendous amount of mystery about this thing. There have been more mental gymnastics performed, more antics and didoes cut up in connection with this thing, more somersaults performed, more changes of sentiment, than in regard to any similar matter that I can recall." As the hours passed and his speech continued, the weary Senator rested upon the arm of his chair. But Simeon D. Fess of Ohio, temporarily presiding, called him to order as Reed Smoot had been called to order in earlier years; if the rules are enforced, Senators must stand upon their feet to talk.

"Am I permitted to drink milk between times?" asked the New Yorker with sarcasm. "Is there anything in the rules that prevents that?"

"That is not a parliamentary inquiry," replied the presiding officer. But the chair thought that, should the rules be strictly enforced, the Senator could be required to stand by his desk rather than roam about the chamber; a speaker might be a diffuse and eccentric orator, but not a peripatetic one. If a Senator insisted upon filibustering he must suffer the consequences of personal inconvenience. The Senator from New York acquiesced. "I am enough of a sportsman," he remarked, "to take my medicine."

Early in the evening, as the speech went on, Charles Curtis of Kansas presented a cloture petition signed by forty-seven Senators, thirty of them Republicans and seventeen Democrats. Obviously the majority intended to fight out the issue. When Copeland yielded the floor at eight o'clock in the evening, Henrik Shipstead of Minnesota carried on the debate for an hour; but opposition was patently hopeless. It could delay, but it could hardly win in the end when so large a majority faced so few opposing Senators. The minority abandoned their purpose and a time for a vote was fixed by unanimous consent. Cloture had proved unnecessary, though its threat may well have been effective; and the treaty was duly ratified.

Less than a year thereafter a filibuster was actually brought to an end by the use of cloture. During the consideration of the World Court Protocol in January 1926, clear evidences of obstruction were discernible. On the 15th Coleman L. Blease of South Carolina began talking and reading with no effort to disguise his purpose. Said he at the outset: "Mr. President, I think if we ever have a contest in the United States to determine who is its poorest reader, that I can easily win the prize. So if any Senator has any other business to attend to I shall not consider it the slightest discourtesy if he declines to listen to my reading." The fiery South Carolinian then proceeded to read from Washington's farewell address, with comments, and also to extemporize upon such topics as evolution, liquor drinking by diplomats in Washington, and the political orthodoxy of Woodrow Wilson.

Even on the next day, as commented by Senator Smoot, talk of cloture was "in the air."[21] Constant talk against the Protocol continued; and it was common knowledge, as Heflin intimated on the floor, that there were "foot tracks of a filibuster in this body." The sally brought an immediate retort from the voluble Blease.

"Mr. President, something has been said about a filibuster." The South Carolinian would not hide his efforts from the light; he would defeat American adherence to the World Court if he could. "I do not know that I exactly understand what that word [filibuster] means,"

[21] *New York Times,* Jan. 17, 1926.

he said, "but . . . I want to say right now that I would to God I had the power to stand here without eating a bite or taking a drink or sleeping a wink until twelve o'clock on the 4th day of March, 1931, if it would keep this iniquitous, infernal machine from being put on the people of America. If you call that a filibuster, then I am guilty, and I am ready for the sentence of the court, whatever it may be."

Senator after Senator talked at great length and read copiously from mountains of documents. James A. Reed of Missouri consumed hours of the Senate's time, and on one day secured unanimous consent for the clerks to read into the *Record* a long article by Andrew Carnegie published in 1893.[22] Even William E. Borah, who declared that he had never taken part in a filibuster and would not do so now, demanded ample time for "substantial arguments upon the proposition" and insisted that no arrangement which would "cramp anybody" be made for agreeing upon a day to vote.[23]

Finally, on the 22nd of January, Irvine L. Lenroot of Wisconsin submitted a cloture petition signed by twenty-four Democrats and twenty-four Republicans. Despite cries of "gag rule" and impassioned protest on the floor of the Senate, cloture was adopted on Monday, the 25th of January, by a vote of 68 to 26. The filibuster was thus brought to an end by a large and determined majority. For the second time cloture had been adopted by the Senate. And for the first time, though its use had been permissible under the rules for nine years, cloture had been effective against an obvious filibuster. The Senate was experiencing new events in the history of obstruction. Two days later the Protocol, with reservations, was approved by a vote of 76 to 17.

Yet cloture could not be easily or frequently invoked to halt the effects of filibuster. The Senate is ever reluctant to depart from unlimited debate, and even in the same session the body illustrated again its preference for the traditional freedom of talk. In the spring of 1926 a substantial majority sought to enact legislation for migra-

[22] 67 *Cong. Record,* pp. 2364-70.
[23] *ibid.,* p. 2298.

tory bird refuges. Opposition speeches, often irrelevant, dragged on for many days; and finally Henry F. Ashurst of Arizona remarked in annoyance that no Senator "is such a babe in the woods as to be oblivious of the fact that there is a filibuster here."

"What is there in this bill," asked Earle B. Mayfield of Texas, "so important as to entitle it to be kept continually before the Senate, denying Senators the right and the privilege of taking up more important measures, such as the soldiers' relief bill, the agricultural bill, and all the other important measures?"

Thaddeus H. Caraway of Arkansas observed that efforts were under way to delay and postpone other legislation by taking up time on the migratory bird issue. The bill, he thought, was being used as a buffer. "The people who make most noise about it are engaged in trying to fight some other measure over this one."[24]

Strong advocates of states' rights were vigorously hostile to the bird bill. The federal government, they believed, should not undertake so many functions. Cole Blease of South Carolina uttered volleys of condemnation. "I think that when God created this country," he said, "He certainly intended to see or at least had an idea that the people should have some rights of self-government. But about the only thing they have left in the country in the way of self-government is how many children the women shall have, and I suppose after a while they will want to regulate even that."

"They are trying to do it now," Mayfield interrupted.

"I am not surprised," Blease affirmed. "Then they will want to take the children and try to rear them according to the way the Government thinks they ought to be reared. . . . Senators get up here and 'cuss' at Mussolini and 'cuss' at some other forms of government, but we are following in their footsteps every day by trying to create here in Washington bureaus to make laws, to make rules, to regulate everything and to regulate everybody."[25]

Other Senators felt that too much time was being devoted to the bird bill. Were there not more important matters awaiting atten-

24 *ibid.*, pp. 10169-70.
25 *ibid.*, pp. 10259-60.

tion? "We are consuming hours and days here," said Heflin, "discussing some desirable and comfortable resting place for a migratory bird, a sanctuary where these wood ducks and teal ducks and canvasback ducks and sandhill cranes may have a pleasant place to sojourn for a season." He reproached his fellow-Senators for neglecting other business. "You have time to provide a temporary habitat or resting place for ducks and geese and cranes, but you do not seem disposed to take the time to lend a helping hand to the farmer and his family who are having a hard time to provide a home and obtain the common necessities of life."[26]

Peter Norbeck of South Dakota, in charge of the measure upon the floor, sought to have the bill brought to a vote. If Senators could vote he was certain the bill would pass. "Notwithstanding misrepresentations through propaganda and by remarks on this floor," he said, "it is nevertheless first and last a conservation measure to prevent extinction of our migratory birds—a problem which the states have found themselves unable to solve, because migratory birds are unconscious of state lines or even international boundaries."[27] To end the obstruction the Senator from South Dakota submitted on the 28th of May a cloture petition with eighteen signatures. But two-thirds of the Senators could not be prevailed upon to favor a policy of shutting off debate. On the 1st of June, after a vote of 46 yeas against 33 nays, the motion for cloture was lost. The bill was dead for the session.

Moreover, cloture again failed of adoption in the next session when it was proposed as a device to end obstruction against the Swing-Johnson Bill for development of the Lower Colorado River Basin. The measure proposed, by means of Boulder Dam, to harness the Colorado River for flood protection and to provide power and reclamation facilities. Yet opponents argued that the suggested distribution of water rights and other advantages among the states involved was unfair and discriminatory; the bill should not be passed if they could help it.

[26] *ibid.*, p. 10273.
[27] *ibid.*, p. 9612.

After the merits of the bill had been explained by its principal Senate sponsor, Hiram W. Johnson of California, the stubborn filibuster began in earnest. On the 21st of February, 1927, disaffected Senators from Arizona, Henry F. Ashurst and Ralph H. Cameron, one a Democrat and the other a Republican, consumed most of the day with prolonged discussion. That night the Senate met by unanimous consent to consider other important business; but on the 22nd, after the customary reading of Washington's farewell address in honor of his birthday, the filibuster was once more in progress.

Johnson of California made it clear that he and the majority would allow no other business to interrupt constant consideration of the Colorado River proposal; even all-night sessions should be held to wear out the embattled minority. Opponents, particularly the Senators from Arizona with Lawrence C. Phipps of Colorado, were ready for the challenge. Cameron took the floor for a speech of such tremendous length and monotony that, after his voice had droned for hours in the Senate chamber, Neely interrupted. "I understood the dam which is contemplated was for the purpose of generating power," ventured the West Virginian. "I think the power ought to be generated down in that section of the country by wind instead of by water."

It was near midnight when the prolix Cameron surrendered the floor and Ashurst took up the fight. "I am hoping," the latter confessed, "that the able Senator from California [Mr. Johnson] will soon move to recess, in order to relieve me from the necessity of speaking, and relieve Senators from the necessity of having a speech from me inflicted upon them."

But Johnson was obdurate. "Mr. President," he replied, "I can not imagine that there could be anything more charming than a speech at this time of night by the Senator from Arizona. I am most anxious to listen to it, and if the Senator from Colorado [Mr. Phipps], who has a speech, will only come in here and deliver it, I would be charmed, too."

In the meantime many Senators, bored and weary, had left the Capitol for relaxation, and an unexpected call for a quorum brought only thirty-six to answer their names. Before talk could be resumed the Senate must assemble a majority of its members to constitute a quorum. Consequently the sergeant at arms was directed to request attendance, and soon the order was given that he should compel absent Senators to come to the chamber. Results were slim. Well after midnight David S. Barry, the sergeant at arms, appeared at the Vice President's desk to report the effect of his efforts. Some Senators had announced that they would come, some were reported ill, others could not be reached. Thomas F. Bayard of Delaware "could not come because he is getting ready to go out of town to attend a funeral tomorrow." Woodbridge N. Ferris of Michigan "says he is tired out and can not come." At the residence of George P. McLean of Connecticut "we reached some one on the telephone, who refused to give him the message." Henry W. Keyes of New Hampshire "is in bed, but says he would think it over." Exasperated Senators clustered in the Capitol ordered that warrants for the arrest of absent Senators be executed forthwith by the sergeant at arms, and that official set out once more on his search. A slow stream of Senators began to trickle into the room, some of them under arrest. Reed of Missouri entered in a rage. "When it shall be in order for me to speak," he fumed, "I intend to express myself regarding what I think is an inexcusable outrage."

A quorum was finally mustered at 2:40, and Ashurst went on with his speech. Until five o'clock in the morning he talked, though, as he confessed to the Senate, "I had to consult a physician late last week with respect to throat trouble and if my words are not painful to others they are painful to me." The issue, he thought, "means the life of a state; and Senators will pardon me if I seem at times to speak with asperity. . . . This is going to be a savage fight. Do not beguile yourselves into the belief that this is going to be a soft-glove affair."

When the Senator from Arizona gave up the floor, the Senate was again without a quorum. Try as he would the sergeant at arms could not bring together a majority of Senators until ten minutes after nine o'clock in the morning. For over four hours the Senate sat helpless, members in attendance fretting about the Capitol or dozing where they could. Yet when a quorum at last assembled Phipps of Colorado was ready with a speech. The Senate remained in session until eleven o'clock that night, and whenever it became necessary opponents were prompt to filibuster against the Boulder Dam project. "When I put my hand to a proposition, there will not be any default or any neglect," said Ashurst in reply to banter from Copeland. "The filibuster, with which the Senator is pleased to charge me, will be successful." Already impatient Senators were clamoring to bring up other matters in the last days of the session, and Johnson was unable to hold the chamber to strict consideration of his measure.

On the next day, while Ashurst held the floor, Johnson rose to submit a motion for cloture; he would try the last resort at his disposal. The Senator from Arizona refused to yield for the presentation of the cloture petition, but Vice President Dawes ruled that a Senator must suspend his remarks for the few moments necessary for cloture to be moved. Ashurst appealed, but the Senate by a vote of 46 to 30 sustained the decision of the chair. The petition for cloture, signed by eleven Republicans and five Democrats, was duly submitted. Not till the second day thereafter could a vote be had on the question of closing debate; and a truce was arranged between the warring Senators to consider other business, for the most part, till the test should come. At the slightest sign that the Boulder Dam project might be brought up for a vote, however, filibustering Senators occupied the floor with inexorable resolution. On the 26th of February, at one o'clock in the afternoon, came the vote on cloture, but not even a majority would support the motion. Limitation of debate was rejected by 32 yeas against 59 nays.

Almost immediately the Senate became embroiled in another filibuster so intense that there could have been no opportunity, in any event, to deliberate upon legislation affecting the Colorado River. One of the fiercest filibusters in recent decades developed over a proposal to extend the life of a special campaign investigating committee headed by James A. Reed, Democrat of Missouri. Those were days in which charges of corruption in the 1926 Senatorial election victories of Frank L. Smith in Illinois and of William S. Vare in Pennsylvania had stirred the country, and further investigations by the special Senate committee of five were pending. That committee had aroused the ire of a few irreconcilable Republicans; and, despite the wishes of many other Republicans and a clear majority of the Senate, the minority refused to permit under any circumstances and at any cost the continuance of the investigation.

The fight against the resolution for extending the life of the select committee was led by stalwart Republicans: David A. Reed of Pennsylvania and George H. Moses of New Hampshire, and later with the cooperating generalship of James W. Wadsworth, Jr., of New York. Their efforts became vigorous on the 1st of March, 1927; but, indeed, it was the result only of an unusual parliamentary situation that obstruction was not begun earlier. On the 28th of February, eager to enact a Prohibition Reorganization Bill before it should become engulfed in wrangling over other matters, the Senate had adopted cloture on that measure, and on the same night the body voted an adjournment rather than a recess.

When the Senators convened on the 1st of March, since they met after an adjournment rather than a recess, "morning hour" with its routine business seemed technically in order. But was morning hour proper, even if the Senate convened after adjournment, when cloture had been previously adopted? Did not the rules of the Senate contemplate that the body proceed, whenever it was in session, with uninterrupted consideration of the measure to which cloture had been applied, each Senator having only one hour for debate?

Under the rules, any motion to consider a measure, made during morning hour, is undebatable. Once pending before the Senate, of course, the issue can be discussed. Only during morning hour, moreover, could such an undebatable motion be made; at any other time even the step necessary to bring a question formally before the Senate can be talked to death. If morning hour were permitted on this occasion, Reed of Missouri could use the opportunity to make an undebatable motion to consider his resolution for further campaign investigations; and all the Senate knew that that motion, if made, would be adopted. Opponents determined to prevent even formal consideration of the hated resolution. To them it was prejudicial to the dignity of the Senate—not to mention that of the Republican party. They argued that such investigations should be conducted by a regular, not a special, committee of the Senate, and they proposed to fight the issue from the start. Reed of Pennsylvania therefore made a point of order that, since cloture had been adopted upon the Prohibition Reorganization Bill, morning business could not be entertained.

Vice President Dawes, announcing his recognition of the importance of the precedent which would be set, submitted the question to the Senate without decision; and the body overruled the point of order by a vote of 61 to 21. Routine morning business was thus declared to be in order even after the adoption of cloture upon a pending measure.

The filibusterers, however, had still another effective trick to prevent the use of morning hour for consideration of the detested resolution. Moses of New Hampshire forced the detailed reading of the journal till the time for morning business had expired. The Prohibition Reorganization Bill, already subject to cloture, was then before the Senate, and for the rest of that day it served as an effective buffer against the campaign investigating resolution.

On the next day, the 2nd of March, the Senate met once more after an adjournment voted the preceding night, and again Moses forced the reading of the journal. But this time the reading consumed less than the full morning hour, and Reed of Missouri made the motion for consideration of his resolution. Undebatable as it was during morning hour, the motion was carried by 56 yeas against 25 nays. The proposal against which the irreconcilables had resolved to wage war was at least before the Senate. Nevertheless, when the time expired for morning business, the Prohibition Bill was again automatically before the Senate as a check against other matters, and it was not passed till later in the day. By strange coincidence filibusterers against one measure had been able to make cloture against another serve their purposes for nearly two days! Such are the possibilities in the complicated Senate rules. For that matter, all parliamentary rules, however devised, could almost certainly be used for obstructive purposes if the proper chain of circumstances should develop.

With the Prohibition Reorganization Bill out of the way, Reed of Missouri was once more able to obtain consideration of his resolution. The filibustering Republicans then set to work with grim determination. It was the afternoon of the 2nd of March, and less than two days must be talked away to assure victory through deadlock. Reed of Pennsylvania took the floor for a long, tiresome speech in which, to the discomfort of weary Senators, he discussed election statistics state by state.

Before many hours it was apparent that Republican obstructionists would have the cooperation of the doughty Blease of South Carolina, who was disgruntled because the Senate had recently applied cloture, departing for the nonce from the tradition of full debate unless limited by unanimous consent. Moreover, as a staunch advocate of states' rights, he sternly disapproved Senatorial interference with state elections.

Blease rose to relieve Reed of Pennsylvania. "Some Senators here voted for cloture the other day," he recalled. "They got scorched for that, and they are going to get burned later. I do not mean in the hereafter; I mean right here. . . . Why should we have cloture? There was no reason in the world, there was no excuse in the world for it. It was the application of the power of might, not right." Indignation rose in the Senator as he proceeded. "Personally," he shouted, "I have never bowed to any lash. Personally I have never bowed to any party or any power, and I never expect to. I expect to vote for what I believe is right on the floor of the Senate, regardless of the source from which it comes."

Turning to the business of elections, Blease boasted that South Carolina conducted hers as she pleased. "When a state holds its election," he argued, "when three managers supposed to be honest men count those ballots, make out a return, and sign it right there while it is fresh, and send it in to the commissioners of election, it ought to be accepted." He doubted whether charges of corruption hurled in some states were valid. Senators had talked of precincts in which one candidate had received all the votes. That was not necessarily an evidence of fraud, he felt; South Carolina had many ballot boxes of that kind. Could not the people of a precinct render a unanimous choice? Of the near unanimity of South Carolina he was proud. "I think Mr. Coolidge received 1,100 votes in my state," he admitted with evident regret. "I do not know where he got them. I was astonished to know that they were cast and shocked to know that they were counted."

That night Ralph H. Cameron of Arizona, his service in the Senate within a few hours of expiration, read to the Senate an excruciatingly long address entitled "The Copper-Mining Industry and Boulder Dam." Neely of West Virginia attempted to establish a precedent, for which there was a possible basis of argument from a former ruling of Vice President Thomas R. Marshall, that a Senator, against objection, might not read a paper prepared by someone else. Willis of Ohio, temporarily the presiding officer, overruled the point of order. "When a Senator is referring to a manuscript," he remarked, "the presumption is that it is his own manuscript." "I presume," questioned the caustic Reed of Missouri, "that presumption continues and abides even if the reader can not pronounce the words?"

When Cameron had at last concluded, Robert N. Stanfield of Oregon, also retiring from the Senate—denying that he participated in the filibuster—talked on "The Countryside and the City—National Solidarity." The hour grew late and Senators exhausted, but proposals to arrange a time for a vote by unanimous consent were invariably rejected. Not only was the stubborn filibuster killing the resolution for campaign investigations; it was slowly strangling urgent legislation for deficiency appropriations, public buildings, and other matters of national import.

Finally Reed of Missouri agreed to offer the Senate a sporting proposition. Let other important measures be saved; there remained more than a day in which to accomplish it. Let the Senate proceed to the consideration of important public bills, by unanimous consent limit debate upon those bills, pass them, then revert to consideration of the pending resolution for campaign investigations. Upon the latter measure there would be no limitation of debate. It would still be subject to filibuster, but other great items of legislation before the Senate would be saved. Without such an agreement, all legislation still pending before Congress would certainly be killed upon the automatic adjournment of the short session at noon on the 4th of March.

Blease of South Carolina objected to the agreement. "If I do not die, I will never consent," he shouted. Nothing could move him; no appeal could reach him. William H. King of Utah attempted to convince the belligerent South Carolinian that the proposed agreement would be better even for his position, that it would simply postpone consideration of the campaign resolution and shorten the final fight against it. "We will pass four or five important measures, consume eight or nine hours, possibly get a little sleep," King pleaded. But Blease was adamant; in the remaining hours, too few in number to make possible the application of cloture under any circumstances, he would give the Senate a taste of what it might mean to use cloture at all in that body. "I know this is not pleasant to some Senators," he proclaimed. "It was not pleasant for me on the World Court matter, when they put cloture on me, but I said then I would make some people pay for it, and I am doing it, and I am going to keep it up."

At four o'clock in the morning of March 3, the Senator from South Carolina asked how many more hours of the session remained. "That," replied the presiding officer, "is not a parliamentary inquiry; it is a mathematical calculation." Blease persisted. "I am very poor at mathematics; so I shall have to get somebody else to figure it out for me." Informed that thirty-two hours remained, he proposed to Wadsworth: "I will use sixteen hours if the Senator from New York will use the other sixteen hours." But Wadsworth felt that the recently rejected unanimous consent agreement should be entered into; it would salvage many important bills about to die. Moreover, he would accept even the resolution for campaign investigations if the authority of the special committee should be restricted to the states of Pennsylvania and Illinois. He and other Senators objected particularly to the roving commission which the resolution proposed for the committee—authority to conduct investigations in any state.

With time before final adjournment ever growing shorter, Senators could reach no agreement. After Blease had read at length about the life of Jefferson Davis, and after Walter E. Edge of New Jersey had read long passages from a Supreme Court decision, Reed of Pennsylvania submitted a proposed agreement similar to that which had already met objection, to displace the pending resolution for a time, limit debate on certain important bills still unpassed, and after disposing of them recur to the campaign investigation resolution without change of its parliamentary status. Like others in the chamber, the Pennsylvania Senator felt that something should be done to rescue great measures to which there was no bitter opposition. But his determination never to consent to the investigating resolution, cost what it might, remained unshaken and unshakable.

This time, however, objection came from George W. Norris of Nebraska. For two major reasons he would not consent to the proposal for unanimous consent. "It means the more certain defeat, if such a thing can be possible, of the resolution that is now pending. It eases up, by the hours that are devoted to the other bills, debate that otherwise would have to go on upon this bill." His second objection he considered even weightier. Such an agreement, he thought, "is the worst kind of cloture or gag upon the other bills mentioned." Because they could be considered only for a limited time Senators must vote upon amendments and upon the measures themselves without adequate discussion or explanation. "To my mind," protested Norris, "that is absolutely the worst method of legislation that can possibly be proposed or devised."

To the Senator from Nebraska the proper remedy for such situations was the adoption of his constitutional amendment to abolish the short session of Congress and its fixed date for adjournment. He recognized the importance of the numerous bills about to be defeated. Nevertheless, he stated, "I think, after all, it will be one good lesson, if all of these things fail. . . . It will call to the attention of the country the impossibility of Congress properly legislating because of the handicap of a constitutional kind which that amendment would remedy."

The parliamentary situation in the Senate had become an impossible snarl, an obstinate knot which no arrangement could be made to loosen. The majority would not allow the pending resolution to be displaced in favor of other matters without some limitation upon debate and assurance that the campaign investigation would again be considered. Such an agreement could not be obtained. Moreover a motion by Reed of Pennsylvania to take up the deficiency appropriation bill for unlimited consideration was defeated by 24 yeas to 33 nays. Only stalemate seemed feasible in the current temper of the Senate.

J. Thomas Heflin undertook to denounce the filibuster and the "three musketeers" who led it. "I sat here last night and watched the proceedings," he said. "The Senator from New Hampshire [Mr. Moses] was on the job. He had a filibuster going on here all night long. He was a good general. . . . This diplomatic, smooth artist from the State of New Hampshire had his forces well trained. One time we asked one of his filibusterers over here to withdraw. He said, 'Wait a minute,' and then walked over to the Republican side and talked to the Senator from New York [Mr. Wadsworth] and the Senator from Pennsylvania [Mr. Reed], and it looked as if they were about to become ashamed of the long filibuster that they had participated in, and they showed signs of weakness. Just at that juncture the big general walked by with his hand up to his mouth and said softly, 'Stand by your guns.'"

Why should meritorious legislation be defeated in a parliamentary jam? Why should special campaign investigations in Pennsylvania and Illinois be stopped? The real motive of obstreperous Republican filibusterers was purely political, Heflin intimated. "You are opposed to this committee's work," he jeered, "and you are saying in your hearts:

> Committee, spare that campaign boodle tree,
> Touch not a single bow;
> In election times it shelters me,
> You must not harm it now.

"That is what is back of it. You know that is true. An honest confession is good for the soul. Why do you not make it?"

"Who is in the confessional—the Senator from Alabama?" asked Moses.

"I am trying to call you Republican sinners to the mourners' bench," came the answer, "and all of you who participated in the miserable filibuster that has kept me up for two days and a night."

Half seriously, half in jest Heflin railed at the Republicans. Yet his remarks took up the time of the Senate, and filibusterers hoped to make the most of it. Questions, relevant and irrelevant, poured in upon the speaking Senator, and with each fresh incentive he turned his remarks to a new tack. Obligingly enough he discussed Negroes in politics, and related in detail circumstances which had caused him years before to shoot at a Negro from the window of a Washington streetcar in order to defend a white woman from "insults and insolence." Nor did he neglect, in his long diatribe, to denounce the Roman Catholic Church; he had become notorious in the Senate and in the country for opposition to that faith, and the occasion was not one to be missed. The Senator from Alabama was against the filibuster, but he contributed effectively to the delay.

"The country is going to say," finally announced Senator Willis, "that the Senate is unable to function, and that it gets into a 'cat and dog' fight in the last few hours of the session and lets important legislation fail while we quibble over nothing."

Reed of Pennsylvania felt no such qualms. "The people of the country," he predicted, "are going to say that we won the 'cat and dog fight,' as the Senator calls it, and they are going to cheer us for doing it."

"We think that this resolution is a force measure being put upon us," insisted Moses, "and we can not do other than resist it."

Nothing could be accomplished in the deadlocked Senate. Finally, at 12:02 on the morning of March 4, after continuous turmoil for thirty-seven hours, exhausted Senators took a recess till 8:30 o'clock.

Reassembling after some eight hours of rest, leading Senators strove desperately once more to salvage a few important measures. Reed of Missouri offered to allow the deficiency appropriation bill to come up under a unanimous consent agreement for an immediate vote. Reed of Pennsylvania promptly announced that he would object if such an agreement would also allow amendments to be offered to the appropriation bill. Frankly he revealed his apprehension that under such an arrangement the campaign investigating resolution might be attached as a rider to the appropriation measure. The Senator from Missouri then agreed to include in his proposal a definite stipulation that only amendments already approved in committee be considered.

To that the Pennsylvanian was ready to assent. But instantly Blease interposed that he had a personal amendment supplying $50,000 for an industry in his state and that he would never agree to the arrangement unless his amendment was included. Robert B. Howell of Nebraska expanded the threat of extortion by making a similar but somewhat more subtle announcement. He intended to see adopted an amendment to appropriate $12,000,000 for improving the Missouri River.

Angrily David I. Walsh of Massachusetts objected to any arrangement at all. "As one Member of the Senate I do not propose that appropriation bills or any other bills shall pass without debate in the midst of a filibuster. . . . This is civil war against the Government with a third of the membership of this body denying to the other two-thirds the opportunity to express a judgment. . . . I congratulate the Senator from Pennsylvania [Mr. Reed] and the Senator from New Hampshire [Mr. Moses]. They think they have achieved a fine triumph. . . . They assumed that in the last hours of the session, after we had stood here fighting for a principle, fighting for the right of two-thirds to express themselves, fighting for the right of the Senate to remove political corruption from its own membership, that when an appropriation bill was offered we would retreat. They gambled on our cowardice at the eleventh hour. But, if I stand alone, victory shall not be theirs."

Walsh would mince no words. To him the whole filibuster situation was indefensible. "Mr. President," he said, "this is political blackmail. It is legislative banditry. If this were not a legislative body, such conduct as we have witnessed here, if perpetrated by a minority outside of this Chamber, would be considered tyrannical and criminal."

The Senate clock reached the hour of twelve on the 4th of March. The Vice President rose to declare the Senate of the 69th Congress adjourned sine die, but he would end the unseemly tumult with a word of reprimand. "The Chair," he said, "regards the results of the present legislative session as primarily due to the defective rules of the Senate, under which a minority can prevent a majority from exercising their constitutional right of bringing measures to a vote. This is the only great parliamentary body in the world where such a situation exists."

The session closed with Senatorial buccaneering once more supreme. Few sessions of the Senate had culminated in more acrimonious contention. The resolution for which an overwhelming majority had suffered and sacrificed remained unpassed, and important bills were strangled in the fight.

CHAPTER VI

TURMOIL

CHAPTER VI

TURMOIL

GEORGE W. NORRIS had argued, in the midst of the fierce dead-locks which closed the 69th Congress in 1927, that the remedy could be found in his constitutional amendment to end the notorious short or "lame duck" sessions. Biennially Congress met for approximately three months after many of its members had been defeated at the polls; and in that short session, with its fixed adjournment on the 4th of March, organized filibusters frequently, almost regularly, brought business to a standstill. Abolish the short session, urged Senator Norris, and successful filibusters could no longer exist.[1]

Men wary of political conclusions might have asked whether the Senator had fully examined experiences of the past. And there was soon to be evidence anew, if it were needed, that the Nebraskan's assurance was not altogether warranted. The first session of the next Congress also ended in filibuster, and yet it was not subject to an automatic date for adjournment. Members of Congress wanted to leave Washington for political battles at home, and their insistent demands for an end of the deliberations forced an adjournment sine die. Congressional clamor for ending the session proved to be fully as effective an encouragement for filibusterers as a fixed date for adjournment.

Again, as it happened, the question of Boulder Dam was before the Senate, and again obstruction dominated the situation. The great controversy over power development, water supply, and flood control in the Lower Colorado River Basin remained an issue for legislative hostilities. Hiram W. Johnson of California was determined

[1] cf. 68 *Cong. Record*, p. 5503.

to secure action upon the measure; Senators from Arizona in particular were equally resolute that no action should be taken. Johnson had sought constantly for months to push forward the bill, and as the hours of the session grew short he strove desperately to obtain a final vote. Such a vote, he was convinced, would pass the measure. On the 28th of May, 1928, with the filibuster developing apace, the Senate voted 40 to 40 on a resolution to adjourn sine die at five p.m. on the 29th. That resolution, if passed by both Houses, would give determined filibusterers almost certain victory. Vice President Dawes by his casting vote rejected it.

But obstructionists, however great the obstacles, had no intention of relinquishing their tactics. Henry F. Ashurst of Arizona boasted of his "superb physical strength," yet acknowledged the savage pressure upon a minority fighting with its back to the wall. "You can take the heart even out of an elephant, the stomach out of an ostrich, and you may finally pierce the hide of a rhinoceros," he protested, "if you keep at him so great a time as the long and weary months that I have been practically on the gridiron, trying to prevent the great injustice this bill would perpetrate upon Arizona." Yet he and his friends would fight on; all night their lengthy speeches continued. Carl Hayden, also from Arizona, occupied hours, and even Cole Blease of South Carolina contributed to the fanfare of delay. On the next day, with prospects for a protracted filibuster becoming ever more alarming, the Senate voted once more upon a resolution to adjourn sine die, this time at five-thirty p.m. on the same day. By 46 yeas against 36 nays the resolution was carried, and all chance of passing the Boulder Dam bill before adjournment was lost.

Johnson nevertheless insisted upon parliamentary maneuvers which would make the measure the unfinished business at the next session of Congress; sooner or later he would win passage for his bill. Over his efforts such dissension arose that the Senate became a house of bedlam. William Cabell Bruce of Maryland held the floor to delay action, and to prevent him from speaking Senators yelled, "Vote! Vote! Vote!" Joseph T. Robinson of Arkansas and other Senators sang out a refrain: "Yeas and nays! Yeas and nays!" Incensed at these tactics, young Robert M. La Follette, Jr., who had succeeded his fighting father in the Senate, rose to rebuke his colleagues and to demand order. "This body has a certain dignity to maintain," he admonished.[2] The Senate at length yielded to propriety; and, while the disputed bill remained technically the unfinished business, other matters were considered by unanimous consent. The filibusterers had defeated the Boulder Dam measure for the session and had forced a strong majority to submission. Not until the following December, when determined legislators brought up the issue with a full session before them, did Boulder Dam at last win Congressional approval.

True to form, the short session of the same Congress ended, on March 4, 1929, in a filibuster. Indeed, various obstructive forays marked the closing weeks of the session. Wrote Vice President Dawes: "The most determined obstructionists are fawned upon, cajoled, flattered—anything to get their acquiescence that the Senate may do its constitutional duty—but so far in vain. It is a shameful spectacle—and yet so common that it passes here as a matter of course."[3]

On February 21 there were signs of filibuster against a naval appropriation bill, but the prospective obstructionists were few in number and abandoned their intention under a threat of night sessions and the possibility of cloture.[4] Cole L. Blease persistently blocked consideration of legislation to create additional federal courts to relieve congested dockets until at last, on the 23rd of February, the Senate agreed to award him a new judgeship for South Carolina.[5] Hope for consideration of a bill to reapportion representation in the House was abandoned when Pat Harrison of Mississippi let it be known that he and others would filibuster against the measure.

Moreover, an incipient filibuster broke out against the second deficiency appropriation bill when Clarence C. Dill of Washington,

[2] *New York Times,* May 30, 1928; 69 *Cong. Record,* p. 10513.
[3] Charles G. Dawes, *Notes as Vice President 1928-1929* (Boston, 1935), p. 287.
[4] *New York Times,* Feb. 22, 1929; Dawes, *op. cit.,* p. 288.
[5] See 70 *Cong. Record,* p. 4121; cf. Dawes, *op. cit.,* pp. 287-9, 291-2.

opposed to the continuance of Marines in Nicaragua, held the session by prolonged talk on the night of February 27-28 till 2:40 o'clock in the morning. Finally the obstruction was called off when compromise arrangements made it possible to fix a time for a vote.[6] The same Senator, however, gave the chamber further indications of filibuster on the 1st of March against a survey for a Nicaraguan canal. Yet tactics of delay were again given up, probably because Senator Dill feared that his efforts might kill the Federal Radio Commission Bill, in which he was much interested.[7]

Before the Radio Bill could be acted upon by the Senate, however, filibuster played a part in modifying its terms. Upon the measure, which proposed to extend the life of the Radio Commission till March 16, 1930, Senators Copeland and Blease talked for hours, and even George W. Norris had books and pamphlets piled high on his desk.[8] Blease especially had no patience with radios or with radio legislation. "Now they want to put a radio back here right behind me so as to broadcast what is going on in the Senate," he expostulated. "I do not know anything about radios; I never listened to one of them in my life. . . . I do not know what they might do, and that is what I want to ask Senators." What danger might lurk in such an instrument, for instance, at the time of the inauguration, now only three days distant? "They might fill that thing up with gas," he warned, "some deadly gas, and just about the time the crowd assembled in this Chamber, everybody in control of the Government of the United States, some fellow might turn on a machine down here and just gas out the whole business."

The Senator from South Carolina wanted to be frank. "I do not care very much about the radio bill," he admitted. "I will be honest about it. I am opposed to it. I was the only man who voted against it when it came up. I have rather peculiar ideas, I guess, and perhaps a lot of people think they are fool ideas. . . . But to save my life I

[6] 70 *Cong. Record,* pp. 4573-608, *passim;* Dawes, *op. cit.,* pp. 298-300.
[7] *New York Times,* March 2, 1929; 70 *Cong. Record,* pp. 4881-3.
[8] *New York Times,* March 2, 1929.

can not see what right we have to control the air that God Almighty gave the people."

Sponsors of the bill recognized that they must compromise to avert further filibuster, and when they agreed to extend the life of the Radio Commission only till December 31, 1929, obstruction was over. Copeland agreed to the modification, and Blease closed his remarks. "My friend from New York," said he, "now informs me— and I suppose he knows what he is doing—that I may yield the floor, and so I do."

The filibuster which closed the session was led by David A. Reed of Pennsylvania, who talked on the morning of March 4 to prevent passage of a resolution to postpone national-origins provisions in the immigration laws. Congress had earlier enacted a statute applicable principally to persons coming from outside the Western Hemisphere and in effect fixing a total annual quota of approximately 150,000 immigrants from countries included in the act. The quota for each nation affected by the law would be fixed in proportion to the number of inhabitants of the United States in 1920 having that national origin, but no quota would be less than 100. The maximum number of immigrants to be admitted from such countries would thus be slightly more than 150,000.

Drastic restriction of immigration was an important issue for a decade after the World War. Labor representatives objected to the dangers of economic disruption from mass migrations to America. Patriotic organizations feared the spread of foreign political doctrines. Passed in 1924 and intended to be effective in 1927, the national-origins plan had been twice postponed by Congress. In spite of difficulties in computing exact quotas, the law would at last become effective in 1929. There was particularly strong opposition from friends of Germany and of the Irish Free State because of material quota reductions for those countries under the new plan. For several days a Senate majority sought a vote upon the postponing resolution, but Senator Reed was determined that the national-origins provisions should become effective as scheduled by law.

On Saturday the 2nd of March Senators had hoped for a vote upon the issue, but late at night the Senate by a close vote recessed until Sunday morning. When Senators were called to order on Sunday, Robinson of Arkansas lamented the prospect of "a prolonged and probably fruitless contest in this body on the Lord's Day." He moved a recess until Monday. Though the Senate had often met in the past on Sunday, particularly at the end of a session, he argued that "another desecration" was unnecessary. "Making no pretense to the possession of a sanctimonious disposition, but respectfully conforming to the traditions, the sentiments, and feelings which are deep grounded in the hearts and consciences of the men and women of this Republic," he declared, "I enter a solemn protest in all sincerity against the proposal that is now imminent to compel the Members of this body to violate their conscientious convictions, desecrate and dishonor the Sabbath, and engage in what is likely to become an unseemly filibuster." By a vote of 39 to 36 the Senate recessed till eleven o'clock on Monday morning, the 4th of March. The session would end at noon, and the national-origins provisions therefore could easily be saved. The speech of Reed of Pennsylvania to consume time on the morning of the 4th occupies less than two pages of the *Congressional Record,* but it nevertheless constituted an effective filibuster.[9]

Likewise, in 1931, the short session of the 71st Congress came to an end amid scenes of obstruction. For three days in January Elmer Thomas of Oklahoma had talked at length against the use of moneys from an Indian fund and had thereby delayed a vote upon the administration bill for Interior Department appropriations.[10] On the night of March 2-3 a persistent group of Senators kept the body in session until 2:55 in the morning while in effect delaying a copyright bill.[11] But these incipient filibusters were minor in comparison with the closing hours of the session, occupied by Thomas of Oklahoma.

---

[9] 70 *Cong. Record,* pp. 5222-3; *New York Times,* March 5, 1929.
[10] cf. *New York Times,* Jan. 21, 1931.
[11] *ibid.,* March 3, 1931.

Senator Thomas was deeply vexed because legislation had not been passed to protect the oil industry, and he proposed to talk until he could force the creation of an investigating commission to study the oil situation. On the night before final adjournment he consumed the time until recess at 1:10 o'clock in the morning; and when the Senate convened at nine on the 4th, he held the floor for three hours before the session expired. The Senator from Oklahoma claimed as the reason for his action the interests of humanity. Dramatically he exhibited to the Senate an old, worn, ragged, and much-patched pair of overalls. For the men who wear such garments he would demand relief. "In a favored land, with storehouses bulging with food," he cried, "our people are hungry; with warehouses crowded with clothing, our people are naked and cold; and with our banks overflowing with money, our people are penniless."[12] The Senator would act, and he would coerce the Senate to action if he could. Opponents of the filibuster offered a vote on the resolution; but Thomas, knowing that a vote would be unfavorable, refused to yield the floor without assurance that his proposal would be adopted. Such assurance was not forthcoming, and the session ended in develop.

Before the Senate witnessed such episodes again the renowned Huey P. Long had arrived for his meteoric career. Filibusters of the past, exciting, spectacular, and even ludicrous though they sometimes were, paled in the brilliance of his restless energy. In drama and in virulent satire Huey Long transcended competition. His Senate speeches were ever galling to his political opponents; and many of his bitterest enemies were, like the Senator from Louisiana himself, enlisted under the banners of the Democratic party. He minced no words; he spoke with a freedom, with a jeering raucousness, with a slang invective new and disturbing to the august assemblage. Senators found him impervious to sarcasm, and no man could silence him.

[12] 74 *Cong. Record*, pp. 7307, 7315.
[13] *New York Times*, March 5, 1931.

Perhaps not since the time of John Randolph of Roanoke, a man whose idiosyncrasies are little remembered in modern times, had the Senate been treated to such a jargon of words. Proud of his nickname, "the Kingfish" barraged the Senate with rambling thoughts, speaking without respect for the majority of his colleagues and completely without subservience to the celebrated dignity of the chamber.

The unaccountable Louisianan had been in the Senate almost a year before the first of his major experiences with filibuster. But early in 1933 he participated as a leading figure in extended obstruction of the important Glass Banking Bill. That measure was brought before the Senate on January 5 and became the chief business of the body on the 10th. Senator Long vigorously dissented from provisions permitting branch banks, and he took the floor to oppose the bill at length. It was typical of the Senator to quote the Bible in support of his position, and he lost no opportunity to apply Scripture to the banking bill.

"Woe unto them that join house to house," he read from the fifth chapter, eighth verse, of Isaiah, "that lay field to field, till there be no place, that they may be placed alone in the midst of the earth!" That passage could be made applicable to bankers—and to the Senate. "All that it is necessary to put in there," he shouted, "are the words, 'banking house to banking house and woe be unto them.'"

It was clear that the Senator from Louisiana would block action if long speeches could serve the purpose. He challenged the Senate and the country with passage after passage of Scripture: "Go to now, ye rich men, weep and howl for your miseries that shall come upon you." On he went, quoting from the fifth chapter of James. "You do not hear that read in the pulpit today," he exclaimed. "If you do, the man will not be in the pulpit very long."

"Concentration and Decay" the fiery Senator entitled the first of his filibustering speeches against the bill. "We must distribute wealth," he warned. The dangers of concentration had been recognized, but what progress was the Congress making toward a solution? "Now we come and try to relieve the country from this system of concentration of wealth and power in the hands of a few, and how do we propose to remedy the situation? By imposing a condition that means twofold more trouble on top of what we have already. . . . We are proposing to concentrate now, to close the door so that there will be eternal trouble with a situation that admits of no correction, regardless of the promises made to the people of this country." Such laws would never be passed even with the tacit consent of the Senator from Louisiana.

The next day Long was up and speaking again, dragging out the proceedings of the Senate. But even he needed rest, and finally he asked that the clerk read a resolution from a bankers' association. Carter Glass of Virginia rose at once to protect his bill; he would force the filibustering Senator to speak in person. "I object, Mr. President," he snapped. "We so much prefer to hear the mellifluous voice of the Senator from Louisiana that I am not willing to have the harsh voice of the clerk disturb us." The Senate supported the caustic Virginian; by a formal vote permission for the clerk to read was refused.

Long was unperturbed; a mere Senatorial reproof could never affront him. "Mr. President," he began derisively, "I thank Senators for this great expression of fealty which they have toward having my vocal strains resound through this Chamber. . . . I do not know of anyone who has been told in the Senate, even against his own will, that the Senate desired to hear him, as I have been here this evening. It is a compliment which I truly appreciate. I shall carry with me, in what few days or few years I have in this body, appreciation for the Senator from Virginia; but I will read the resolution myself."

Carter Glass told the Senate with asperity that it was again "confronted with the question as to whether or not it shall be permitted to legislate." For his part, he intended that it should, and he demanded longer sessions.

Yet on the 12th Long blandly assured the Senate that "we will take our time about this thing." He would reveal to the country the evils in the proposed legislation, and he would not be turned from his purpose. Hiram Bingham of Connecticut asked to interrupt that he might make a plea for the poor in the District of Columbia; only immediate passage of a deficiency appropriation could provide needed funds for further relief. But Long could be cavalier. "I decline to yield to any Senator who has not a good record in behalf of the poor people or the kind of a poor people's record that I have. Whenever I am forced to get any advice about taking care of poor people, I want it to come from somebody who is in actual touch with the condition of the poor people."

Long was not alone, however, in his opposition to the Glass Banking Bill. Thomas of Oklahoma was ready to cooperate in the filibuster. As the days passed the white-haired Oklahoman, deliberate in action and diction, contributed thousands of words to the delay. It was no deep secret, indeed, that Republican leaders recently defeated at the polls, especially James E. Watson of Indiana and George H. Moses of New Hampshire, were encouraging and abetting the obstruction. They hoped, for political reasons, to force upon the incoming Democratic administration, a special session of Congress.[14] Yet Huey Long remained the spectacular center of filibustering action. He hugely enjoyed the showmanship, the byplay, and the battle of wits.

When President Hoover's veto of Philippine independence was brought before the Senate on the 14th of January, that too was used by the Louisiana Senator as a convenient topic for discussion. Any subject that would take up time and thus prevent passage of the Glass bill was agreeable to Senator Long. Upon certain conditions, he told Senators responsible for the bill, the Senate would be allowed to legislate; "if they have arrived at the view that they will sidetrack the chain bank bill, if they have decided that they are willing to let the hand of imperial finance rest where it is for a while rather than to consolidate everything into the hands of these

[14] 76 Cong. Record, p. 2078; James E. Watson, As I Knew Them (Indianapolis, 1936), pp. 305-6.

few masters of fortunes and wreckers of nations I am ready to talk turkey."[15]

James Hamilton Lewis of Illinois suggested that the predicament of the Senate "is bringing upon this body the contempt of the Nation and the disrespect of mankind."[16] Millard E. Tydings of Maryland truculently announced to the press that he would resign his seat in the Senate if filibustering could not be abandoned in favor of legislative business.[17] Joseph T. Robinson presented a petition signed by twenty-nine Democratic Senators asking for cloture upon the banking bill. Carter Glass addressed the Senate to "brush away some of the rhetorical rubbish and elocutionary misrepresentations of the various provisions of the measure."[18]

However, the Senate displayed its usual reluctance to apply cloture. Thomas of Oklahoma openly proclaimed that so long as the cloture motion was pending—and thereafter if it should be adopted—he would retaliate by preventing business by unanimous consent.[19] On the 19th of January cloture was defeated by the margin of a single vote. It was understood, however, that Long was willing to agree to a unanimous consent arrangement to limit debate on the bill and its amendments; without such an understanding, cloture would probably have been adopted.[20] Still, Robinson of Arkansas was furious at the outcome. "The question involved," he said, "is whether at a time when the country is suffering from a depression unparalleled in its history, at a time when legislation is badly needed, the Senate will demonstrate its unfitness and its incapacity to do business. Why not debate these issues, determine them upon their merits, and let a majority of the Senate decide?"

Though Robinson was floor leader of the Democratic party, Long refused to allow such a view to go unchallenged. "The Senator from Arkansas, Mr. President, is not speaking the sentiments of

[15] 76 Cong. Record, p. 1843.
[16] ibid., p. 1844.
[17] New York Times, Jan. 17, 1933.
[18] 76 Cong. Record, p. 1935.
[19] ibid., p. 1988.
[20] New York Times, Jan. 20, 1933.

the Democrats of the United States; he is not speaking the sentiments of the Democrats of the South; he is not speaking the sentiments of the Democrats of Louisiana; he is not speaking the sentiments of the Democrats of Arkansas in the statement he has made here this morning." The election returns, said Senator Long, had justified his pronouncement.

Yet the Senate did grant unanimous consent, as proposed by Borah of Idaho, to limit each member to speeches of one hour upon the bill and thirty minutes upon any amendment. So many amendments were offered, however, that for nearly a week discussions continued virtually unabated. "Of course," said Glass, "the unanimous-consent agreement under which we are now operating is not worth the paper upon which it is written."

Obstruction had delayed the banking measure for more than two weeks, but the majority of the Senate at last had its way. The opposition relented and allowed a vote. Prolonging the delay was a strenuous task, and on the 25th of January Thomas of Oklahoma proposed an arrangement for strict limitation of debate by unanimous consent. Yet he could not refrain from a final gibe at the majority and its program. "In some sections it is claimed," he said by way of preface, "that those who oppose the passage of the Glass branch banking bill are engaged in a filibuster." If that term was correct, he continued, "then it is a filibuster against a scarcity of money, a filibuster against the absence of credit, a filibuster against hunger, cold, and want, a filibuster against the failure of the Senate leadership in even trying to ascertain the causes of the depression." With alacrity the Senate agreed to limit further time to be consumed by the bill. Amendments should be offered not later than seven o'clock that evening, no Senator should speak more than ten minutes upon any amendment, and the body should remain in continuous session until final disposition of the measure. The filibuster was then abandoned and the bill was passed.

The next filibustering adventure of the dynamic Huey Long was positive in character. On the last day of the second session of the 73rd Congress, June 18, 1934, he undertook to force adoption of a conference report on a farmers' bankruptcy bill—and succeeded. Without enthusiasm from administration leaders, Congress voted that overdue mortgages could be paid in installments.

Through some legislative mischance, accidental or intentional, the original copy of a conference report was lost after it had been signed by the conferees but before it could be presented to the Senate. Senator Long, fearful that administration leaders would arrange a final adjournment before the report could be voted upon, began talking in the Senate with the avowed intention of blocking last-minute legislation until the bankruptcy bill could be passed. The report had been lost in the House, he argued; but it would have to be found and acted upon. "There is something miraculous about this. There is a malignant influence pursuing the House every time it deals with the farm bankruptcy bill. They are all set, ready to go, and, lo and behold, they have lost the papers again." He intended, by filibustering, to provide an incentive for finding them.

Administration leaders recognized the danger of a legislative jam. Robinson of Arkansas sought to smooth over the situation. "I have just been informed," said he, "that the papers to which the Senator refers are on their way to the Senate now."

"Glory be!" exclaimed Long. But he would not stop talking on that account; other bills would have to wait until legislation for farmers was certain. "It will not hurt Congress to wait a while and listen to me. Do not be in a hurry. Many people have gotten into their buggies and have driven forty miles to hear me, back home. If Senators do not desire to hear me, they can retire to the cloak-room. I am not going to talk so as to disturb anyone out there."

Finally, after much bickering, Robinson of Arkansas gave definite assurance as Democratic leader that there would be a vote prior to final adjournment, and Long yielded the floor. Soon thereafter the missing conference report, newly prepared, was submitted to the Senate and agreed upon. Whether or not such tactics were really necessary to force final passage of the legislation, the obstruction had succeeded. The Congressional struggle had ended, but eminent Justices of the Supreme Court later wrote a sequel by unanimously invalidating the statute.

One filibuster seemed merely to encourage another, for the day was not to pass without a new outbreak. That evening, the Senate having already arranged for adjournment sine die not later than midnight, Daniel O. Hastings of Delaware held the floor to oppose a railway labor bill. Intended to prevent railroad companies from interfering with union membership of employees, the measure had received the approval of the administration and its friends. Privately the Senator from Delaware assured friends that he would talk if necessary till the hour of midnight; but finding that his views clashed with those of virtually the whole Senate he gave up the fight[21]—after extorting a unanimous-consent agreement that matters other than the railway bill and conference reports would not be considered over a single objection.

Another filibuster was waged successfully by the irrepressible Mr. Long on March 8, 1935. The Senator was determined that no vote should be taken on the disputed "prevailing wage" amendment to the administration $4,880,000,000 work relief bill before the effects of a forthcoming radio address by Father Charles E. Coughlin should be felt in the Senate.[22] The Louisiana Senator disagreed with the administration; if possible he would require the government to pay relief wages equivalent to wages offered by private employers. Accordingly he talked at length and with blithe irrelevance upon the then pending War Department appropriation bill.

"The fact of the case is," he admitted, "I do not know what the War Department bill is." Senatorial freedom of speech he found most helpful. He could talk about what he pleased. Unlike more subtle filibusterers in the Senate, he was ever engagingly frank. At last, recognizing the purpose of the obstruction, Carter Glass agreed that if Long would permit passage of the pending bill no action would be had upon controversial amendments to the work relief

21 ibid.; June 19, 1934.
22 ibid., March 11, 1935.

bill before Monday. Long, having won his technical point, ended
his palaver instantly.

"All right. I agree. O. K."

Two weeks later the Senate was enmeshed in another filibuster
revolving about the work relief bill. Upon this occasion Elmer
Thomas of Oklahoma, whose reputation as an obstructionist was
already well established, proposed to force adoption of an amendment for currency inflation as part of the relief program. Preferably
he would combine inflation with extensive governmental purchases
of silver. For five and a half hours on the 22nd of March he occupied the floor in behalf of his cause; efforts to limit debate by unanimous consent were fruitless. On the next day it was still impossible
to limit debate because of the objection of Thomas, but on motion of
Senator Robinson the currency amendment was laid on the table.
Thomas promptly offered a modified amendment, and it was clear
that filibustering was certain to continue.

Worse than that, news arrived that Senator Long, absent for the
nonce, was taking a plane from the South.[23] Should the loquacious
Louisianan arrive before passage of the measure, days might be consumed in dilatory debate.

Hastily Senator Glass sought a compromise. "I am desperately
anxious to expedite action on the pending joint resolution," he said.
"For nearly a month now there have been pathetic appeals in the
Senate to save millions of people from starvation and other millions
from freezing for lack of clothing; and I think they will all starve
and freeze to death before we get through with this joint resolution
if it shall not be speedily enacted. Therefore, for myself I am willing to accept this amendment and let it go to conference." Thomas
agreed, undoubtedly knowing that the amendment would be eliminated by conferees, as it subsequently was. The obstruction ended
in compromise none too advantageous for the filibusterer.

A month thereafter the Senate faced an organized filibuster upon
the perennial question of federal antilynching legislation. Senators
Edward P. Costigan of Colorado and Robert F. Wagner of New

[23] *ibid.*, March 24, 1935.

York undertook to secure consideration for such a measure on the 24th of April, 1935. Immediate Southern opposition even to consideration arose, and Costigan merely succeeded on that day in explaining the bill.

On the following day, after Wagner had spoken briefly, Senators Tom Connally of Texas and Josiah W. Bailey of North Carolina consumed the rest of the session. The next day, Friday, April 26, Bailey continued to attack the bill, section by section, with hammer and tongs. To him and to other filibustering Senators it was a force bill, aimed at the South for political reasons. "The American people cannot be coerced," Bailey asserted with heat. "They may be led, they may be persuaded, and there are those who think they can be fooled. We can work with them, we can deliberate with them; but, by the eternal gods, neither the Federal Government nor the State government nor the powers in heaven nor the powers in hell can coerce an American citizen. He will not yield."

Senator Robinson, the Democratic leader, stood with his Southern brethren upon the issue. That afternoon he moved that the Senate adjourn; his strategy was simply to sidetrack the pending measure. But the party leader was defeated by 33 yeas against 34 nays, and the majority in favor of an antilynching law forced the Senate to recess. Recess, by continuing the legislative day, technically kept the pending business before the chamber. On Saturday, however, Tom Connally was ready with a speech. Robinson again sought an adjournment, for the same strategic purpose, and was again defeated: only 28 voted with him, 37 against him.

When the Senate convened on Monday, Hugo L. Black of Alabama and James F. Byrnes of South Carolina consumed the time; Southerners were adamant that the bill should never pass. Once more, at the end of the day, Robinson was defeated in an effort to adjourn. Even the inevitable delay of a soldiers' bonus bill could not prevail upon the majority to abandon legislation against lynching. The motion to adjourn was lost by 37 to 38, and the Senate recessed.

For two days thereafter John H. Bankhead of Alabama held the floor. Nothing could be done in the Senate, and at times the chamber neared a state of confusion. In a tangle of motions Thomas of Oklahoma intimated that there seemed to be several questions before the Senate at the same time. "Let us debate them all," suggested "Cotton Ed" Smith of South Carolina. The South would not be downed. Southern Senators would stand upon state rights, and they would talk and talk and talk.

At last, on the afternoon of May 1, after almost six days of filibuster, proponents of the bill became convinced that it could never be enacted. Moreover, important legislation was piling up in an increasingly uncomfortable jam. When Robinson moved in the middle of the afternoon to adjourn for a few minutes in order to displace the motion to consider the antilynching bill, his leadership was followed by a vote of 48 to 32. The North had capitulated to the South.

A filibuster more petulant than important was undertaken by Huey Long on May 21, 1935. It was frankly an effort to prevent passage of a concurrent resolution for a joint session of the two Houses of Congress on the 22nd of May to hear President Roosevelt read his bonus veto. Frederick Steiwer of Oregon argued that the Constitution does not countenance the return of a vetoed bill to both Houses instead of to one; and later Long rose for a rambling tirade against the proposition and against the President.

As usual the Senator from Louisiana, to the great amusement of the galleries, had no respect for relevancy. In the course of his remarks derogatory to the President he chanced to mention the State of Tennessee. Leaping angrily to his feet, Kenneth McKellar lashed out: "I think the Senator had better confine his statement to Louisiana. He has nothing to do with Tennessee, and he had better let Tennessee alone. I am telling the Senator for about the last time that I am tired of hearing him talk about Tennessee." McKellar went on to assert that Long had no influence in the Senate. "I do not believe the Senator could even get the Lord's Prayer endorsed in this body if he undertook to do so. . . . The Senator from Louisiana has an idea that he is a candidate for President. For Heaven's sake!"

"The occupants of the galleries are not in order," protested Connally, and the presiding officer admonished spectators to maintain quiet.

Alben W. Barkley of Kentucky interrupted. "I appeal to the Chair," he begged, "not to be too harsh with the occupants of the galleries. When people go to the circus they ought to be allowed to laugh at the monkey."

"Now, Mr. President," retorted Long, "I resent that statement about my friend from Tennessee."

The leadership determined to "sit out" the one-man filibuster. Senator Robinson is reported to have said, "I want to see just how long he intends to make an ass of himself."[24] But Long was undaunted. For hours he talked, skipping from one subject to another until there were many Senators who thought privately what McKellar said openly. "He does not know anything about a fact," the Senator from Tennessee said in the presence of the filibusterer. "His mind is not capable of taking in anything about a fact. . . . I desire to say that I think it would be a great deal better if the Senator from Louisiana were not a Member of this body. It would be better for the Senate and better for his State and better for the Nation."

After talking almost five hours, Senator Long made the parliamentary mistake of leaving the chamber during a quorum call. A point of order was at once made and sustained that he had surrendered the floor. Technically, because of earlier proceedings, he had now held the floor twice on the same legislative day on the same subject, and a second point of order was sustained against him when he sought to regain it. Having had the floor twice, he could not take it again while the same question was pending, even to make another motion on which he could speak. Because the Senate rules were strictly enforced and because the Senator from Louisiana had failed to be wary of technicalities, the filibuster was lost.

The most celebrated of the Long filibusters was staged from shortly after noon on June 12 till early in the morning of June 13, 1935. For fifteen and one-half hours the remarkable harangue con-

[24] *ibid.*, May 22, 1935.

tinued, interrupted by only two roll calls to establish a quorum and by occasional questions. It was a feat of physical endurance never excelled in the Senate. The Senator from Louisiana sought to attach to a pending joint resolution, the proposed extension of the National Industrial Recovery Act, an amendment proposed by Thomas P. Gore of Oklahoma to require that personnel receiving more than $4,000 per year be appointed by the President and confirmed by the Senate. That amendment, through which patronage would become essentially Senatorial, had been adopted by the body on June 11, but on the 12th there was pending a motion to reconsider and opponents of the policy now had mustered enough votes to remove it from the measure.

The National Industrial Recovery Act had been declared unconstitutional by a unanimous decision of the Supreme Court. "Thank God for that!" was the sentiment of Huey Long. "If America lives twenty years from this day it will owe its life to the nine men on the Supreme Court of the United States who saved this country from Fascism and Bolshevism when they annulled that detestable, contemptible, despicable blue-buzzard N. R. A." The Senator had no wish for the extension of even a skeletonized N. R. A., but if such a law must be passed by the Congress it should contain provisions which would modify the evil. Upon that ground he would fight, flamboyantly, pertinaciously, and even wildly.

He would give the Senate a lecture about the Constitution. In these times it was a vanishing subject, a collection of "ancient and forgotten lore"; but, he informed his audience, "these things which are ancient, these things which are more or less a matter of mythology, are engaging, they are enticing, they are interesting." For hours he read from the Constitution, expatiating upon its provisions in a loud voice and with incredible volubility.

"With great deference to the Senator," said Sherman Minton of Indiana, "may I suggest that he do not talk so loudly? A number of people around here are asleep."

"I am sorry I awakened the Senator from Indiana," Long apologized. "We would have been better off if he had not waked up. The best thing the Senator from Indiana can do is to go back into the cloakroom and go right back to sleep."

Undaunted by the inattention of his colleagues, the Senator undertook a detailed explanation of the "chicken-coop case" in which the Supreme Court had invalidated the N. R. A. The legal proceedings had arisen because of a shipment of chickens, he declared. "In that coop there were some 'dominicker' roosters, a plymouth rock, a buff cochin, white leghorns, and some common chickens that nobody knows by any name except chickens, hill-billy chickens, and various other kinds of chickens." And what had been the violation of the law? A purchaser had "proceeded to get the chicken that he wanted, regardless of the law and the code"; the purchaser was convicted because he had not taken the chickens as they had come; he had discriminated between chickens. At last the Justices of the Supreme Court had passed upon such a law. " 'Hold on,' " they had said. " 'All the crazy people are not in the insane asylum.' " They held unanimously "that a man has the right to any kind of a chicken he wants to eat."

"What is the N. R. A.?" demanded Senator Long, and proceeded to answer his own inquiry. "The national racketeers' arrangement," he shouted. "That is what they are talking about putting back on the books. N. R. A.—Nuts Running America. N. R. A.—Never Roosevelt Again."

At one point in his long-drawn-out proceedings the filibustering Senator was called to order for violating the rules by reflecting upon other Senators, and the Senate thereupon voted on the question whether he should proceed in order. The "noes" seemed to have it, but on a division demanded by Gore a majority voted that he be allowed to continue. Had the vote been in the negative, the filibuster could have been ended; but the spirit of the Senate was not yet for limitation of Senatorial privilege to talk.

Hours of constant speaking were desperately fatiguing even to the indomitable Huey Long. In the midst of his persistent discourse he sipped milk, ate candy, and nibbled at a sandwich. Boyishly he tossed chocolate caramels to Senators near by and sought diversion in jumping up and down to exercise his aching limbs.[25] Could he obtain a respite by asking that the clerk read the Democratic platform? Several Senators hastily objected. He should have no rest till the end of the obstruction.

"Can you beat that?" Long responded, upon objection to hearing the platform read. But he would make a last effort; he would test his influence with the body, recalling no doubt Senator McKellar's remarks on the subject. Would the Senate allow the Lord's Prayer to be read? A chorus of objections answered the request, the voices of Guffey of Pennsylvania, Schwellenbach of Washington, and Moore of New Jersey ringing lustily above the others. "All right," said Long resignedly. " 'The guilty flee when no one pursueth.' " He would then continue his remarks.

Lewis B. Schwellenbach of Washington, speaking on behalf of a group of new members of the Senate, had issued an ultimatum: "We are no longer going to permit the Senator from Louisiana to run the Senate, and we are not going to consent to any unanimous-consent agreement so far as the Senator from Louisiana is concerned."

In one respect the filibuster developed genuine parliamentary significance, marking one more step in the interpretation of the rules to the disadvantage of filibusterers. Earlier practice had been that when a Senator yields for a quorum call he does not surrender the floor. During the tempestuous Huey Long filibuster upon the N. R. A., however, the President pro tempore (Key Pittman of Nevada) declared that a quorum call is the transaction of business and that Senators who yield for that purpose lose the floor. Whenever the rules are strictly enforced under such an interpretation, a speaker yielding twice for quorum calls (if they are in order) while the same question is before the Senate is unable to regain the floor on that question during the same legislative day. A new deterrent to the activity of filibusterers, even if relatively minor in character, was thus brought into being.

[25] *ibid.*, June 13, 1935.

About four o'clock in the morning, exhausted after his protracted adventure in continuous talking, Senator Long finally yielded the floor. Merely to print his speech in the *Congressional Record* cost the public several thousands of dollars.[26] Yet the Senator did not wish to be "hoggish" about the time of the Senate. "I will solicit a conference with the rebellious element in this body," he said in conclusion, "and undertake to get harmony and understanding." In the meantime, he knew, Thomas D. Schall of Minnesota would speak. That Senator rose, but Bennett Champ Clark of Missouri in the chair quickly put the question on the motion to reconsider the amendment for which Long had fought. Clark declared that the "ayes" had carried it. Protests against the haste with which the chair had put the question were unavailing, but Schall sought to launch an attack against the N. R. A. in general. Totally blind, he asked that the clerk read his address, but McKellar interposed an objection. Charles L. McNary of Oregon, the Republican floor leader, came to the rescue and moved that the clerk read as requested; by a vote of 38 yeas against 17 nays the Senate extended the courtesy. Obstruction was still in progress but weakening hour by hour. At the conclusion of Schall's contribution and after a vain effort by Pat McCarran of Nevada to bring before the Senate the social security bill, Barkley moved to table the controversial Gore amendment. The motion carried, and all hope for the filibuster was gone.

In August another filibuster, undertaken by a group of Senators, was successful almost immediately after it had become incipient. The danger of war in Europe seemed imminent, and many influential legislators demanded a statute calculated to promote American neutrality. Prospects for such legislation seemed none too certain, but in the midst of consideration of a coal bill, on August 20, Homer T. Bone of Washington began to speak at length about neutrality. Plainly he intended to talk, with the help of other Senators known to be ready to cooperate, till assurance should be given that a neutrality measure should be brought before the Senate. Democratic leader Robinson insisted that the Foreign Relations Com-

26 cf. *New York Times*, June 14, 1935.

mittee had met even that morning to authorize the report of such a bill. But the filibusterers were not to be put off with promises; they demanded action. Finally Chairman Key Pittman of the Foreign Relations Committee came to the chamber and reported a neutrality bill, and it passed the Senate the next day.

Two days afterward, on the 23rd of August, Millard E. Tydings of Maryland, who had once threatened to resign if Senate obstruction did not cease, resorted to the practice of filibuster. Disapproving enormous appropriations in a flood control bill he talked for two and one-half hours. "Men may throw money away," he cried, "but, oh, there will be a different story when the time comes to write a tax bill." He would illustrate in detail the exorbitant items, "the glaring and outrageous and unconsidered and unjustifiable items," in the measure. Moreover, said he, "I am not going to give any recipes for potlikker; but I am going to give a recipe to the taxpayers of the country as to whom they should and whom they should not elect to Congress if they want less taxes." Finally it was agreed to postpone the issue, and the Senate voted to recommit the bill with instructions that the Committee on Commerce report it at the next session.

The much obstructed session of Congress came to a close, as did the Senatorial career of Huey Long, with a determined filibuster by the energetic Louisianan. For two months he had not imposed upon the Senate his peculiar talents for delay, but on the night of the 26th of August, 1935, he was busy again. It had been agreed that Congress would that day stand adjourned sine die, and the hour of adjournment was thus fixed for not later than midnight. A deficiency appropriation bill including funds for the social security program had yet to be passed and leaders were eager to hurry it through. Senator Robinson announced that because of the parliamentary situation in the House it would be impossible to pass the bill with the Senate amendments in effect guaranteeing to farmers minimum prices of 12 cents a pound for cotton and 90 cents a bushel for wheat. He moved therefore that those particular amendments be stricken from the bill.

In these amendments Senator Long was interested. At six-thirty in the evening he took the floor to talk until the leadership in the Senate and in the House should agree to find a way to save them. "I challenge all sides and beg all sides, the high, the mighty, the powerful," he shouted, "to let the House have a chance to vote. That is all I ask." Without a House vote upon the amendments, so far as he was concerned there would be no deficiency appropriation.

Robinson propounded a rhetorical question: "If the Congress shall not pass the deficiency appropriation bill, carrying items for old-age pensions, old-age insurance, crippled children, railroad pensions, and the dependent blind, it will be four months, will it not . . . before any of these measures can be carried into effect?"

Under such conditions, Long replied to the majority leader, "the thing for the Senator to do is to move to reconsider the vote by which he has undertaken to adjourn Congress." His own position was clear and unchangeable: if Congress must hasten to adjourn without action by the House upon the cotton and wheat amendments, he would block legislation till the bitter end. Yet when a point of order was made and sustained that he had violated the rules of the body by referring by name to a member of the House, the Senate refused to vote him from the floor. Even the provocation of a Huey Long was not great enough to make the solemn Senate forget its tradition of unlimited speech.

Again and again Black and Schwellenbach interrupted, under the guise of parliamentary inquiries, to ask in tones of stinging rebuke whether the Senator by his filibuster would force suffering and misery upon the poor, the aged, the crippled, and the blind. Senators implored the Louisianan to allow appropriations for social security to be carried. But to both threats and entreaties he was unyielding. For five and one-half hours he waved his arms and shouted in the chamber, and the majority could find no effective way to silence him.

"This stand for principle will mean something in this country pretty soon," he predicted. "It may preserve legislative government. Remember what I am telling you: It may preserve legislative government, which is nearly gone."

"It may also destroy the right of free speech in the Senate," said Black. "The people of the country may become so disgusted that they will cut off the right of free speech here."

Long thought otherwise. "No they will not. This is one time the country will approve me. I challenge Senators to find out anything I have ever stood for in this body that has not been popular among the people."

"I know the Senator has always thought it was popular," Black continued, "but he is going to be mistaken this time."

"Am I?" Long yelled. "Then go down and help beat me. I come before the electorate in Louisiana in four months, and I challenge the whole dad-gummed kit and barrel of the Democratic Party to come down and beat me. I want them to beat me if they can on this issue."

Crimson with rage, he was defiant to the last. The tirade, torrential and irrelevant, went on; the hour of midnight came; the session closed. For the time both the appropriation and the amendments failed. Long had deadlocked the session but had lost the parliamentary battle. He dashed out a side door and away. And before the Senate and the country had recovered from his barrage of words, this buccaneer unrivalled in Senate history was dead, assassinated in the capitol of his own Louisiana domain.

Although Huey Long had gone forever, the next session of Congress ended in a similar débâcle. In a preliminary skirmish Bennett Champ Clark and others were easily successful in forcing the House of Representatives to pass a measure for ship subsidy. On the 19th of June, 1936, the Senators, with Clark as principal speaker, shrewdly filibustered against Treasury and Post Office appropriations. The latter included funds for continuing contracts with shipping interests, virtual subsidies authorized under a law passed in 1928. If such funds were voted without delay, the House would probably refuse to consider direct subsidy legislation intended eventually to supersede the mail contract system.

Clark and his fellow obstructionists were eager to stop the policy of lavish mail grants, and to accomplish their purpose they would accept a direct subsidy law. Under the leadership of President Roosevelt, Democrats were reversing their historic policy of opposition to ship subsidies. The regulatory features connected with the outright subsidy made it a desirable measure, Clark asserted; and under the threat of defeat for important appropriations the House yielded on the night of the 20th.[27]

By the 20th of June there was tremendous pressure for final adjournment from tired members busy with election worries. That evening, when the Senate was considering a coal conservation bill, Rush D. Holt of West Virginia rose for prolonged opposition. "I realize that many Senators have stayed late tonight to hear the discussion on the coal bill, and I appreciate that consideration," he began; "but I wish to read them tonight from the volume called Aesop's Fables." First, however, he would read from a book about miners and mining written by John L. Lewis. In addition he would discuss the Works Progress Administration and the political situation in West Virginia.

"Will the Senator tell us now whether he expects to support the Democratic nominee for Senator in West Virginia?" asked Minton of Indiana.

The feud within the ranks of the Democratic party between the young Senator Holt and his veteran colleague, M. M. Neely, had more than once enlivened the battles of the Senate, and the filibusterer was not averse to continuing it. "If I should say what I thought of him," he replied, "I would be violating the rules of the Senate, because I am not allowed to talk about my colleagues in that way."

Indeed, the coal bill itself had been pressed in the Senate by no less hardy politicians than Joseph F. Guffey of Pennsylvania and M. M. Neely. The Supreme Court had invalidated earlier legislation enacted to regulate the coal industry, but the two Democratic Senators and their supporters now proposed a new measure omitting labor features which the Court had criticized. That bill would not

[27] *ibid.*, June 21, 1936.

be passed if Rush Holt could talk it to death, but he would annoy his colleagues as painlessly as possible. He would read Aesop's Fables. But Senators must listen in order to draw the morals. On and on, from fable to fable, the Senator droned: the wolf and the shepherd; the elephant and the assembly of animals; the eagle, the cat, and the wild sow; the ass that carried the image.

"Is it the Senator's intention to continue his address?" asked Robinson.

"I have a great many of Aesop's Fables to read," Holt replied.

"The Senator would not be willing to yield for a vote on the bill?"

"Oh, I would have to read all these fables. I desire to read them."

"Very well," Robinson rejoined. He himself would yield to the filibuster and to the pressure for adjournment. Upon his motion the Senate concurred in a resolution already passed by the House that at the end of the day the two Houses stand adjourned sine die. Obstruction had been fully successful, for it was clear that the Senator from West Virginia could easily hold the floor for many hours. After desultory debate and a few formalities, the body adjourned. The youngest of its members, by the use of time-honored tactics, had won the legislative victory.

Still more recent among the Senate's many episodes of extended filibustering is a series of sectional conflicts over an issue already famous as an incentive for obstruction. Twice in 1937 and again early in 1938 there were determined efforts to enact federal anti-lynching legislation, although to raise that question in the Senate is virtually to assure a filibuster.

On August 11, 1937, the antilynching issue came unexpectedly before the Senate. The Democratic leader, Alben W. Barkley of Kentucky, had arranged that after the passage of a bill regarding helium any one of three Senators should be recognized by the chair to bring up other business. But Robert F. Wagner of New York sprang from his seat, obtained the floor, and moved to consider the bill to punish the crime of lynching. Barkley protested that the motion was premature, that it was "unfortunate at this particular juncture that an exceedingly controversial matter should be brought forward now." The situation was delicate; the legislative program of the administration might be disrupted. Even Vice President John N. Garner felt called upon to make some explanation. He had recognized the Senator from New York because no other Senator was on his feet; discretion lay with the chair only when several Senators were seeking recognition. When he had been Speaker of the House, he admitted, he had enjoyed more latitude; it had been possible to "recognize a member in his seat and ask him to stand up."

Wagner had been too quick for his Senatorial colleagues, and he was convinced of the importance of his measure. "I do not want to disarrange any program," he said, "but I shall not yield on this proposal."

The Senate was in confusion. Many favored the antilynching bill, while others regarded it as unconstitutional. Southern Senators could be counted on to filibuster against it, and even Borah of Idaho threatened to oppose it with all his physical strength.[28] Barkley sought to displace the subject and moved to adjourn. Wagner opposed that motion, and the Senate rejected it by 27 to 35. By adopting a motion to recess immediately thereafter, the issue was kept before the body. On the next day Tom Connally of Texas was on the floor; he had been selected to fire the opening guns of a filibuster, and for hours he talked and talked. A compromise was the objective of the administration leadership, eager to save its legislative program. At last Barkley hit upon a formula, and the Senate agreed by unanimous consent to make the antilynching bill the unfinished business of the next session of Congress, after the disposition of farm legislation. The thunder clouds of filibuster then rolled away, and the Senate went on with its business.

In the brief special session which convened in November, however, farm legislation was delayed and Senators favoring an antilynching bill decided to press it for immediate consideration. When Southern Democrats became aware of that strategy, signs of filibuster preceded even the first move of antilynching advocates. During morn-

[28] *ibid.*, Aug. 12, 1937.

ing hour on November 16, 1937, James F. Byrnes of South Carolina occupied the floor to preclude the making of a motion (undebatable at that time) to consider the bill against lynching. His
strategy was successful. and it was not until later in the day that
Wagner could move to bring up his measure.

Once the motion was made, Connally promptly took the floor.
Why should not Senators consider farm legislation, for which they
had been called into session? Why should not the committee pre-
paring agricultural proposals report to the Senate? "It probably
would bring in just as good a bill tomorrow as it would bring in a
month from now." If the Senate would not carry out its pledges to
the farmer, he would occupy the time; and it developed that he could
do so very effectively. At a moment when the majority were off
guard, he shrewdly obtained unanimous consent for the reading of
a speech about the lynching problem delivered during the filibuster
of 1935 by Hugo L. Black of Alabama. That expedient consumed
the rest of the day and part of the next. For hours the Senate clerks
read to an almost empty chamber.

In many respects Southerners welcomed as a political godsend
an opportunity to talk against a measure which they deemed in-
tensely unpopular among their constituents. The organized obstruction suffered no dearth of cooperation. Essentially, however, the
filibuster was uncontested; each evening recess was voted at a
reasonable hour, rules were not strictly enforced, and little hope of
passing the measure in special session was entertained. If the issue
afforded the minority a new opportunity to demonstrate sectional
loyalty, it also offered to the majority an occasion to display before
the country politically valuable efforts in behalf of the cause. The
Senate remained in good temper. Beneath the appearance of struggle was political profit for all.

Yet there were moments when anger rippled across the good
humor of Senate proceedings. On the 19th of November Connally
walked into the chamber and noticed upon the wall a poster depict-
ing the lynching of Negroes. "I should like to know by whose
authority this placard was placed on the wall of the Senate Cham-

ber," he demanded. The Texan had no objection to the custom that
Senators might use the walls for hanging maps and charts to illustrate their speeches but he was not prepared to suffer this display
in silence.

The placard had been placed at his request, Senator Clark announced. "I can very readily understand how it may be irksome to
the Senator from Texas to have these exhibits presented. It may
cause some faint flurry of that conscience for which the Senator from
Texas used to be renowned, but which his conduct this week has led
most of us to believe has become calloused." He added caustically
that the placard seemed already to have served its purpose.

"Of course it has," retorted Connally, rapidly becoming so infuriated that he violated the rules of the Senate with his language.
Its purpose, he declared, was to make headlines and get into the
newspapers the name of the Senator who arranged it. "I know that
is what it is for, but I protest against the Senate being made a sewer
for the vaporings of the Senator from Missouri."

For five calendar days, during the Senate sessions, the filibuster
was in full swing. Even the new Senator from Alabama, Dixie Bibb
Graves, recently appointed by her husband the governor, contributed
a brief address. "I shall not speak to consume time," she said. But
she went on to register her opposition to a federal antilynching
bill. "To punish deliberately innocent citizens is a new departure in
Americanism, and a most unwelcome one. . . . A general wrong
avenging a particular wrong is all wrong."

On the 23rd of November, the sixth day of session after the beginning of the filibuster, Wagner withdrew his motion to consider
the bill against lynching in order that farm legislation might have
priority. With comparative ease Southern Democrats had blocked
the hated measure, at least for the time.

After the disposal of farm legislation, however, under the terms of
the agreement in the Senate during the summer, the antilynching
question became the unfinished business. But the special session
was drawing to a close, and Senators preferred postponement to
further filibuster. On the 20th of December Barkley and the prin-

cipal advocates of the bill arranged an agreement by which January 6, 1938, after the next session should have convened, was set as a date for renewed consideration.

When the proposal came before the Senate at the later date proponents planned a vigorous fight for enactment. Filibustering broke out at once, and Connally moved to adjourn and thus to displace the measure. It was a test vote: the yeas stood at 18 as against 52 nays. Clearly an overwhelming majority of the Senate favored the bill, but to make progress against organized obstruction was a perplexing undertaking.

Early in the parliamentary battle Senator Borah threw his weight against the bill, thus aiding the filibuster though not directly participating in it. Southern Senators talked in relays for days, obviously relishing their forensic opportunities. But it remained for Hattie W. Caraway of Arkansas to perpetrate once more a siege of reading by the clerk, for in the midst of her own remarks she was able unobtrusively to secure unanimous consent for the reading of a voluminous document prepared by the minority members of a Senate committee in 1887. Meanwhile visitors to the Senate galleries, watching the activities of these men and women who proudly called themselves members of the world's greatest legislative body, were at once amused, indignant, and disillusioned.

From the 14th to the 20th of January, with one day out for Sunday, Allen J. Ellender of Louisiana alone consumed most of the hours in the sessions of six calendar days. With astonishing fortitude he read statutes on matters of racial discrimination from many states, and after going through a sheaf of such papers he read for days from the histories of Egypt, India, and Haiti. Yet he would not end his remarks without a discussion of contemporary America, and for nearly a day he edified the Senate with comments about Father Divine, Negro religious leader, known to his followers as "God." He spoke at length about Father Divine's "angels": Sweet Angel Faithful Mary, Jesus the Christ, and others. And the Senator from Louisiana was frank in announcing that he stood for white supremacy and would tolerate nothing less. The white men and women of the South had fought for it, he shouted; he would not abandon it. "The struggle was costly; it was bitter; but oh, how sweet the victory! Let us not reward the deeds of those men and women with a crown of thorns, but, instead, let us perpetuate their memories with this challenge, 'We shall at all cost preserve the white supremacy of America.'" But at last the prodigious speech was ended.

Exasperated at what he called "the snail's pace we have been making in regard to the consideration of this bill," Barkley announced for the majority that he would expect the Senate to meet earlier and to sit at night. Accordingly, on the 24th and 25th of January the Senate met at night. On the 25th a cloture petition with seventeen signatures was submitted by Senator Neely. After that day, however, night sessions were abandoned; members of the majority were in no mood to endure the repeated inconvenience of long hours of Senate attendance.

On the 27th, with the filibuster still in full progress, Senator McNary as the Republican leader announced that he would vote against cloture. All Republicans in the Senate save two, he stated, sincerely favored the bill. They were willing "to remain here from sunrise to evening star and from evening star to sunrise in order to have the bill passed. . . . But, Mr. President, I am not willing to give up the right of free speech and full, untrammelled opportunity for argument. That right is the last palladium; it is the last impregnable trench for those who may be oppressed or who are about to be oppressed; it may be the last barrier to tyranny." With the Democratic membership hopelessly split upon the antilynching question, there was no chance for a two-thirds vote for cloture. When the test was taken, the Senate decisively rejected it: 37 yeas against 51 nays.

The filibuster continued, but on the 31st of January and the 1st of February it was shelved by common consent for consideration and passage of a conference report on the administration housing program. With the adoption of that report obstructionists renewed their activities, and Theodore G. Bilbo of Mississippi held the floor.

"The Man" Bilbo would offer a solution to the whole problem: repatriation of the Negro. In particular he would recommend Liberia; let the Negro go back to Africa. "In offering the solution," he told the Senate, "I repeat that it is not wild; it is not fanciful; it is not fantastic; it is not visionary; but it is really the cream of the judgment and statesmanship of all great men who have gone before." The Senator would develop his plan in detail. "I do not mean that we should deport the Negro. . . . I mean that we are to take him as a friend, carry him back to his homeland, and there colonize him." The Negro's property should be purchased, of course. "It amounts to only about $3,000,000,000, and we spend more than that in one year for relief. We can afford to buy every dollar of property the Negro has in the United States and then spend $2,000,000,000 on top of that in buying the country for him and standing the initial expense of his colonization."

"I am ready to speak for thirty days," the Senator from Mississippi calmly informed his auditors. But there were other Senators who wished to take up time, and proponents of an antilynching law felt that they should explain and defend it. "The support for this bill is rooted, Mr. President," said Senator Wagner, "in a tradition of Anglo-Saxon justice that goes back to Magna Carta—the right of every man accused of a crime to a fair trial by his peers. We seek to vindicate those practices which are the hallmark of any civilized government. We seek to substitute for the rope, the faggot, and the blowtorch the orderly processes of the law." Experience has made it evident, he claimed, that the states cannot end lynching; only a federal law would be effective.

Glass of Virginia moved consideration of appropriations for independent offices. "We have wasted nearly a month of the time of the Senate in discussing an infernal, unconstitutional bill," he observed. Still the majority refused to yield; the motion was rejected by 34 yeas to 52 nays.[29] However, the majority had no desire, by insisting upon consideration of the antilynching bill, to throttle all important public measures. For three days in February the conference report

[29] 83 *Cong. Record,* pp. 1501-2.

for agricultural relief was considered and it was finally adopted. Often, as in this case, minority filibusterers who seek to defeat legislation are glad to yield for any other business which will help take up the time.

On the 14th of February, with the antilynching measure once more before the Senate, Wagner presented a second cloture petition. "I do not think that there is anything unreasonable in the request that this debate be brought to a conclusion," said Barkley. Whenever the bill had been taken up for debate, he pointed out, "every door has swung wide open, because Senators were making an exodus as if a wild beast had been turned loose on the floor of the Senate. And the very desks themselves would have left had they not been screwed to the floor and found it impossible to move."

Yet on the 16th cloture was defeated: 42 yeas against 46 nays. With Republican support of unlimited debate, a two-thirds majority for cloture, even at any time in the future, seemed utterly impossible. Senator Ellender, who had again been speaking for days, continued his remarkable outpouring until the frustrated majority on the afternoon of Thursday, the 17th of February, voted a recess until the following Monday.

When the Senate met again, Barkley rose to confess the impossible parliamentary predicament of antilynching legislation and moved the consideration of relief appropriations. Even Wagner conceded that the situation had reached a deadlock. "There is absolutely no way of ever bringing this bill to a vote except by means of a cloture," he admitted, "because there are too many engaged in the filibuster." To the embarrassment of the retreating majority Holt of West Virginia insisted upon a roll-call vote, and the motion which indicated surrender was carried by 58 yeas to 22 nays.

As a matter of fact, the majority had never converted the filibuster into a fight of intensity. Hiram W. Johnson of California, scornfully deriding the leadership of the antilynching advocates, asserted that the proceedings "might be denominated a 'feather duster' filibuster, a 'pink tea' filibuster."[30] The majority had allowed Senators

---

[30] *ibid.*, p. 2204.

to retain the floor by unanimous consent after numerous technical yieldings; such rules as might be inconvenient for filibusterers were not enforced; all-night or even long-continued sessions were not employed. The spirit of the majority had been weak. From the 6th of January till the 21st of February the filibuster had been the most conspicuous accomplishment of the Senate, but it was an achievement easy for the minority to win. For twenty-nine calendar days of actual Senate sessions the antilynching bill had been before the body. The most prolonged filibuster demonstration in recent years utterly precluded its passage.

A filibuster of a different sort, more ingenious and potentially more discomfiting to the majority occurred on the 29th of March, 1938, when Bennett Champ Clark by clever tactics delayed a vote upon naval appropriations until the following day. Reputedly he acted to obtain an opportunity to speak against the measure at the beginning of a daily session when Senate attendance is larger and more constant.[31] To accomplish his purpose the Missouri Senator, son of former Speaker Champ Clark and one of the ablest parliamentarians in the body, alternated motions with demands for quorum calls. As each motion was defeated business was transacted, and thus a quorum call was in order. With frequent quorum calls, Senators were inconveniently compelled to be present almost constantly in the chamber. The Senate leadership soon agreed that a vote should be delayed till the morrow.

The summer of 1939 brought further interesting episodes in the long story of Senate obstruction. At the outset Senators friendly to the producers of silver banded together to ask a higher price for that commodity and if possible to obtain a $2,000,000,000 inflation of the currency.[32] By the 20th of June their position was strategic. The fiscal year of the federal government would expire at midnight on June 30, and administration policies would be severely handicapped unless monetary, work relief, and tax legislation could be passed within ten

[31] *New York Herald Tribune,* March 30, 1938.
[32] *New York Times,* June 22, 1939.

days. Under the leadership of Elmer Thomas of Oklahoma and Pat McCarran of Nevada, a group of Western Senators resolved to block Congressional business until the price of silver should be raised.

During the consideration of monetary legislation on June 20 filibusterers went into action. The measure proposed to extend Presidential authority, otherwise expiring at the end of the fiscal year, to alter the value of the dollar and to operate a huge stabilization fund of $2,000,000,000 for the purpose of controlling foreign exchange. McCarran and William H. King of Utah began the oratorical efforts of the silverites, but Robert R. Reynolds of North Carolina provided welcome relief by speaking at length on the immigration and deportation of criminal aliens.

The next day, with Senator Thomas holding the floor and illustrating an extended discourse with maps and charts, McCarran argued vehemently in the cloakrooms on behalf of the silver cause. Would he and his friends admit, came the inquiry, that a filibuster was under way? But "filibusterer" is a name which Senators often do not wish to acknowledge. "I am a bronco-buster," replied the elderly Senator from Nevada, dexterously covering evasion with facetiousness. "A filly is a little thing. A bronco is a full-grown horse."[33]

Filibusterers had no wish, however, to antagonize unduly their colleagues and the administration. On the 22nd of June a legislative truce made possible Senate passage of the important tax measure, and the monetary bill was again considered. Henry F. Ashurst quickly took the floor to talk half seriously, half jocosely on the subject of copper. The following day Lynn J. Frazier of North Dakota and Key Pittman of Nevada renewed the obstructive battle, and late in the afternoon with few Senators in attendance the eloquent Josh Lee, junior Senator from Oklahoma, consumed the time.

"Mr. President," he began, "I am not responsible for the seats in the Senate Chamber not being filled. I am reminded of the preacher,

[33] *ibid.*

who, after preaching a while, said to one of the ushers, 'Wake Brother Brown up.' The usher replied, 'Wake him up yourself; you put him to sleep.' "

Empty seats and inattentive Senators could not prevent him from speaking. "We have heard an able discussion of gold by the Senator from Colorado, Mr. Adams," he continued. "We have heard a learned speech on silver by the Senator from Nevada, Mr. Pittman. We have heard a glowing tribute to copper from the Senator from Arizona, Mr. Ashurst, and now I propose to put in my nickel's worth."

Senator Lee had observed that those with least wealth usually know most about the money question, and he therefore regarded himself as fully qualified to speak with authority. "In spite of the fact that it is said that more people go crazy over money than any other subject," he announced, "I shall venture a few observations on the subject of money."

"I should like to inquire just the implication of the Senator's remark," said Senator Schwellenbach. "Does he imply that he has already gone crazy or that he expects us who listen to him to go crazy?"

Filibustering activities continued through a poorly attended session on Saturday. On Monday, June 26, events turned in a new and remarkable direction. Conservatives who wished to abolish the power of the President to devalue the dollar formed a coalition with the filibustering silverites. Party lines were shattered. By a vote of 47 to 31, the Senate adopted an amendment to end the authority of the President over the value of the dollar and by 48 yeas against 30 nays voted in effect to raise the price of domestic silver from 64.64 cents an ounce to 77.57 cents.[34] Although stabilization fund provisions were retained in the monetary bill, the astonishing coalition of conservatives and silverites had delivered a stinging rebuke to the administration of President Roosevelt. But devastating as was the defeat, the President refused to consider it final. Bluntly he labelled

[34] *ibid.*, June 27, 1939; 84 *Cong. Record*, pp. 7867-8.

the blow at his power over the dollar an attempt to transfer currency control from Washington to Wall Street.[35]

The administration exerted tremendous pressure to reverse the situation. Loyally the House of Representatives refused to accept the monetary bill with Senate amendments, and the measure was sent to a committee of conference. Meanwhile conservatives and silverites threatened a joint filibuster if conferees should strike out the controversial amendments.[36] Administration strategists, however, sought to break the peculiar coalition responsible for their downfall, and they were equal to the occasion. Senate and House conferees agreed to restore the President's power over the dollar and to fix the price of domestic silver at approximately 70 cents,[37] and it was soon apparent that the concession to the silverites would induce them to desert the coalition and vote to accept the conference recommendations. For the conservatives, however, the net result of adopting such a conference report would be anything but pleasing. In reality they were opposed to the higher price for silver which their own strategy had nevertheless helped to effect. And in the renewal of the President's authority over valuation of the dollar they would lose every vestige of compensation for their policy. Republicans were particularly disgruntled at the prospect.

Rumors were soon current that the monetary bill would be talked to death on the night of June 30. The President's dollar authority and the stabilization fund expired at midnight. Many observers contended that should continuing legislation fail to pass before the hour of expiration an entirely new bill must be introduced, recreating rather than extending the Presidential powers. The Democratic floor leader, Alben W. Barkley of Kentucky, agreed with that view. "We can revive them," he said, "by new legislation just as we could create them in the beginning; but when they have once expired, we cannot, in my judgment, revive them simply by continuing what does not exist."[38]

35 *New York Times*, June 28, 1939.
36 *ibid.*
37 *ibid.*, June 30, 1939.
38 84 *Cong. Record*, p. 8193.

Early in the evening of June 30 the conference report on the monetary bill was presented to the Senate for consideration. The important work relief bill had been approved by the chamber and the body was ready for uninterrupted controversy on the money issue. The action of the conferees was first attacked by two Senators young in service, Democratic D. Worth Clark of Idaho and Republican Robert A. Taft of Ohio. The conservative Democrat, Alva B. Adams of Colorado, a conferee who had refused to sign the report, protested the failure to carry out the mandate of the Senate. Two administration Senators pointed to the need for action and defended the report. Republican conferee John G. Townsend, Jr., of Delaware, who had also refused to sign the conference recommendations, exclaimed in indignation, "Mr. President, in all my ten years in the Senate I have never known of a single instance when the will of the Senate was so completely ignored and cast overboard by a conference committee as was the case yesterday with reference to the monetary bill. . . ."

With Townsend's denunciation Republicans began to talk against time. Arthur H. Vandenberg of Michigan at the conclusion of a long speech rejoiced "that in one hour and fifty minutes from now there will be no concentrated power to control the money of America in any one man's hand, anywhere." W. Warren Barbour of New Jersey also denounced the delegation of monetary control to the President. Before the hour of midnight Democratic Millard E. Tydings of Maryland, whose renomination had been vigorously opposed by the President in the famous "purge" of the preceding year, rose to cooperate in killing the administration measure. The bill would die that night if obstruction could do the deed. The Senator from Maryland did not think that "the end of the world" would come because of it. "I have a feeling—I may be wrong—that even in New York City overnight grass will not be growing in the streets. I have a feeling that the banks will all open, that all the merchandising establishments will have their wares on display; that people will be going back and forth to the world's fair; and that down in North Carolina Mount Pisgah in all its glory will kiss the first refulgent rays of the golden rising sun."

Midnight came, and triumphantly he talked on. Believing that victory was ever more certain, minute by minute, as the long hand of the Senate clock moved slowly downward from the numeral twelve, the Senator became too exultant to be overly concerned with the month or the day. "Mr. President," he shouted, "I was always fond of the number 17, always have been fond of it, and looking at the official clock . . . I see that it is now seventeen minutes past twelve o'clock midnight January [laughter]—I mean July 1, 1939. No Senator on this floor will dispute that. Do I hear that denied? No one rises to deny it. What I have said has met with the approval of all present, at least no Senator has dared to contradict me that it is now eighteen minutes after midnight, January the 1st [laughter]—"

For the moment the President was frustrated. He had sat in the White House in readiness to rush across the city to sign the monetary bill in the Capitol itself if the measure could be passed before midnight.[39] How could executive authority over money now be salvaged from the legislative entanglement which filibusterers had wrought?

In the Senate Taft undertook to drive home the point that Presidential monetary authority had expired and could not be revived save by new legislation.

"I should like to ask the Senator from Ohio," inquired Schwellenbach, "if he and those with whom he is associated are so confident as to their position, why they keep on talking on into the night?"

As a matter of fact, Republicans had been disturbed to discover that administration leaders had changed their minds. When Taft read aloud Barkley's earlier statement expressing the view that the legislation would be dead unless passed prior to midnight on the 30th of June, the Democratic leader was ready with a bland reply. "That proves," he said, "that frequently lawyers in expressing curbstone opinions may be mistaken. Upon further investigation of the law and the decisions I have reached the conclusion that the opinion I expressed on yesterday was a mistake, that it did not state the law, that the law is not dead, and that the adoption of the conference

[39] *New York Times*, July 1, 1939.

report would be as valid tonight or tomorrow as if it had been adopted yesterday."

Taft sought to learn for himself and his colleagues whether President Roosevelt had also changed his mind, for reports had been circulated that he too had agreed that the bill to be effective must be passed before the midnight now gone. "I should like to ask the Senator from Kentucky, since he has eaten his own words," said Taft, "if he knows whether the President also has eaten his."

Barkley would not be committed on that point. "I can speak only for myself," he responded, "and if I have eaten my words, and even if the President has eaten his, neither finds them unpalatable."

Republican Henry Cabot Lodge, Jr., of Massachusetts had scarcely begun an address which promised to be long when Barkley interrupted with a proposal for a holiday adjournment over the 4th of July. His suggestion was coupled with the condition that when the Senate should meet on the 5th debate should be limited by unanimous consent to one speech not longer than thirty minutes for each Senator and that a final vote on the conference report should be had that day not later than five o'clock. Republicans had talked over the proposition and had decided that further contest upon the validity of the conference report, if adopted, could if necessary be settled in the courts.

Said Warren R. Austin of Vermont, speaking for the Republican minority: "I wish to have it understood that if no objection should be interposed by us, and if the unanimous-consent agreement should be entered into, we who are opposed to the conference report do not by our silence admit anything; that we do not waive any claims or any rights. . . ."

The agreement was made, and the Senate prepared to adjourn. At Barkley's request a clerk read an opinion from the recently appointed Attorney General, Frank Murphy of Michigan, written at the request of the President and expressing the view that monetary powers could be continued if the conference report were adopted at any time after midnight on June 30. Senators voted adjournment in full knowledge that the President would insist upon adoption of the report and would fight to retain his authority.

When the Senate met again, on the 5th of July, debate was immediately resumed. But the administration had the votes, and the conference report was accepted by 43 yeas against 39 nays.

A month later the session adjourned sine die, but not until threatened filibuster had forced Senator Key Pittman, chairman of the Committee on Foreign Relations, to abandon a joint resolution authorizing government sale of military and naval equipment to any other American republic. The Senator from Nevada would have the United States assist South American republics in their problems of defense. Would not such a policy be that of the good neighbor? Arthur H. Vandenberg informed the Senate that he thought otherwise. Declaring himself in full sympathy with the efforts of the State Department to promote friendly relations throughout the Americas, he insisted that he did not believe it wise to make "an arms huckster out of Uncle Sam." It soon became evident that the Senator from Michigan was prepared to argue at some length that good will could not be promoted in that fashion.

"Does the Senator feel that he can conclude his remarks within thirty minutes?" asked Barkley, who as Democratic leader was responsible for guiding the program of the session.

Vandenberg saw no need for such brevity. On the contrary he assured the majority leader that "the subject merits the extended consideration which some of us intend it shall have. . . ."

Senator Pittman was of course aware that a filibuster was impending, although he admitted that Vandenberg had not used the "obnoxious word." Clearly, further insistence upon the military and naval equipment proposal would be at the expense of other important legislation. "Naturally I would not want to engage in a futile undertaking," he announced, as he reluctantly allowed the joint resolution to be relegated to a place among bills which could not be considered.

Obviously filibustering is still a successful instrument in the Senate of the United States.

CHAPTER VII

THE DILEMMA

CHAPTER VII

THE DILEMMA

STRATEGY to curtail the devastating effects of clever filibustering has given no little concern to Senate parliamentarians. Most of them have been forced to acknowledge ruefully that, at least so long as the rules are observed, obstructionists have a decided advantage. During the first ninety years of its history the Senate could rely for the most part upon dignity, courtesy, and custom to hold within bounds the practice of filibustering. There was obstruction but at the same time there was usually a deep respect for the prestige of the Senate, a deference which contrasts sharply with the brazen defiance so common in subsequent years. Since the early 1880's filibustering has had a tremendous vogue and a remarkable effectiveness in the Senate, and until 1908 virtually no significant parliamentary devices were contrived and put in operation primarily to curb the almost unrestricted power of filibusterers.

Obstruction as it is practiced in the United States Senate is often, indeed characteristically, complex in motives, in techniques, and in participating personnel. There is a popular tendency to think of filibustering simply as an attempt to *defeat* measures by long speeches and by other means of delay. That this conception is both inadequate and inaccurate needs little demonstration after a survey of the long history of Senate filibusters.

The purpose of delay is often far from negative. For instance, the final filibuster of Huey P. Long, in 1935, was not intended to defeat a deficiency appropriation bill carrying funds for the social security program. He favored, or professed to favor, that measure; his purpose was simply to force inclusion of amendments in behalf of cotton and wheat. In effect he proclaimed that if amendments were adopted the deficiency appropriation bill might be passed at once. Without amendments, there would be no legislation. The action which the Senator took was negative in character and result. By talking for hours he defeated the deficiency appropriation. Yet his purpose was positive, and in the defeat of the measure he failed in his ultimate aim.

Of course many filibusters are primarily negative in purpose, but it is very doubtful whether any of them, unless it be of the most petulant and personal sort, is exclusively so. In virtually every filibuster undertaken to defeat measures before the Senate there are additional considerations, perhaps incidental but none the less inseparable from a true and full picture of the parliamentary situation. The famous barricades of oratory against antilynching proposals, for example, have had principally a negative purpose; it was a major aim of Southern Senators to make enactment of such legislation impossible. It was also the wish of the obstructionists to assure their constituents that they would stand foursquare for the interests of the South as they saw them; it was their intention to obtain political capital in their own states; and it may well have been in part their purpose to focus national attention upon the legislation and if possible to convince national opinion that the measures were undesirable.

In respect to participants, three types of filibustering are discernible: one-man, cooperative, and organized.

Examples of filibustering by a single Senator are not so common as the casual observer of the Senate might suppose. It is probable that obstruction by Huey Long on May 21, 1935, against a concurrent resolution for a joint session of Congress to hear President Roosevelt deliver his bonus veto, was a one-man undertaking; and it is claimed that the forced postponement of a vote upon naval appropriations on March 29, 1938, engineered by Bennett Champ Clark, was also a one-man project.

Most filibusters which are apparently conducted by a single Senator are in reality cooperative enterprises. Two of the most famous so-called one-man filibusters in Senate history are those of Thomas

H. Carter of Montana against the river and harbor bill of 1901 and of Edward W. Carmack of Tennessee against a ship subsidy measure in 1907. In the first instance, Senator Carter actually had cooperation on the floor from George L. Wellington of Maryland. It was widely reported that the Montana Senator acted with the full approval and support of President McKinley, whose administration forces could certainly have mustered further filibustering assistance had it been necessary. In 1907 Senator Carmack plainly acted for Democratic Senators, who probably preferred that defeat of the ship subsidy should not become too clearly a party responsibility. In each instance the principal obstructionist was ending his service in the Senate and could afford to relieve his colleagues from apparent responsibility for tactics which might conceivably produce embarrassing results.

The cooperative filibuster is conducted by large or small groups of Senators with tacitly or informally arranged strategy. A recent example is the incipient filibuster, on August 20, 1935, to force action on neutrality legislation. A group of Senators, variously estimated from six to a dozen, were ready to participate, but it is generally understood that Homer T. Bone of Washington actually began the obstruction upon his own responsibility.

The line of distinction between cooperative and organized filibusters is not sharp and not easy of demarcation. The difference is genuine, however, for in some instances of the latter type discipline as effective as that intensifying party cohesion is attempted. The organized filibuster is likely to be characterized by definite floor leadership and carefully planned strategy. Caucuses may be arranged to harmonize views of procedure and to determine the general outlines of obstructive technique to be employed.[1] Indeed, organized filibusters are at times undertaken as party measures, and behind the strategy of delay is thrown every facility of already organized party representation in the Senate.[2] Filibusters equally well organized may

[1] cf., e.g., *New York Times*, Jan. 23, 1938.
[2] cf. *New York Times*, Feb. 24, 1917.

be and are erected upon sectional, economic, or other common interests. Often such organized obstruction transcends party lines.

Aside from the number of Senators participating in a filibuster, there is ever to be considered the personality traits of Senators who undertake obstruction. The Senate has known preeminently dominating personalities who would unhesitatingly force their wills upon their colleagues through the unrestrained use of every parliamentary device which ingenuity could fashion. Even in a body of supposed leaders there are always those to whom others tend to defer. For that matter, daring and persistent obstruction by ingenious use of parliamentary tactics is probably beyond the personality resources of most Senators acting as individuals.

It has been reported, for instance, that Daniel O. Hastings of Delaware, on the night of June 18, 1934, announced privately that he would filibuster against a railway labor bill until the session should end in hopeless deadlock; but when he found himself pitting his will against virtually the whole Senate he abandoned his intention. Dominating personalities of the caliber of Huey P. Long and the elder La Follette were not so considerate of the susceptibilities of their colleagues. Particularly in the past half century, when considerations of courtesy and esteem of colleagues have been of little concern to many Senators of strong will, have daring filibusters throttled the business of the Senate.

Obstruction is undertaken in a legislative body, obviously enough, only to secure advantages in influence or power. From this viewpoint three types again may be discerned: filibusters over issues, partisan filibusters, and publicity filibusters. The three brands are by no means mutually exclusive.

Filibusters over issues are the most common. The issue in dispute ordinarily involves the enactment or defeat of legislation, the ratification or rejection of a treaty, or the confirmation or rejection of a nomination. As it happens, antilynching proposals and merchant marine bills have been the most common issues.

The partisan filibuster is designed to gain political advantage in or out of the Senate, or both. Notable examples are the battles over organization and the election of officers of the Senate in 1881, various efforts to block Presidential appointments for the purpose of acquiring "spoils," and the Republican tactics early in 1919 intended to force President Wilson to call a special session of Congress to meet during the Paris Peace Conference.

Doubtless few filibusters are conducted solely for the benefits of publicity which may result. Yet Elmer Thomas of Oklahoma has declared in effect that through prolonged consumption of time in the Senate consequent press mention of the question discussed may bring a changed attitude upon the subject. In speaking of the effects of his 1931 filibuster in behalf of Indians the Senator said: "When the Government, as the guardian of the Indians of this Nation, was proceeding to rob them by law, I took time upon the floor to speak for those defenseless people. . . . The support I received I got throughout the press of the country. I got none here. . . . As a result of the time taken upon this floor upon the Indian question two committees were appointed to investigate Indian affairs throughout the United States."[3] The spread of information and the forming of public opinion are undoubtedly significant effects of filibustering.

Broadly speaking, men filibuster when the cause at stake is desperate—or when they think it is. Ordinarily Senators do not undertake obstruction unless their design has some chance of success, but there is rarely a time in the Senate when the attempt is hopeless.

It has become axiomatic that filibusters can be conducted with greatest effectiveness for a given quota of exertion near the time for final adjournment, and for that reason they are most frequent at the ends of sessions. Yet even successful obstruction is by no means confined to days immediately prior to adjournment sine die. It is true that if a filibuster must be extended for a prolonged time to achieve its purpose the participants must be more numerous than that number (perhaps only one) ordinarily necessary for success at the conclusion of a session. But a group comprising one more than a third of the body (two-thirds being necessary for cloture) could theoretically continue obstruction without limit. Indeed, with care-

[3] 76 *Cong. Record*, pp. 2286-7.

fully planned strategy, as few as one-fifth of the body could filibuster virtually indefinitely—always assuming that the rules would not be overridden by an outraged majority.

The Constitution guarantees that upon demand of one-fifth of the members present in either House the yeas and nays shall be entered upon the journal. After cloture becomes effective new amendments are not in order save by unanimous consent; but a minority equal to one-fifth of the membership, foreseeing the use of cloture, could introduce in advance thousands of amendments and later force a roll call upon each one. Moreover, under the rules of the Senate as they are now interpreted, an additional roll call to ascertain the presence of a quorum could be demanded after every vote. Literally months could thus be consumed by continuous calling of the roll. In all its history the Senate has been subjected only to samples of the obstructive possibilities of such tactics. Yet, for example, on the 28th of February, 1917, a Republican minority consumed an entire evening, nearly five hours, by demanding consecutive roll calls.

To be realistic, however, it must be recognized that there is a limit beyond which public opinion itself would not tolerate further obstruction. No man knows what that limit is, and it would vary with the exigencies of the time. But practical politicians, and most Senators are in the class, are not disposed to outrage public opinion so persistently that their careers will be buried in universal odium. Nearly every filibuster is conducted with at least some popular support, and Senators are usually careful that the home sector shall form part of the approving chorus.

No filibuster in the history of the Senate has ever approached the indefinitely extended duration conceivable under the rules. Public wrath has occasionally been great, but it can hardly be said to have reached at any time a pitch so intense that further obstruction in the Senate was impossible. If popular anger should ever use other than parliamentary means or social disapproval to silence any group of filibusterers operating with genuine support in a considerable section of the country, violence and civil strife might easily be the consequence. That widespread violence, in or out of the Senate chamber, has never resulted from the most bitter of parliamentary feuds is evidence of the quiet but controlling power of public opinion.

Filibustering as a technique is likely to be successful for the purpose employed (1) when the end of a session is so near at hand, either because of an advance arrangement for adjournment or because of pressure among members to stop work, that complete deadlock in the Senate is achieved by consumption of a relatively brief time; (2) when, at any time during a session, public business of great urgency is suspended until a filibustered measure can be disposed of; or (3) when the participants are sufficiently numerous and have enough determination, endurance, and parliamentary skill to continue the tactics as long as may be necessary.

If the presiding officer is sympathetic with filibusterers to the extent that they will be given all possible latitude under the rules a material advantage is at hand; conversely, there is a decided handicap if the chair undertakes strict interpretations of the rules. It is very difficult for a presiding officer to be altogether neutral, however much he may strive to be so, because he cannot always sit in the chair if sessions become long-continued. In the very selection of Senators as temporary occupants of the chair a Vice President or President pro tempore is in danger of aiding or inconveniencing a filibuster.

In prolonged obstruction parliamentary skill is so important that one filibusterer or group of filibusterers might succeed when under like circumstances another would fail. The famous Aldrich-Vreeland Currency Bill obstruction of 1908 was ended when blind Senator Gore sat down with no other Senator immediately at hand to continue filibustering. Huey Long lost the floor and with it his filibuster against a resolution to hear President Roosevelt in joint session when he failed to give proper regard to parliamentary technicalities which might be and were used against him. Purely physical endurance may also be a factor of no mean importance in the success of a filibuster, particularly if the obstruction is carried on by one man or by a very few men.

A filibuster of primarily negative purpose has less to overcome than has one of positive purpose. To defeat a measure a minority need merely prevent a vote; to force passage of a measure through the filibuster device a minority must compel Senators to sacrifice their opinions in respect to a disputed point in return for action on other matters. Not always are members of a majority willing to yield their position in return for cessation of filibuster. It has already been mentioned that Huey Long was unable to force through Congress amendments favorable to cotton and wheat on August 26, 1935, and as a result killed important legislation without accomplishing his purpose.

No man will ever learn how many or what proportion of measures before the Senate are passed or defeated because of the coercive *threat* of filibuster. The potential use of the instrument is ever lurking in the background during Senate proceedings. Former Vice President Charles G. Dawes has declared that in his experience the tacitly or privately expressed threat of filibuster accounts for the defeat or passage of far more measures than does actual use of dilatory tactics.[4] It is often remarked that, especially near the end of a session, Senators grow frightened at the mere hint of filibuster and are consequently ready for major concessions to appease extortionate obstructionists.

Two basic techniques have always been available even to the most scrupulous strategist seeking to oppose and to counteract filibuster tactics. They are (1) full utilization of the rules and (2) prolonged sessions of the Senate.

The second procedure involves less complicated expedients than the first. The Senate may simply be required to meet early, to sit at night, or even to remain in continuous session for days. The device of recessing rather than adjourning from day to day is essentially similar, for by retaining the same legislative day no time is devoted after reassembling to the routine business of morning hour.

The purpose of the prolonged session, as it is used by opponents of a filibuster, is patently to inconvenience and if possible to exhaust

---

[4] *Notes as Vice President 1928-1929* (Boston, 1935), pp. 55, 70.

the obstructionists and to increase the burden of their responsibility for delay. Unless the number of filibusterers be very small the prolonged session is actually more spectacular than effective. Newspaper readers are thereby given the desired impression that herculean efforts to break up the filibuster are under way; but any experienced maneuverer in the Senate knows that a determined group of filibusterers, before they are themselves exhausted, can usually manage to wear out the patience and the endurance of the majority.

If the obstructionists can find excuses for demanding a roll call to ascertain the presence of a quorum—and they usually can—opposing strategists must corral a majority of Senators to answer. Less than a quorum may request or even compel the attendance of absent Senators, and members of the body who are in no way interested in the struggle may find the sergeant at arms or a deputy at their homes in the middle of the night insisting upon their attendance. Senators in the filibustering contingent not on floor duty for the time may find opportunity to vanish for needed rest to places of vantage even beyond the searching ingenuity of the sergeant at arms. But if too many Senators nominally opposed to the filibuster also disappear a quorum cannot be held, the Senate cannot continue its deliberations, and the very purpose of the prolonged session is defeated. Strategists leading the forces opposed to obstruction naturally seek to hold a quorum within call. By the whole process the members of the majority are frequently more inconvenienced than the filibusterers. And men who think of themselves as dignitaries have little relish for sleeping fitfully in army blankets in the Senate chamber.

It is notorious that the Senate rules are rarely enforced save in times of urgency or great controversy. The tradition of the body encourages laxity of regulations in deference to the importance and convenience of Senators. Unanimous consent is constantly asked and obtained to proceed in a manner otherwise contravening the rules, or to obtain favors and concessions. Senators who have the floor yield to others for extended statements or for all kinds of business and are still considered as retaining the floor. Points of order supposedly undebatable (until an appeal is taken) and privileged motions not debatable according to the rules are often liberally discussed by tacit unanimous consent.

When a filibuster becomes intense it is usually considered to the advantage of opponents of obstruction to abandon the laxity of normal times, to enforce the rules, and to refuse courtesies allowable by unanimous consent. Parliamentary strategists who undertake such firmness must be very sure of the support of their followers else precious votes will be sacrificed. If a Senator secures unanimous consent to consider and to pass some favorite measure, a respite, however brief, is afforded the filibusterers. Opponents of the obstruction may consider it unfortunate to grant the truce, yet under some circumstances refusal might alienate indispensable support in their own fight. Even too severe pressure upon the filibusterers may bring unwanted retaliation. If obstructionists are consistently refused consent to have read at the desk even short papers, reprisal may prevent every other Senator from obtaining the much-asked-for permission to have items printed in the *Congressional Record*. Use of the rules against filibusterers is thus often a delicate matter demanding the most adroit maneuvering.

Despite only relatively minor changes in the text during the course of Senate history, strict enforcement of the rules has involved different interpretations of their meaning. In 1891 Senator Nelson W. Aldrich of Rhode Island strove to secure an interpretation of the rules which would declare undebatable an appeal from a decision of the chair, thus indirectly breaking a filibuster, but his scheme was never fully tested and certainly did not achieve success. As a matter of fact, as has been stated, until 1908 no important interpretation of the rules primarily designed to oppose filibustering was adopted.

In that year, in the significant filibuster against the Aldrich-Vreeland Currency Bill, three important developments arose, two of them new interpretations of the rules and the third an old provision now to be enforced with effect: (1) the chair might count a quorum, if one were physically present, even on a vote, whether or not the Senators would answer to their names; (2) in ordering quorum calls (which cannot be demanded consecutively without intervening business), mere debate would not be considered business; (3) Senators could be restrained from speaking on the same subject more than twice in the same legislative day. In 1914 the Senate at first agreed and then, with swift reversal, declined to add another interpretation which would further have curtailed the freedom of filibusterers, to the effect that Senators could not yield even for a question without unanimous consent.

Since 1908, in addition to the regular application of the virtual innovations then established, there have been at long intervals two further developments in the rules, one an important alteration and the other a significant new interpretation by the chair, which reduced the dominance of filibusterers in the chamber. These were respectively, the famous cloture provision of 1917 and the pronouncement during the Huey Long filibuster of June 12-13, 1935, that Senators yielding for purposes other than the asking of a question, even for a quorum call, will lose the floor. A third development since 1908, accomplishing a number of objectives and incorporating provisions expected to reduce filibustering, is the Twentieth Amendment to the Constitution, proclaimed by the Secretary of State on February 6, 1933. A fourth, oddly enough, is the Reorganization Act of 1939.

Prior to the 1917 introduction of cloture provisions in the rules, the Senate had had in its experience no arrangement even approaching effective limitation of debate except by unanimous consent. Breaking off a filibuster, under any conditions, was thus virtually impossible. It is common knowledge among persons interested in Senate procedure that until 1806 the rules provided for a previous question, but about the nature of that motion there is often misunderstanding. The previous question as it is generally known today is an undebatable motion which, if carried, will close debate. In the early Senate the motion was itself debatable. Thomas Jefferson in his famous *Manual* rendered the judgment that even after the previous question had been moved (not carried) further amendments could be offered and debated.[5] The Senate form of the previous question, dropped from the rules in 1806, was rarely invoked even in its mild form.

Jefferson in his *Manual* incorporated the view that "no one is to speak impertinently or beside the question, superfluously, or tediously."[6] Leaving aside matters of impropriety, however, who is to decide whether a Senator's remarks are superfluous or tedious, whether, in short, they are relevant to the business at hand? Early practice was not entirely uniform, but for the most part it was long the custom for the chair to require Senators to remain within the bounds of relevancy. Vice President Calhoun, on the other hand, held the view that under the rules then existing the chair should not initiate action calling Senators to order but should await initiative taken from the floor.

As late as August 12, 1848, the Senate voted a member out of order because of irrelevancy. Senator David L. Yulee of Florida in the chair had ruled in order Henry S. Foote of Mississippi, whose relevancy was questioned, but on appeal the Senate reversed the chair by 2 yeas against 27 nays.[7] Two days later, however, the President pro tempore, David R. Atchison of Missouri, refused to rule out of order Hopkins L. Turney of Tennessee, whose irrelevancy was complained of by Daniel Webster. No appeal was taken.[8] On February 29, 1872, the relevancy of Charles Sumner was questioned by John Sherman; but Vice President Schuyler Colfax declared that "the chair decides that under the practice of the Senate he cannot restrain a Senator in remarks which are, in the opinion of the Senator himself, pertinent to the issue before the Senate." Upon Sherman's appeal the Senate sustained the chair by 28 yeas to 18 nays.[9]

In later years the regular practice, now firmly a part of the Senate spirit and tradition, has been that no Senator may be taken from the

[5] *Jefferson's Manual of Parliamentary Practice*, Sec. XXXIV, in *Senate Manual* (Washington, 1938), pp. 292-4.

[6] *ibid.*, Sec. XVII, at p. 265.

[7] *Journal of the Senate*, 30th Cong., 1st Sess., p. 588.

[8] *ibid.*, p. 592; *Cong. Globe*, 30th Cong., 1st Sess., pp. 1083-4.

[9] *Cong. Globe*, 42nd Cong., 2nd Sess., pp. 1293-4.

floor for irrelevancy in debate. Obviously a ruling that a speaker is irrelevant must in some degree be arbitrary, for no man can say with certainty that a remote digression may not be drawn in as an illustration bearing upon the subject at hand. If relevancy were too strictly construed Senators might under some circumstances be severely handicapped in the presentation of supporting arguments.

Although the rules of the Senate provided no better means of limiting debate than the device of unanimous consent, the chamber had from time to time no dearth of Senators who believed that means for further limitations should be found. A mere list of proposals to amend the rules for that purpose, submitted in a multitude of forms in the long course of Senate experience, would fill many pages.[10] Prior to 1917 not one of those suggestions received the formal approval of the body.

Of the many abortive propositions for alteration of the rules to limit debate perhaps the plan for majority cloture pressed by Senator Aldrich during the Federal Elections or "Force" Bill filibuster of 1890-1891 came nearest to adoption. His proposal was designed to be applicable only during the session then current. However, like the measure it was expected to further, the cloture resolution died with the triumph of the great filibuster. Other notable instances of prolonged obstruction, particularly the silver repeal fight of 1893 and the Republican opposition to the Ship Purchase Bill of 1915, brought forth extensive discussion of cloture; but not till the Senate reassembled after the fierce Armed Ship filibuster of March 1917, did words become transmuted into action.

Despite the fact that limitation of debate is possible only after a delayed two-thirds vote, the adoption of cloture provisions in the rules, on March 8, 1917, is the most important potential and actual curtailment of filibustering ever undertaken by the Senate. Yet the process arranged is slow, cumbersome, and rarely undertaken.[11]

[10] For a compilation submitted in 1915 by Senator Robert L. Owen, with data on limitation of debate in state legislatures and abroad, see 52 *Cong. Record,* pp. 3717-36.
[11] See George H. Haynes, *The Senate of the United States* (Boston, 1938), Vol. I, pp. 404-9.

From the outset parliamentarians and even politicians recognized that modified cloture could be useful only in circumstances approaching an emergency. Even the Democratic national platform of 1920 by implication branded the cloture provision as inadequate, for the San Francisco convention approved a statement identical with that in the platform adopted at Saint Louis in 1916: "We favor such alteration of the rules of procedure of the Senate of the United States as will permit the prompt transaction of the Nation's legislative business."[12]

In the twenty-two years since cloture has been possible, the Senate has voted upon its application only thirteen times, and on only four occasions has the motion been adopted. In the case of all but three of the votes, however, the motion would have been carried had a simple majority been sufficient. But there are many Senators who look upon cloture as an unwise infringement of the traditional freedom of debate and who are therefore willing to countenance it, if at all, under only the most unusual circumstances. Moreover, there are tacit understandings in the Senate, bearing a close resemblance to "logrolling," by virtue of which minority elements often combine against cloture even if only a few are strongly opposed to the measure upon which it is moved. The attempts to adopt cloture in 1938 upon an antilynching bill presented the interesting spectacle of approximately two-thirds of the Senators ready to vote for the measure but less than a majority willing to close debate. A tabular picture (on opposite page) of Senate experience in voting upon motions for cloture is illuminating.

Cloture would be most likely to be effective when employed against the activities of a small coterie of filibusterers at a time of crisis. Before a vote upon cloture, of course, a calendar day must elapse after presentation of the motion. Although in practice the Senate has voted upon thus limiting debate after meeting in the late morning or at noon, in great emergencies the body could convene upon the turn of midnight. The possibility of thus hurrying action

[12] Kirk H. Porter, *National Party Platforms* (New York, 1924), pp. 384, 417.

CLOTURE MOTIONS VOTED UPON BY THE SENATE

ISSUE	PETITION	VOTE			ADOPTED?
(With date of vote)	SIGNATURES	YEAS	NAYS	NOT VOTING	(By 2/3 vote)
Versailles Treaty November 15, 1919	30	78	16	1	Yes
Emergency Tariff Bill February 2, 1921	34	36	35	25	No
Fordney-McCumber Tariff July 7, 1922	52	45	35	16	No
World Court Protocol January 25, 1926	48	68	26	2	Yes
Migratory Bird Bill June 1, 1926	18	46	33	17	No
Pepper-McFadden Banking Bill February 15, 1927	58	65	18	12	Yes
Swing-Johnson Bill to Develop Lower Colorado River Basin February 26, 1927	16	32	59	4	No
Retirement Bill for Disabled Emergency World War Officers February 26, 1927	28	51	36	8	No
District of Columbia Public Buildings Bill February 28, 1927	17	52	31	12	No
Prohibition Reorgani- zation Bill February 28, 1927	22	55	27	13	Yes
Glass Banking Bill January 19, 1933	29	58	30	8	No
Wagner-Van Nuys Antilynching Bill January 27, 1938	17	37	51	8	No
Wagner-Van Nuys Antilynching Bill February 16, 1938	18	42	46	8	No

was recognized by Vice President Dawes in answer to a hypothetical question posed in the Senate.[13]

The minimum time lapse before a vote upon a cloture motion is slightly more than twenty-five hours, if the motion is presented just before a midnight. If it is submitted earlier in the day, as would be likely, the minimum is correspondingly longer. While each Senator is entitled to speak for one hour after the adoption of cloture, it is highly improbable that any occasion would find every Senator availing himself of the privilege. Proponents of the pending measure, especially, might be counted upon to be brief in their remarks or silent altogether.

The difficulty of invoking cloture because of the necessity for a two-thirds vote has promoted extensive discussion in and out of the Senate respecting the need for a more stringent rule favorable to the limitation of debate. When one considers the many filibusters which have raged since 1917 it is obvious that cloture by a two-thirds vote is inadequate for overcoming obstruction. Of various proposals to augment the rules by means of additional devices to be used against filibusterers, those of Vice President Charles G. Dawes have been the most vigorous and the most publicized.

Dawes opened his campaign to alter the Senate rules with a forensic bombshell. Having taken the oath as Vice President on March 4, 1925, he rose before a brilliant assemblage of members and visitors in the Senate chamber—President Coolidge, members of the Supreme Court in their black judicial robes, the diplomatic corps resplendent in uniforms, and the major dignitaries of Washington—supposedly to utter an essentially perfunctory appreciation of his new honors and responsibilities. Instead he launched a scathing attack upon the Senate rules, declaring that "under them the rights of the Nation and of the American people have been overlooked. . . ."

Standing on the Senate rostrum clad in faultless morning attire, his voice rising to an excited falsetto, Vice President Dawes shook his finger at his audience like a schoolmaster and asserted that "under the inexorable laws of human nature and human reaction, this

[13] 70 *Cong. Record*, p. 4852.

system of rules, if unchanged, can not but lessen the effectiveness, prestige, and dignity of the United States Senate." He assured his amazed listeners, uncertain whether to laugh or to applaud, that "the rules can be found, as is the custom in other deliberative and legislative assemblies, to fully protect a Senator in his right to be heard without forfeiting at any time the greater right of the Senate to act."

Startled Senators were indignant at the outburst, Robinson of Arkansas declaring the performance "ridiculous." Ashurst commented that "it was the most acrobatic, gymnastic speech I have ever heard in the Senate." Pat Harrison remarked to a reporter, "If I gave a statement of what I think it would set your paper on fire." Others feared that any hope of changing the rules had been dimmed.[14]

Moreover, the Vice President's unprecedented inaugural remarks were followed by other occurrences unfortunate for his prestige. When recently elected Senators, four at a time, came forward with customary dignity to take the oath, Dawes soon became impatient and marshalled before him all the remaining Senators-elect in a body; and when ceremonies had been concluded in the Senate he waved his arms as if to "shoo" out the whole crowd. James A. Reed of Missouri declared on the floor the next day that the Senate did not recess or adjourn but "simply broke up."

To make matters worse, the Vice President failed to return after the formal inauguration of President Coolidge to preside over the Senate for the day's concluding business. Tension was partly eased when Frederick Hale of Maine explained that he had mistakenly advised the Vice President to go with the President to a reviewing stand.[15] But on the 10th of March Dawes was again absent from the Senate at the critical moment when the vote upon confirmation of Charles Beecher Warren for Attorney General stood tied,[16] and by this remissness the administration lost one of its major officers. Two

14 *New York Times,* March 5, 1925.
15 67 *Cong. Record,* pp. 4-8.
16 *ibid.,* pp. 101-2; *New York Times,* March 11, 1925.

days later, with Dawes in the chair, George W. Norris gave expression to the general attitude of the Senate by reading a satirical poem upon the latest exploit of the new presiding officer.

In spite of uncertain prestige Dawes retained his convictions and his courage. Moreover, he had support in the Senate. Oscar W. Underwood of Alabama introduced a much-discussed proposal for the previous question to be adopted by majority vote, with each Senator entitled to speak only an hour.[17] The Vice President favored cloture by majority, but recognizing that he had not enough support in the Senate to carry his point, he determined to take the issue to the people. Whenever opportunity afforded he spoke upon public platforms, both in the East and in the West. Never before had the power of filibuster, protected by the nature of the Senate rules, received so extended and so open a pummelling. Hitherto occasional wrath had swept the country against filibusterism, but now for the first time Senatorial obstruction was made the issue of a concerted campaign.

Although Dawes aroused a great amount of public interest in the Senate rules and their alteration, still against the placidity of the Senate he and his supporters made little progress. By way of compromise he suggested that majority cloture be applicable to revenue and appropriation bills;[18] if the first step could be taken, perhaps majority cloture upon all measures might be a later development. For all the Vice President's energetic campaigning and suggesting, however, his cause achieved no success. So far as the rules were concerned, filibusterers retained their influence undiminished. The Senate would not be convinced that tradition should be altered by action.

Among the opponents of majority cloture, for which General Dawes so enthusiastically campaigned, was the senior Senator from Nebraska, George W. Norris. Believing that filibustering should be discouraged, nevertheless he denounced curtailment of free speech and limitation of extended argument in the Senate as dangerous to

[17] 67 *Cong. Record*, p. 9.
[18] cf. *New York Times*, Feb. 7, 1926.

sound and well considered legislation. To him the remedy was an amendment to the Constitution ending the biennial short session of Congress with its fixed date for adjournment.[19]

Before many years had passed, the Nebraska Senator had his way respecting an amendment to the Constitution. The short or "lame duck" session of Congress, with its automatic adjournment upon the 4th of March in odd years, was brought to an end by the Twentieth Amendment. But there has not been an end of filibustering. There has not even been an end of filibustering at the close of sessions. As under the old arrangement for an automatic cessation of business, there have been last-minute rushes of legislation before final adjournment. Business piles up because men seem by nature to work under increasing pressure near a deadline, and the deadline is now supplied, not by legal compulsion, but by demands within the membership of Congress to be permitted to stop legislating and go home. Filibusterers employ their techniques to block or to extort, and sessions often expire under the domination of a few daring and obstructing Senators. The short session has been abolished, but it may be taken as significant that the final session of both the 73rd and 74th Congresses, the first two to operate under the Amendment, ended in filibuster.

If the experience of the Senate since the constitutional alteration is a reliable indication of the normal run of events, the effect of the Twentieth Amendment as a deterrent to filibustering has been exaggerated. Yet, like other developments since 1908 unfavorable to filibustering, the Amendment has added to the difficulty of successful obstruction by one man or by very few men.

To the solitary obstructionist or to a small group, a definitely fixed adjournment beyond which efforts need not be exerted is certainly a goal more encouraging to success than the now indeterminate and possibly shifting date at which members of Congress will insist that they have had enough and intend to go home whether the constituted leadership wills it or not. It is conceivable that, despite

[19] cf. George W. Norris, "Mr. Dawes and the Senate Rules," *The Forum*, Vol. LXXIV (Oct. 1925), pp. 582-6.

impatience of members to be off, Congress could be held in session long enough to allow adoption of cloture in the Senate upon some obstructed measure; but that process is actually so slow and the tendency for all minority groups to combine against cloture is so great that the possibility for its effective use in the last hours of a session is usually little better than at the end of the former short sessions. In the odd years under the old arrangement the arrival of the 2nd of March made cloture virtually impossible. Today, as the rules exist, after enthusiasm for final adjournment has begun to move the membership, cloture could be adopted only under circumstances most extraordinary.

The Twentieth Amendment has made Senators less subject to fright at the suggestion of filibuster in the last regular session of a Congress, at least in the early days of that last session. The Amendment has lessened, though it has not destroyed, the power of a single Senator to coerce his colleagues into acceptance of favorite bills and amendments under the threat or the practice of obstruction. But it has not ended the day of the successful filibuster nor even the day of the successful one-man filibuster.

That the Senate is becoming fully alive to the possible dangers and disadvantages of filibustering is strikingly revealed in the Reorganization Act of 1939. By that legislation, effective until 1941, the President is authorized under certain conditions and with certain exceptions to transfer, consolidate, or abolish governmental agencies; but no reorganization plan of the President shall become effective for sixty days after being transmitted to Congress. Moreover, such a plan may not become effective if, during the sixty-day period, Congress should pass a resolution expressing its disapproval.

Framers of the statute were faced with the possibility that Senatorial friends of the President, finding themselves in a minority, might prevent the opportunity of Congressional disapproval by staging a filibuster. If a dozen Senators should filibuster for sixty days, a Presidential plan would become law even against the will of a majority in Congress. What could be done to obviate the risk? By an unprecedented arrangement limitation of debate upon a resolution to disapprove a Presidential reorganization proposal was made a part of the statute itself. In express terms, applicable in each House, debate is limited to ten hours, to be divided equally between those favoring and those opposing the resolution.[20]

By concurring in such legislation, approved by President Roosevelt on April 3, 1939, the Senate agreed to limit the verbosity of its members with a tranquillity little short of amazing in a tradition-bound body noted for its almost unbending insistence upon unrestricted speech.

The Constitution grants to each House of Congress the power to frame its own rules of procedure, and the Reorganization statute expressly recognizes the power of either House to alter the parliamentary rules set forth in the act. But the fact remains that the Senate has consented, without even a parliamentary battle, to an advance limitation of discussion in a fashion which breaks sharply with the past. The circumstances were admittedly unusual; the Reorganization Act itself contemplates a legislative veto which is a departure from Congressional precedents. Yet the once virtually unbridled power of Senate filibustering has been curtailed. What innovations will next develop in the Senate rules? The query is inescapable and unanswerable.

The continuance of filibustering as an instrument of policy depends, of course, upon the willingness of members to abide by the Senate rules. Wholesale and high-handed infractions by an actual majority, especially through their power to interpret the rules by means of repeated appeals from decisions of the chair, could blast the hopes of the most ardent filibusterers. The presiding officer might himself take the initiative, through arbitrary rulings, to make effective obstruction impossible. Yet any arbitrary action, to be successful, must ultimately be supported by a Senate majority. Such a majority would be difficult and ordinarily impossible to find.

There are many men, potential filibusterers themselves, who want to see the rules preserved against a day of need as effective implements of delay. And, moreover, there is ever in the Senate a nucleus

[20] Reorganization Act of 1939, Public No. 19, 76th Cong. 1st Sess.

of men who will place the letter and spirit of the rules above partisan advantage; they will not tolerate deviations from precedent unless the Senate in calm deliberation agrees upon formal modifications. Rules, they believe, are made to protect minorities and ought to be obeyed. The very fact that filibustering continues because the rules are observed is an evidence of American loyalty to order and regular procedure.[21]

There is, however, a sharp division of respectable opinion upon the question of whether the Senate rules should be altered to prevent filibustering. For generations there have been discussions upon the subject, critical and uncritical, profound and naïve. No one, apparently, defends obstruction in all its excrescences; but there are those who argue persuasively that its potential use safeguards important functions of the Senate. It must be the purpose here to select and to summarize: to choose from a vast mass of verbiage the principal arguments of those who have attacked or defended dilatory tactics.

Arguments against filibustering may be reduced to four major categories: (1) that the majority should rule; (2) that the Senate should legislate efficiently, with responsibility only to the people; (3) that experience abroad and in the state legislatures indicates that debate can be limited without undemocratic results; and (4) that, on the basis of a constitutional argument, an issue should be decided when the yeas and nays have been properly demanded.

Whether or not there exists a full theoretical justification for the principle of majority rule, there is everywhere heard in America the dictum that if a decision is to be reached it should come from the majority, not the minority. To Americans the majority should have what it wants and should not be compelled to have what it does not want. Under the practice of filibustering, runs the argument, the whole basic American tenet is set at naught. By means of it the minority, not the majority, rules. Not only is the majority

[21] No filibuster in the Senate of the United States has resulted in such disorderly procedure as that, for instance, which rocked the Rhode Island Senate during obstruction in 1924. In that State Senators and spectators were driven from the legislative hall by the use of a "stink bomb." For details see C. C. Hubbard, "Legislative 'War' in Rhode Island," *National Municipal Review*, Vol. XIII (Sept. 1924), at pp. 479-80.

thwarted in its purpose to enact public measures, it is also coerced
into acceptance of measures for which it has no desire or approval.
The Senate rules, declared Vice President Dawes, place "in the hands
of one or of a minority of Senators a greater power than the veto
power exercised under the Constitution by the President of the
United States. . . ."[22]

If the Senate is to be efficient, time should not be wasted in unnecessary delay. There should be opportunity for deliberation, for both
the majority and the minority to be heard, but no man or group of
men should be allowed to consume time merely for the sake of
obstruction. The time devoted to specific items of business should
be reasonable, though that is a limitation difficult of exact definition.

Henry Clay, whatever his personal practice, once approved the
statement that no man could talk "sensibly or usefully on any topic
for more than a quarter of an hour."[23] Vice President Marshall
wrote in his memoirs that Senator Albert B. Cummins of Iowa
once expatiated upon the thought that a man could contribute in
an hour everything of value that he might say upon a bill, but when
the Senator had concluded his remarks it was found that he had
consumed two hours and thirty-five minutes.[24]

If there is a conflict between the time for debating and a time
for voting, Senator Lodge once declared, action is a higher duty
than debating.[25] "The public business must, in some way or other,
go forward," Alexander Hamilton asserted in a strong denunciation
of minority rule.[26]

Moreover, there should always be a reasonable proportioning of
the time devoted to various matters before the Senate. Too much of
it should not be consumed upon a few measures because of stubborn
minorities, leaving other important items upon the calendar to be
passed with little or no consideration or to be lost because there is

[22] 67 *Cong. Record*, p. 3.
[23] *Cong. Globe*, 27th Cong., 1st Sess., p. 203.
[24] *Recollections of Thomas R. Marshall* (Indianapolis, 1925), p. 294.
[25] Henry Cabot Lodge, "Obstruction in the Senate," *The North American Review*,
Vol. CLVII (Nov. 1893), at p. 527.
[26] *The Federalist*, No. XXII, Lodge ed. (New York, 1904), p. 130.

no time for them. Because of filibustering, special sessions of Congress are at times made imperative if the nation's affairs are to be conducted, and with the special sessions come unnecessary expense to the people and business uncertainty in the country.

Not only does filibustering encourage extravagance in fiscal legislation—because much of it must be enacted after time available for careful consideration has been consumed with a few bills—but the practice and its threat also add to the nation's financial burden because Senators can coerce their colleagues into acceptance of new and exorbitant items. Indeed filibustering adds to the multiplicity of laws, for, inasmuch as Senators as individuals or in small groups threaten to block the legislative process, much legislation is successful which otherwise would never be enacted.

Under a popular government subjected to filibuster, it can be argued, responsibility to the people is destroyed. The majority can offer no other excuse to their constituents than that the minority have prevented action. Patently it is difficult for a popular majority in the country to hold responsible a minority in the Senate. But with too frequent disruption of public business by parliamentary antics, it has been predicted again and again, the Senate will finally lose the respect and confidence of the people. Woodrow Wilson, John Sherman, and Charles G. Dawes are notable among those who have used the argument that the Senate should adduce lessons from comparative government and should recognize that other great parliamentary bodies have been able to limit debate with beneficial results.

Americans are fond of seeking constitutional grounds for the political policies which they advocate. Against filibustering a constitutional argument, more ingenious than convincing, was once offered by Senator Robert L. Owen of Oklahoma. He looked upon that portion of the Constitution which declares that "the Yeas and Nays of the Members of either House on any question shall, at the Desire of one fifth of those Present, be entered on the Journal"[27] and insisted that in that clause the Constitution guarantees an imme-

27 Art. I, Sec. 5.

diate record upon the demand of one-fifth of the members. A filibuster, he contended, therefore ought to be and could be ended whenever a request for the yeas and nays has been properly seconded.[28] The word *immediate* is of course an interpolation by Senator Owen. The same section of the Constitution empowers each House to make its own rules of procedure, and it is to be supposed that the time for a vote can be determined on the basis of those rules rather than by constitutional mandate. It is reasonably certain, whatever the constitutional guaranty, that there could be no appeal beyond the Senate itself; the courts have been most unwilling to interfere with rules of procedure adopted by the coordinate legislative branch.

The Owen proposal, if utilized, could destroy virtually all debate in the Senate. A minority equal to one-fifth of the membership, for instance, could refuse to allow an explanation of a bill even by the chief spokesman of the majority.

The principal defenses offered by the supporters of the practice of filibustering are: (1) that minorities have rights which no majority should override; (2) that a Senate majority does not necessarily represent a majority of the people or even of the states; (3) that it has become the special duty of the Senate carefully to inspect legislation, a duty not readily performed without freedom of debate; (4) that filibusters really do not prevent needed legislation, because no important measure defeated by filibuster has been enacted later; (5) that it is the peculiar function of the Senate to act as a check upon the executive, a responsibility too easily thwarted if Senators could be prevented from speaking fully upon all matters; and (6) that the constitutional requirement for recording the yeas and nays is a protection of dilatory tactics.

The principle that minorities have rights is no less an American tenet than the principle that the majority should rule. It is not an unfamiliar cry that government is constituted to protect minorities against majorities. Indeed, most Americans would uphold the argument that there are rights of individuals which a majority must respect. Natural rights, inalienable and inherent, are still significant

---

[28] 52 *Cong. Record*, p. 3718.

in American thought. The Constitution contains great guaranties of minority freedom from oppression. Many defenders of the filibuster argue that when a great constitutional guaranty is being trampled by an unheeding majority the minority should obstruct with all the vigor at its command. John Sharp Williams of Mississippi declared that Senators represent states as ambassadors and that it is their duty to protect the rights of states even by filibuster.

It is contended that if a minority cannot be protected by parliamentary means the forces restrained through majority pressure may well overturn the majority at the next election or may burst out even in violence or revolution. Filibusters are almost always supported by minority opinion bearing at least some strength in the nation, and if the issue is great enough that minority may never yield short of physical conflict. Filibustering is part of the democratic system to force compromise, the conserving possibility in great controversy.

Often Senate majorities do not conform to the opinion even of the popular majorities which they purport to represent. Frequently popular opinion upon a question has not been formulated, or if it has been, it is often not effectively expressed. For the formation and expression of public opinion, information, discussion, and time are necessary. Those indispensables are supplied in part by prolonged debate in the Senate, and filibuster may prevent hasty majority action which would be out of harmony with genuine popular will. Legislative obstruction apprises the public of proposals with which they may be out of sympathy and which perhaps are close to enactment without popular awareness. If the public is actually sympathetic with the proposition, time is afforded for consideration of factors perhaps overlooked and for a clear popular mandate. That time should elapse before a final decision is said to be a reasonable minority demand.

An existing Senate majority may have been repudiated at the polls. In the former short sessions of Congress, sitting (prior to the Twentieth Amendment) after an election, that was frequently the case. Even today such "lame duck" sessions of Congress might be called between the date for the Congressional elections and the following 3rd of January, and in such sessions a Senate majority might be unrepresentative both of popular will and of the will of a majority of the states. Moreover, only one-third of the Senatorial terms expire after each election. After an election in which candidates favoring an issue had been defeated by the people with unmistakable intent, a majority for that issue might still remain. The objection might have particular validity regarding ratification or rejection of a pending treaty which had been an issue. The House, more responsive to election returns, would have no voice in the matter and could not check the Senate.

It is complained that at any time a Senate majority may represent a minority of the people in the nation. Because of the equal representation of the states that possibility is unavoidable. On the other hand a relatively few Senators from populous states may represent a majority of the American people, and at times such Senate minorities have been led to feel that they should have a determining voice in the public business. It has also been pointed out that in critical circumstances, when a division in the Senate is close, existing vacancies in representation may give the majority only a temporary lease upon control of the situation. Unrepresentative and temporary majorities, it is argued, are justifications for filibuster.

A clear majority in the Senate may act under compulsion from a minority of leaders or from outside influences, and defenders of filibustering contend that under such conditions proposed legislation should be resisted with every parliamentary device. If a caucus system prevails, formally or informally, a mere majority of the majority party, perhaps a distinct minority of the entire Senate, may seek effectively to control the action in the chamber.

At present it is possible, under certain conditions, for members of the Democratic conference in the Senate to bind party followers, although the arrangement is rarely used. There is no procedure in the Republican conference by which Senators can be bound. Yet the committee system itself may enable a few Senators to exert great influence upon all the members of their party. Committee members of the majority party may so commit their party to a course of action that only insurgents will refuse support. Often members of a Senate majority learn that in order to obtain legislation of their own they must consent to measures proposed by other majority Senators even if they do not approve of them. Legislation can thereby come to final passage supported by a majority of whom very few are genuinely in favor of the whole bill; it has been a matter of accepting the undesirable in order to retain highly valued provisions or to win support for other measures. Compulsion upon a majority also may come from outside the chamber, particularly from an executive who uses his power of patronage to drive through the Senate a program of his own. Obstructionists therefore assert that in defeating legislation they often express the inarticulate sentiments of many Senators in the majority.

Since debate and deliberation are now rigidly curtailed in the House of Representatives, the Senate has become the only forum in the national government where unhurried consideration and if necessary long discussion can be employed to perfect laws. The importance of the Senate in revising bills passed in the House is recognized as great. Senators are proud to be entrusted with responsibility for thorough analysis of legislation, and they value the privilege and utility of unlimited speech to enable the presentation of every possible view.

A favorite argument of defenders of obstruction is the statement that no filibuster has ever defeated important legislation deeply desired by the American people. To support the remark it is said that great measures which have been successfully obstructed have not subsequently been enacted into law. But conditions may change to make obsolete a desire for such once-defeated legislation, and often measures are of such nature that however great the demand for them in some quarters passage is obviously impossible because of the inevitable renewal of filibustering should old issues be reopened. Users of such an argument take no account of bills enacted because of minority coercion, or of the multitude of measures indirectly defeated by filibustering because there has been no time to consider them.

There are even those who insist that filibusters do not prevent the Senate from accomplishing the necessary business before it. They point out that a great mass of legislation is enacted by agreement to vote or by unanimous consent and that arrangements have been made in the rules for regular times to consider unobjected measures. And after all, it is contended, the only real sanction behind the rules, whatever they are, is honor. Through a sense of honor and responsibility both the majority and the minority cooperate in the process of legislation. Business in the Senate cannot be conducted upon a plane higher than the caliber and integrity of its membership.

It has been argued persuasively that it is the peculiar function of the Senate, by the nature of the constitutional system, to check the executive. The Senate alone has been endowed with prerogatives of advice and consent upon matters pertaining to appointments to office and to the ratification of treaties. Through its power of investigating policies of governmental agencies, combined with the privilege of Senators to discuss without hindrance what they please, the Senate constitutes the only great check upon the activities of the executive branch. Without the potentiality of filibusters, that undiminished power to check would be gone. Senators who believe that something is wrong in the government are free to dilate upon it and to present such evidence as they may elect. If the policy or condition complained of is flagrantly improper, its investigation or correction is difficult to avoid without embarrassment. Indeed, Senators may by their sheer ability to block business force investigations distasteful to a majority and perhaps also to an executive. Free speech in the Senate, by encouraging publicity in the affairs of government, is a safeguard to liberty.[29]

Finally, in accordance with an American characteristic, proponents of obstruction are not to be outdone in relying upon the Constitution. They, too, point to the provision which requires the yeas and nays to be recorded in the journal at the desire of one-fifth of

[29] cf. Lindsay Rogers, *The American Senate* (New York, 1926), especially Chaps. VI-VIII.

the members present and declare that it is an intentional safeguard allowing the minority to delay proceedings.

There is certainly some evidence that the framers of the Constitution were aware of the obstructive possibilities in demanding the yeas and nays. In the convention of 1787 Gouverneur Morris on August 10 moved to adopt a provision requiring the yeas and nays in either House upon the demand of one member. Several objections were raised. Nathaniel Gorham declared that he had known the device to be abused in Massachusetts "in stuffing the journals with them on frivolous occasions."[30] The provision as it was finally drafted, making mandatory a record of the yeas and nays when requested by one-fifth of the members present, appears in that clause of the Constitution requiring publication of the journal (except for such portions as demand secrecy); and it would seem likely that the primary purpose of the whole clause is publicity of legislative proceedings. The Constitution does not stipulate that the vote by yeas and nays shall be upon the final question but upon "any question." The minority, by multiplying questions through amendments and dilatory motions, can postpone indefinitely the final question. Whatever the intent behind the words, the Constitution affords obstructionists a technical advantage.

In the face of these admittedly powerful arguments[31] upon both sides of the issue, students of government may be led to seek a solution which would preserve intact the peculiar functions of the Senate but which would at the same time avoid flagrant abuses of the privilege of unlimited debate. It has been demonstrated that in 1908 the initial steps were taken in a new movement toward restraining the unregulated power of filibusterism and rendering the practice of

[30] James Madison, *The Debates in the Federal Convention of 1787*, Hunt and Scott ed. (New York, 1920), p. 379.

[31] For other discussions see Joseph P. Chamberlain, *Legislative Processes* (New York, 1936), pp. 183-5; Thomas C. Donnelly, "Freedom of Speech in the Senate," *Social Science*, Vol. VII (July 1932), pp. 225-36; Haynes, *op. cit.*, Vol. I, pp. 415-26; Robert Luce, *Legislative Procedure* (Boston, 1922), pp. 296-302; Rogers, *op. cit.*, pp. 182-90; W. F. Willoughby, *Principles of Legislative Organization and Administration* (Washington, 1934), pp. 493-500.

obstruction more difficult. This movement has been fourfold. It has included interpretation of the Senate rules, alteration of those rules, an amendment of the Constitution, and a rule-making statute.

The Senate was already a venerable institution when the crisis in the long, slow process was reached; but filibustering as a successful and fiercely used parliamentary weapon did not actually become an acute problem in the Senate until near the close of the nineteenth century. It should not be forgotten, however, that previous unsuccessful attempts to put an end to unlimited debate, especially the efforts in 1891 and 1893 for majority cloture, were more drastic in intention than any actual development even to this day.

That a definite strengthening of the trend to discourage filibusterers began as long ago as 1908 is in many ways remarkable when one remembers Senatorial pride in tradition. Many considerations perhaps explain this impetus given to the slow movement: the very fact that the proposals adopted were not so drastic as previous suggestions for majority cloture had been; that no filibuster between 1893 and 1908 had so incensed the majority as did the Aldrich-Vreeland Currency Bill obstruction during which steps for control were taken; that the filibusterers were fewer in number than had often been the case; that the parliamentary situation (consideration of a conference report) was especially favorable to attempts to stop the filibuster; and finally that the leaders of the Senate majority were unusually prone to take action.

Conditions in the twentieth century have apparently been conducive to filibustering. Sharp conflicts in the social order have arisen, complicated by an increasing quantity and variety of legislation, less reverence in the Senate for traditional dignity and politeness, and the election of Senators more daring and more experienced with the use of dilatory tactics. In the past thirty years the practice of obstruction has materially increased. It is improbable, with relatively new measures for control, that there will be a continued increase in the practice, although experience has been too brief for adequate indication. The effectiveness of one-man obstruction has certainly been reduced, but there is no evidence that the number or the success of filibusters by large and determined groups has diminished.

It is doubtful that there will ever be an end of filibustering while the structure and the functions of the Senate remain the same. Senators find that the potential use of the power to obstruct is a parliamentary weapon too useful to forgo.

So far as the rules of the Senate are concerned, it would seem salutary to adopt a system of majority cloture applicable upon a particular measure after unlimited debate for a specified minimum number of days. Such an alteration would not end obstruction. It would, however, make action by the Senate less difficult and more responsive to the will of a majority.

The problem of dilatory tactics will exist to some degree so long as there are conflicts between majorities and minorities. The solution, whatever it is, will never be found to lie wholly in a set of rules. It must rest in part upon the election of legislators with a keen sense of public responsibility, men who will never allow political strife to thwart a need for action.

INDEX

INDEX

Adams, Alva B., monetary bill, 201, 203.
Adams, John Quincy, 19.
Aesop's Fables, read to Senate, 8, 190-1.
Aldrich, Nelson W., on cloture, 53, 55-7, 221; banking bill abandoned, 76; Aldrich-Vreeland Currency Bill, 83-90.
Aldrich-Vreeland Currency Bill, 5, 83-91, 99, 215, 218, 239.
Allen, William V., on Silver Repeal, 60, 62.
Ames, Fisher, on early filibusters in House, 14.
Anthony, Henry B., 46.
Antilynching bills, (1922) 133-7; (1935) 179-81; (1937-1938) 5-6, 191-9; 210.
Apportionment, 167.
Arizona, bills for admision, (1902-1903) 73-6, (1911) 91-3.
Armed Ship Bill, obstruction, 115-23.
Armor plate, filibuster over, 68-9.
Arms sale, obstructed, 206.
Army appropriation bill, filibuster against election rider, 35-9.
Arthur, Chester A., 44, 46.
Ashurst, Henry F., pleasantry, 3; on Indian bill, 116-17; on migratory bird bill filibuster, 148; filibusters on Colorado River development, 150-2, 166; monetary bill, 200-1; on Dawes, 225.
Atchison, David R., relevancy, 220.
Austin, Warren R., monetary bill, 205.

Bacon, Augustus O., 89.
Bailey, Joseph W., charges against, 6; on river and harbor amendments, 76-7; Arizona-New Mexico admission, 91, 93.
Bailey, Josiah W., antilynching bill, 180.
Baker, Ray Stannard, cited, 97n.
Bankhead, John H., 107.
Bankhead, John H., 2nd, antilynching bill, 181.
Bankruptcy bill, farmers', 176-8.

Barbour, W. Warren, monetary bill, 203.
Barkley, Alben W., pleasantry, 182; antilynching bill, 191-2, 194-6, 198; monetary bill, 202, 204-5; arms sale, 206.
Barry, David S., 151.
Bate, William B., 66.
Bayard, James Asheton, 32-3.
Bayard, Thomas F., 151.
Benton, Thomas H., on expunging censure of Jackson, 20; against dismissal of printers, 21; against limitation of debate, 23-4; altercation with Foote, 27.
Berry, James H., 55.
Beveridge, Albert J., on omnibus statehood bill, 72-5.
Bilbo, Theodore G., antilynching bill, 196-7.
Bingham, Hiram, rebuff by Long, 174.
Black, Hugo L., antilynching bill, 180, 193; social security funds obstruction, 188-9.
Blaine, James G., against elections rider to army appropriation bill, 35-6, 38; appointed to Cabinet, 44.
Blair, Henry W., on federal education bill, 51-2; on parliamentary procedure, 56.
Blease, Coleman L., 8; filibuster on World Court Protocol, 146-7; on migratory bird bill, 148; campaign investigation resolution, 155-8, 161; Colorado River development, 166; judgeship, 167; radio bill, 168-9.
Bone, Homer T., on neutrality, 186, 211.
Borah, William E., Labor Department Bill, 94; 108; on World Court Protocol, 147; 176; antilynching bill, 192, 195.
Boulder Dam (see Colorado River development).
Bowers, Claude G., cited, 75n.
Brandegee, Frank B., on parliamentary issue, 98-9.

Bristow, Joseph L., 94.

Brooks, Preston S., assault on Sumner, 30.

Brown, Joseph E., on filibuster strategy, 47.

Bruce, William Cabell, 166.

Bryan, Nathan P., on parliamentary issue, 98-9.

Buchanan, James, against dismissal of printers, 21.

Burton, Theodore E., on Wilson appointment, 95; river and harbor bill obstruction, 100; 108; on filibustering, 110, 114.

Butler, Andrew P., denounced by Sumner, 29-30.

Butler, Matthew C., 55; on compromise, 61; 66.

Byrnes, James F., antilynching bills, 180, 193.

Calhoun, John C., addressed by Randolph, 16; on questions of order, 18-19, 220; against expunging censure of Jackson, 20; against dismissal of printers, 21; against limitation of debate, 23; quoted by Butler, 61.

California, admission of, 27-8.

Camden, Johnson N., 107.

Cameron, James Donald, 57.

Cameron, Ralph H., filibuster on Colorado River development, 150; campaign investigation obstruction, 156.

Campaign investigation, obstruction, 152-62.

Cannon, Joseph G., 72.

Caraway, Hattie W., antilynching bill, 195.

Caraway, Thaddeus H., ship subsidy filibuster, 140; on migratory bird bill, 148.

Carmack, Edward W., against ship subsidy, 78-9, 211.

Carnegie, Andrew, article by, 147.

Carpenter, Matt, 44.

Carter, Thomas H., filibuster against river and harbor bill, 69-72, 210-11.

Caucus system, 235-6.

Census director, appointment delayed, 95.

Chamberlain, Joseph P., cited, 238n.

Chandler, William E., 70.

Clapp, Moses E., on majorities, 108-9; 122.

Clark, Bennett Champ, in chair, 186; ship subsidy, 189-90; colloquy with Connally, 194; naval appropriations, 199, 210.

Clark, D. Worth, monetary bill, 203.

Clarke, James P., on filibuster for cotton, 102-3; on Ship Purchase Bill, 107; quotes Hoar on unlimited debate, 113.

Clay, Henry, against expunging censure of Jackson, 19-20; challenged to duel, 22; on Fiscal Bank Bill and limitation of debate, 22-4; on Compromise of 1850, 27-8; on length of speeches, 231.

Clayton Antitrust Act, 96.

Cleveland, Grover, on Silver Repeal, 58-9.

Cloture, rule for, 7, 127-8, 219, 221-4; applied on Treaty of Versailles, 131-2; Emergency Tariff, 132; Fordney-McCumber Tariff, 133; petition on Isle of Pines Treaty, 146; on World Court Protocol, 146-7; migratory bird bill, 149; Colorado River development, 152; Prohibition Reorganization Bill, 153-5; Glass Banking Bill, 175; antilynching bill, 196, 198; table of Senate votes on, 223.

Coal conservation bill, 190-1.

Cockrell, Francis M., 66.

Colfax, Schuyler, on relevancy, 220.

Colombian Treaty, filibuster against, 77.

Colorado River development, obstruction, (1927) 149-52; (1928) 165-7.

Compromise of 1850, extended debates on, 27-8.

Conkling, Roscoe, against elections rider to army appropriation bill, 36-9; resignation, 50.

Connally, Tom, antilynching bills, 180, 192-5.

Constitution, Federal, filibuster of opponents in Pennsylvania legislature, 13-14.

Constitutional provisions, 6, 61, 111, 227-9, 232-3, 237-8.

Coolidge, Calvin, Blease on, 156; inauguration, 224-5.

Copeland, Royal S., Isle of Pines Treaty obstruction, 144-6; 152; radio bill, 168-9.

Copyright bill, 170.

Costigan, Edward P., antilynching bill, 179-80.

Cotton legislation, filibuster for, 101-3.

Coughlin, Father Charles E., 178.

Cowan, Edgar, 32.

Crawford, Coe I., 100.

Culberson, Charles A., 84.

Cummins, Albert B., on filibustering, 114; 122; on length of speeches, 231.

Curtis, Charles, cloture petition, 146.

Dangerfield, Royden J., cited, 144n.

Davis, David, as independent, 44-5.

Davis, John, defeats appropriation for Mexican territory, 26.

Dawes, Charles G., crusade for limiting debate, 144, 162, 224-6, 231-2; parliamentary issues, 152, 154, 224; casting vote, 166; on obstructionists, 167; cited, 167n., 168n.; on filibuster threats, 216.

Dawes, Henry L., 47, 50.

Debate, unlimited, 6-7, 231; Clarke, quoting Hoar, 113; Dawes on, 224-6; Gallinger on, 113; Lodge on, 60, 113; Norris on, 226-7; Owen on, 110-11; Pepper on, 141-2; Root on, 104-5; Sherman on, 64-5; Teller on, 60-1; Turpie on, 61.

Deficiency bills, 130-1, 167-8, 187-9.

Democrats, for elections rider to army appropriation bill, 35-9; on Senate organization, 44-51; Federal Elections Bill, 52-7; against ship subsidy, 78-9; on Ship Purchase Bill, 103-15; Emergency Tariff, 132; Fordney-McCumber Tariff, 132-3; opposition to ship subsidy, 137-42; new attitude on ship subsidy, 190; on Senate rules, 222.

Dial, Nathaniel B., relief claim, 134-5.

Dill, Clarence C., 167-8.

Dillingham, William P., 110.

Divine, Father, 195.

Dolph, Joseph N., on Silver Repeal filibuster, 63.

Donnelly, Thomas C., cited, 238n.

Douglas, Stephen A., on admission of California, 28; for admission of Kansas, 28.

Dubois, Fred T., against Silver Repeal, 59, 66; refusal to vote, 63-4.

Edge, Walter E., campaign investigation obstruction, 158.

Education, bill for federal obstructed, 51-2.

Elections (see Federal Elections Bill).

Ellender, Allen J., antilynching bill, 5-6, 195-6, 198.

Emergency Tariff Bill, Democratic obstruction, 132.

English Parliament, obstruction, 13.

Eppes, John W., 15.

Expunging censure of Jackson, filibuster against, 19-21.

Fairbanks, Charles W., on Aldrich-Vreeland Currency Bill, 84-5, 87.

Faulkner, Charles J., long filibuster of, 54.

Federal Convention of 1787, 13, 238.

Federal Elections or "Force" Bill, 6, 52-7, 113.

Federal Radio Commission Bill, 168-9.

Federal Trade Commission Bill, 96.

Fendall, Philip Richard, 19.

Ferris, Woodbridge N., 151.

Fess, Simeon D., parliamentary issue, 145.

Filibustering, defined, 5; longest examples, 5-6; techniques, 8; chief arguments against, 9, 230-3; chief arguments for, 9, 233-8; curtailment, 209, 216-18; purpose of, 209, 212-13; classified by participants, 210-12; duration, 213-15; success, 215-16.

Filibusters, principal, against N.R.A., 3-5, 182-6; Aldrich-Vreeland Currency Bill, 5, 83-91, 99, 215, 218, 239; antilynching bills, (1922) 133-7, (1935) 179-81, (1937-1938) 5-6, 191-9; Silver Repeal, 6, 58-68; Federal Elections or "Force" Bill, 6, 52-7, 113; organization of Senate in 1881, 6, 44-51; Federal Constitution, in Pennsylvania legislature, 13-14; discourses of John Randolph, 16-19; against expunging censure of Jackson, 19-21; against dismissal of printers, 21-2; Fiscal Bank Bill, 22-5; Oregon, termination of "joint occupancy," 25; appropriation for Mexican territory, 25-7; Compromise of 1850, 27-8; Kansas, admission of, 28-30; against indemnification for suspension of habeas corpus, 30-4; reconstruction of Louisiana, 34-5; army appropriation bill, elections rider, 35-9; Hayes appointments, 43; education, federal, 51-2; armor plate, 68-9; river and harbor bills, (1901) 69-72, 211, (1903) 76-7, (1914) 97-101; omnibus statehood bill, 72-6; Colombian Treaty, 77; ship subsidy bills, (1907) 78-9, 211, (1922-1923) 137-42, (1936) 189-90; Arizona-New Mexico statehood, 91-3; Taft appointments, 93-4; Labor Department bill, 94; census director, appointment delayed, 95; ship registry bill, 96-7; cotton legislation, 101-3; Ship Purchase Bill, 103-15; Republican filibuster for special session, 115-17; Armed Ship Bill, 115-23; Republican obstruction in 1919, 128-31; Southern filibuster for nitrate purchases, 142-3; Isle of Pines, 144-6; World Court Protocol, 146-7; migratory bird bill, 147-9; Colorado River development, (1927) 149-52, (1928) 165-7; campaign investigation resolution, 152-62; Federal Radio Commission Bill, 168-9; immigration, 169-70; oil industry investigation, 171; Glass Banking Bill, 172-6; farmers' bankruptcy bill, 176-8; railway labor bill, 178, 212; work relief, 178-9; joint session, 181-2, 210, 215; neutrality legislation, 186-7, 211; flood control, 187; social security funds, 187-9, 209-10, 216; coal conservation bill, 190-1; naval appropriations, 199, 210; monetary bill, 199-206.

Fiscal Bank Bill, filibuster against, 22-5.

Fleming, Denna Frank, cited, 129n.

Fletcher, Duncan U., for Ship Purchase Bill, 104, 115.

Flood Control Bill, 187.

Foote, Henry S., altercation with Benton, 27; relevancy, 220.

Foraker, Joseph B., on Aldrich-Vreeland Currency Bill, 85, 89-90.

"Force Bill," (see Federal Elections Bill).

Ford, Henry Jones, on Silver Repeal filibuster, 58.

Fordney-McCumber Tariff Bill, 132-3.

France, Joseph I., general deficiency bill, 130-1.

Frazier, Lynn J., monetary bill, 200.

Friedrich, Carl Joachim, cited, 13n.

Frye, William P., 79.

Gallinger, Jacob H., cloture resolution, 60; for ship subsidy, 78-9; on La Follette tactics, 85-6; on parliamentary ruling, 98; on Ship Purchase Bill, 104-5; 108; on limiting debate, 113.

Gardenier, Barent, long speeches in House, 15.

Garfield, James A., appointments, 43-4.

Garner, John N., reply to Huey Long, 3; on recognition, 192.

Glass Banking Bill obstruction, 172-6.

Glass, Carter, banking bill, 173, 175-6; work relief bill, 178-9; antilynching bill, 197.

Gore, Thomas P., Aldrich-Vreeland Currency Bill filibuster, 85, 89-90, 215; N.I.R.A. amendment, 183; 184.

Gorham, George C., 47-8.

Gorham, Nathaniel, 238.

Gorman, Arthur P., on Silver Repeal, 66.

Graves, Dixie Bibb, on antilynching bill, 194.

Gronna, Asle J., Labor Department Bill, 94; Armed Ship Bill, 119, 122; vote on cloture rule, 127.

Guffey, Joseph F., 185; coal bill, 190.

Guggenheim, Simon, Labor Department Bill, 94.

Habeas corpus, filibuster against bill to "indemnify" President for suspension, 30-4.

Haines, Lynn, cited, 88n.

Hale, Eugene, 90.

Hale, Frederick, on Dawes, 225.

Hamilton, Alexander, on minority rule, 231.

Hamlin, Hannibal, 31.

Hannan, John J., cited, 88n.

Harding, Warren G., Republican filibuster, 117; administration of, tariff program, 132; special session, 133; ship subsidy, 137-8.

Hardwick, Thomas W., 107.

Harris, Isham G., banter with Dolph, 63; on Silver Repeal, 66-7.

Harris, William J., appointment delayed, 95; nitrates filibuster, 143.

Harrison, Pat, Emergency Tariff, 132; Dyer antilynching obstruction, 134-6; ship subsidy filibuster, 140; on apportionment, 167; on Dawes, 225.

Harrison, William Henry, 21, 22-3.

Hastings, Daniel O., railway labor bill, 178, 212.

Hay-Pauncefote Treaty, 95-6.

Hayden, Carl, filibuster on Colorado River development, 166.

Hayes, Rutherford B., on army appropriation rider, 36, 39; appointments obstructed, 43.

Haynes, George H., cited, 127n., 221n., 238n.

Heflin, J. Thomas, Dyer antilynching obstruction, 135; on ship subsidy, 142; on nitrates, 142-3; on World Court Protocol filibuster, 146; on migratory bird bill, 149; campaign investigation obstruction, 159-60.

Hereford, Frank, 38.

Heyburn, Weldon B., Aldrich-Vreeland Currency Bill filibuster, 90.

Hill, Benjamin H., on Mahone, 45-6, 49-50.

Hill, David B., cloture resolution, 60, 66; petition against dilatory motions, 64.

Hitchcock, Gilbert M., 107; Armed Ship Bill, 118-21; cloture petition, 131.

Hoar, George F., on filibustering, 47-8; Federal Elections Bill, 52, 54, 57; article by, 58; cloture resolution, 60; quoted by Clarke on unlimited debate, 113.

Hollis, Henry F., on cloture rule, 127-8.

Holt, Rush D., on Aesop's Fables and coal conservation bill, 8, 190-1; antilynching bill, 198.

Hoover, Herbert, veto of Philippine independence, 174.

House of Representatives, early characteristics, 14-15; since 1890, 15-16.

Howell, Robert B., 161.

Hubbard, C. C., cited, 230n.

Hughes, William, 102.

Immigration, 169-70.

Indian fund, 170, 213.

Indian Territory, 73.

Isle of Pines Treaty, filibuster, 144-6.

Jackson, Andrew, censure of, expunged, 19-21; on national bank, 22.

James, Ollie M., on limiting debate, 112.

Jefferson, Thomas, on John Randolph, 15; on debate in House, 15; on previous question, 219-20; on Senate debate, 220.

Jellinek, Georg, cited, 6n.

Jessup, Philip C., cited, 105n.

Johnson, Hiram W., on Colorado River development, 150, 152, 165-6; antilynching bill obstruction, 198.

Joint session, opposition, 181-2, 210, 215.

Jones, James K., 74.

Jones, John P., on Silver Repeal, 60, 67.

Jones, Wesley L., on filibustering, 108; ship subsidy, 138-9, 142.

Kansas, obstruction against admission, 28-30.

Kenyon, William S., river and harbor bill obstruction, 97-9; 122.

Keyes, Henry W., 151.

King, Preston, 33.

King, William H., campaign investigation resolution, 157; monetary bill, 200.

King, William R., against dismissal of printers, 22; challenges Clay to duel, 22; threatens filibuster, 23.

Kirby, William F., Armed Ship Bill, 118-19, 122-3.

Kirkwood, Samuel J., 44.

Labor Department Bill obstructed, 94.

La Follette, Robert M., record in filibuster against Aldrich-Vreeland Currency Bill, 5, 84-90; Taft appointments, 94; 110; Armed Ship Bill, 120-3; on cloture rule, 127; on mineral leasing bill, 129-30; on Victory Loan, 130;

general deficiency bill, 130-1; on meat packers, 134-5; on ship subsidy, 139; 212.

La Follette, Robert M., Jr., rebuke of Senate, 167.

Lamar, Lucius Q. C., colloquy with Conkling, 37-8.

Lane, Harry, 122.

Lee, Josh, monetary bill, 200-1.

Legislative day, defined, 7-8.

Lenroot, Irvine L., cloture petition, 147.

Lewis, Dixon H., 26.

Lewis, James Hamilton, 108; on Glass Banking Bill obstruction, 175.

Lewis, John L., 190.

Lincoln, Abraham, denounced by Saulsbury, 30-2; reconstruction of Louisiana, 34; 35.

Linn, Lewis F., 22.

Linn, William, 14.

Lodge, Henry Cabot, article by, 58; on Silver Repeal filibuster, 59; on unlimited debate, 60, 113, 231; public buildings bill, 94; 108; cloture on Treaty of Versailles, 131; Dyer antilynching obstruction, 137.

Lodge, Henry Cabot, Jr., monetary bill, 205.

Long, Huey P., filibuster against N.R.A., 3-5, 182-6, 219; defines "potlikker," 4; characteristics, 171-2, 212; Glass Banking Bill, 172-6; farmers' bankruptcy bill, 176-8; work relief bill, 178-9; joint session obstruction, 181-2, 210, 215; social security funds obstruction, 187-9, 209-10, 216.

Louisiana, filibuster against reconstructed government, 34-5.

Luce, Robert, cited, 13n., 58n., 238n.

Maclay, William, on early Senate, 14.

Madison, James, cited, 13n., 238n.

Mahone, William, alliance with Republicans, 44-50.

Majority principle, 230-1, 233-6; Clapp on, 108-9; James on, 112; Teller on, 60-1, 65-6; Williams on, 140-1; filibuster by majority, 120-1.

Manderson, Charles F., 63.

Mangum, Willie P., motion to dismiss printers, 21.

Marshall, Thomas R., on audibility of speeches, 106; adjournment "sine Deo," 131; parliamentary ruling, 156; on Cummins, 231.

Martin, Thomas S., on cloture rule, 127-8.

Mason, George, on quorum breaking, 13.

Mason, William E., on river and harbor act and on Senate rules, 76-7.

Mayfield, Earle B., on migratory bird bill, 148.

McCarran, Pat, 186; monetary bill, 200.

McCumber, Porter J., on Democratic tariff filibuster, 132-3; cloture petition, 133.

McElroy, Robert, cited, 56n.

McKellar, Kenneth D., Dyer antilynching obstruction, 136; ship subsidy filibuster, 140; altercation with Long, 181-2, 185; objection to clerk reading, 186.

McKinley, William, on river and harbor bill, 71, 211.

McLean, George P., 151.

McMaster, John Bach, 58.

McNary, Charles L., motion on behalf of Schall, 186; on cloture, 196.

Mexico, filibuster against appropriation for territory of, 25-7.

Migratory bird bill filibuster, 147-9.

Mineral leasing bill, 129-30.

Minton, Sherman, colloquy with Long, 183-4.

Monetary bill, 199-206.

Moore, A. Harry, 185.

Morgan, John T., on Federal Elections Bill, 57; filibuster against Colombian Treaty, 77.

Morning hour, 153-4, 216.

Morris, Gouverneur, 238.

Morton, Levi P., 54; on parliamentary procedure, 55-6.

Moses, George H., campaign investigation resolution, 153-4, 159-61; Glass Banking Bill obstruction, 174.

Murphy, Frank, opinion, 205.

Myers, Henry L., 134.

National origins, immigration, 169-70.
National Recovery Administration, filibuster against "skeletonized," 3-5, 182-6.
Naval appropriations, 167, 199, 210.
Neely, M. M., banter with Copeland, 145; on Colorado River development, 150; parliamentary issue, 156; feud with Holt, and coal bill, 190; cloture petition, 196.
Nelson, Knute, on omnibus statehood bill, 73-4.
Neutrality legislation, 186-7, 211.
Newlands, Francis G., 108.
New Mexico, bills for admission, (1902-1903) 73-6, (1911) 91-3.
Nichols, Jeannette Paddock, cited, 59n., 64n., 66n., 67n.
Niles, Hezekiah, on John Randolph, 17-18.
Nitrates, filibuster for purchase, 142-3.
Norbeck, Peter, on migratory bird bill, 149.
Norris, George W., Armed Ship Bill, 119-20, 122; campaign investigation obstruction, 158; constitutional amendment, 158-9, 165, 226-7; radio bill, 168; on Dawes, 226-7.

O'Gorman, James A., 107, 122.
Oil industry investigation, 171.
Oklahoma, bill for admission, 73-6.
"Onslow" letters, 19.
Oregon, termination of "joint occupancy," 25.
Organization of Senate, 1881 obstruction, 6, 44-51.
Overman, Lee S., 79; Dyer antilynching obstruction, 137.
Owen, Robert L., filibuster for Arizona admission, 91-3; on audibility of speeches, 106; on filibustering and unlimited debate, 110-11, 232-3; Armed Ship Bill, 120; on Clemenceau, 134; cited, 221n.

Palmer, John M., on Silver Repeal filibuster, 61-2.
Panama Canal, 77; tolls debate, 95-6.
Parnell, Charles Stewart, obstructionist in English Parliament, 13.

"Patrick Henry" letters, 19.
Peffer, William A., 60.
Pendleton, George H., 44.
Penrose, Boies, on Stone, 111; Republican filibuster, 115-17; whispering with La Follette, 129; cloture petition, 132.
Pepper, George Wharton, cited, 131n.; on filibustering, 141-2.
Philippines, tariff, 75-6; independence veto, 174.
Phipps, Lawrence C., filibuster on Colorado River development, 150, 152.
Pierce, Franklin, administration of, supports admission of Kansas, 28.
Pinchot, Gifford, 75.
Pittman, Key, parliamentary ruling, 185; neutrality, 186; monetary bill, 200-1; arms sale, 206.
Platt, Orville H., cloture resolution, 60.
Platt, Thomas C., resignation, 50.
Plumb, Preston B., 53.
Poindexter, Miles, 94; Republican filibuster, 116.
Polk, James K., on Oregon, 25; on Mexico, 25-7.
Pomerene, Atlee, ship registry bill, 96-7; on parliamentary issue, 98; ship subsidy filibuster, 140.
Pomeroy, Samuel C., arbitrary ruling in chair, 32-4.
Poore, Ben: Perley, cited, 16n.
Porter, Kirk H., cited, 222n.
Powell, Lazarus W., 32-3.
Previous question, 15, 219-20, 226.
Printers, dismissal of, 21-2.
Proceedings of Senate, reported, 16.
Prohibition Reorganization Bill, 153-5.
Pugh, James L., on Silver Repeal, 66-7.

Quay, Matthew S., filibuster on price of armor plate, 68-9; on omnibus statehood bill, 72-6; 87.

Railway labor bill, 178, 212.
Randolph, John, reputation in House, 15; rambling discourses in Senate, 16-19; 172.
Reed, David A., campaign investigation resolution, 153-5, 158-61; immigration, 169-70.

Reed, James A., on Ship Purchase Bill, 107-8; cloture resolution, 110, 113; ship subsidy filibuster, 140; World Court Protocol filibuster, 147; anger, 151; campaign investigation resolution, 152-7, 161; on Senate and Dawes, 225.

Reed, Thomas B., count of quorum in House, 15, 85.

Relevancy, in debate, 8, 220-1.

Reorganization Act, 219, 228-9.

Republicans, opposition to army appropriation bill rider, 35-9; obstruct Hayes appointments, 43; on Senate organization, 44-51; Federal Elections Bill, 52-7; Wilson appointment, 95; on currency adjustment, 95; on Ship Purchase Bill, 103-15; filibuster for special session, 115-17; obstruction in 1919, 128-31; for Emergency Tariff, 132; Fordney-McCumber Tariff program, 132-3; for ship subsidy, 137-42.

Reynolds, Robert R., 200.

Rhode Island, legislative "war," 230n.

Richardson, William A., 32.

Riddleberger, Harrison H., 47-8.

River and harbor bills, (1901) 69-72, 211; (1903) 76-7; (1914) 97-101.

Robinson, Joseph T., parliamentary ruling, 98; Armed Ship Bill, 119-20; colloquy with La Follette, 129-30; on ship subsidy, 138, 141-2; demand for vote, 166; on Sabbath, 170; on Glass Banking Bill, 175-6; farmers' bankruptcy bill, 177; work relief bill, 179; antilynching bill, 180-1; joint session obstruction, 182; neutrality, 186; social security funds obstruction, 187-8; colloquy with Holt, 191; on Dawes, 225.

Rogers, Lindsay, cited, 237n., 238n.

Rollins, Edward H., 49.

Roman Senate, obstructionists in, 13.

Roosevelt, Franklin D., bonus veto, 181, 210, 215; ship subsidy, 190; monetary bill, 201-2, 204-5; Reorganization Act, 229.

Roosevelt, Theodore, on Colombian Treaty, 77; on ship subsidy, 78; Isle of Pines treaties, 144.

Root, Elihu, 94; on unlimited debate, 104-5; 108; on filibustering, 109; on Senate rules, 112.

Rules, Senate, nature of and changes in, 6-8, 87-8, 91, 98-9, 185, 217-30, 240; filibustering in defiance of, 64; Dawes on, 162, 224-6; Democratic platforms on, 222; Root on, 112; Wilson on, 121-2.

Sabbath, 79, 170.

Saint Louis post office improvements, 97.

Saulsbury, Willard (1820-1892), denounces Lincoln, 30-2.

Saulsbury, Willard (1861-1927), ship registry bill, 96-7.

Schall, Thomas D., on N.R.A., 186.

Schwellenbach, Lewis B., on N.R.A. obstruction, 185; social security funds obstruction, 188; monetary bill, 201, 204.

Senter, E. G., filibuster in Texas Senate, 6.

Sevier, Ambrose H., 22.

Sheppard, Morris, filibuster for cotton legislation, 103; ship subsidy filibuster, 139-40.

Sherman, James S., 93.

Sherman, John, on unlimited debate, 64-5, 232; relevancy, 220.

Sherman, Lawrence Y., Republican filibuster, 116; vote on cloture rule, 127; on general deficiency bill, 130-1.

Ship Purchase Bill obstruction, 103-15.

Ship registry bill obstructed, 96-7.

Ship subsidy bills, (1907) 78-9, 211; (1922-1923) 137-42; (1936) 189-90.

Shipstead, Henrik, Isle of Pines Treaty, 146.

Shortridge, Samuel M., 134.

Silver Repeal, filibuster against, 6, 58-68.

Simmons, Furnifold McL., 116, 135.

Smith, Ellison D., 108; nitrates filibuster, 143; antilynching bill, 181.

Smith, Frank L., election charges, 153.

Smith, Hoke, filibuster for cotton legislation, 101-3; Armed Ship Bill, 121.

Smoot, Reed, appeal, 98; Ship Purchase Bill filibuster, 106; 135; 145; on World Court Protocol obstruction, 146.

Social security, obstruction of funds, 187-9, 209-10, 216.

Spooner, John C., 74, 113.

Stanfield, Robert N., speech, 156.

Stanley, A. Owsley, on ship subsidy, 138-9.

Statehood bill, omnibus, 72-6.

Steiwer, Frederick, joint session, 181.

Stephenson, Nathaniel Wright, cited, 90n.

Stevenson, Adlai E., on Silver Repeal, 64.

Stewart, William M., 53; on Silver Repeal, 60, 66-7.

Stone, William J., Aldrich-Vreeland Currency Bill filibuster, 89-90; Saint Louis post office, 94; on parliamentary issue, 99; on Ship Purchase Bill, 107-8; on cloture, 111; Armed Ship Bill, 118-19, 122.

Sumner, Charles, assaulted after Kansas speech, 29-30; against reconstructed government of Louisiana, 34-5; relevancy, 220.

Sutherland, George, parliamentary ruling, 89; Ship Purchase Bill filibuster, 106.

Taft, Robert A., monetary bill, 203-5.

Taft, William Howard, on Arizona, 91-2; appointments delayed, 93-4.

Teller, Henry M., on Silver Repeal and unlimited debate, 60-1, 65-6; against Philippine tariff, 76; 89.

Thomas, Charles S., on filibustering, 109.

Thomas, Elmer, Indian fund, 170, 213; oil industry, 171; Glass Banking Bill, 174-6; work relief bill, 179; parliamentary situation, 181; monetary bill, 200.

Thurman, Allen G., on filibuster techniques, 38; on counting a quorum, 39, 85.

Tillman, Benjamin R., debate with Carter, 70-1; on South Carolina claim, 72, 94.

Townsend, Charles E., on Wilson appointment, 95.

Townsend, John G., Jr., monetary bill, 203.

Treaty of Versailles, 131-2.

Trumbull, Lyman, 32-3; on Sumner tactics, 34.

Turney, Hopkins L., relevancy, 220.

Turpie, David, on unlimited debate, 61.

Twentieth Amendment, 219, 227-8, 234.

Tydings, Millard E., fair play demand, 3; resignation threat, 175; flood control, 187; monetary bill, 203-4.

Tyler, John, on Fiscal Bank Bill, 23-4.

Underwood, Oscar W., Emergency Tariff, 132; Fordney-McCumber Tariff, 133; Dyer antilynching obstruction, 134-7; previous question, 226.

Vandenberg, Arthur H., monetary bill, 203; arms sale, 206.

Vardaman, James K., 107; Armed Ship Bill, 122-3.

Vare, William S., election charges, 153.

Vest, George G., 66.

Victory Loan, 130.

Von Holst, H., 58.

Voorhees, Daniel W., for Silver Repeal, 59-60, 62, 66-7.

Vreeland, Edward B., 83.

Wadsworth, James W., Jr., campaign investigation resolution, 153, 157-9.

Wagner, Robert F., antilynching bills, 179-80, 191-3, 197-8; cloture petition, 198.

Wall, James W., 32-3.

Walsh, David I., campaign investigation obstruction, 161-2.

Warren, Charles Beecher, 225.

Warren, Francis E., on reservoirs, 71-2.

Watson, James E., tariff bill, 132; Glass Banking Bill obstruction, 174.

Webster, Daniel, against expunging censure of Jackson, 20; 220.

Weeks, John W., 115.

Wellington, George L., 71, 211.

Whigs, dismissal of Senate printers by, 21-2; advocate Fiscal Bank Bill, 22-4.

Williams, John Sharp, on river and harbor obstruction, 99-100; remarks on Penrose and Poindexter, 116; on filibustering, 140-1, 234.

Willis, Frank B., ship subsidy filibuster, 140; parliamentary ruling, 156; campaign investigation obstruction, 160.

Willoughby, W. F., cited, 238n.

Wilmot, David, offers Proviso, 25-7.

Wilson, Henry, 32.

Wilson, Woodrow, appointment delayed, 95; on Panama Canal tolls, 96; on ship registry bill, 97; hasty trip to Capitol, 101-2; 108; on Armed Ship Bill, 115, 118; quoted by Norris, 120; on Senate rules, 121-2, 232; veto of Emergency Tariff, 132; 137; 146; 213.

Windom, William, 44.

Wolcott, Edward O., 57.

Woodbury, Levi, against dismissal of printers, 21.

Work relief, 178-9.

Works, John D., 122.

World Court Protocol, filibuster, 146-7.

Wright, Silas, against dismissal of printers, 21.

Yulee, David L., against admission of California, 28; 220.

Zeis, Paul Maxwell, cited, 79n.

Zimmermann note, 118.